MIKE H

# Congo Mercenary

MW00698918

# MIKE HOARE

# Congo Mercenary

Greenhill
Books

*Congo Mercenary*

Originally published in 1967 by Robert Hale, in 2008 by
Paladin Press and in 2019 by Partners in Publishing
This paperback edition published in 2022 by Greenhill Books,
c/o Pen & Swords Books Limited,
47 Church Street, Barnsley, South Yorkshire, S70 2AS
www.greenhillbooks.com
Author website: www.madmikehoare.com

ISBN: 978-1-78438-871-3

All rights reserved

Copyright © 1967, 2008, 2019, 2022 Mike Hoare

The right of Mike Hoare to be identified as author of this work
has been asserted in accordance with Section 77 of the Copyright
Designs and Patents Act 1988.

A CIP data record for this title is available from the British Library

Printed and bound in England by
CPI Group (UK) Ltd, Croydon, CR0 4YY

MIX
Paper from
responsible sources
FSC    FSC® C013604
www.fsc.org

# FOREWORD

Joseph Désiré Mobutu was born near Lisala, a small town on the north bank of the Congo River, on 14 October 1930, and was educated at the Christian Brothers boarding school at Coquilhatville. He joined the Belgian colonial army at age 19 and rose to the rank of sergeant-major, the highest rank possible for him in colonial days. In the late 1950s, he worked as a journalist and joined the nascent Congolese National Movement in 1959. When the Congo became independent on 30 June 1960, it was renamed the Democratic Republic of the Congo. Joseph Kasavubu became its first president and Patrice Lumumba its first prime minister. Lumumba chose Mobutu as his private secretary and, soon afterwards, appointed him army chief of staff with the rank of full colonel.

Five years later, on 25 November 1965, Mobutu staged a coup and overthrew President Kasavubu without a shot being fired. Mobutu proceeded to rule the Congo with an iron hand. In May 1966, six months after he had seized power, he arrested four former ministers of state for plotting to murder him. They were tried by summary court martial and, after five minutes deliberation, sentenced to death.

On 2 June 1966, the four men were hanged in the Grand Place of the capital Leopoldville, now named Kinshasa. The crowd was estimated at more than 50,000. During the execution, an incident took place that illustrates the power that witchcraft and superstition exert over the people of Zaire even to this day. One by one the condemned men ascended the gallows to be hanged by the neck until they were dead. The last was Evariste Kimba, a former minister in the independent state of Katanga in 1963 and prime minister of the Congo in 1965.

A ripple of suppressed excitement ran through the crowd as a black bag was pulled over Kimba's head. Every person there knew that Kimba came from a family of witch doctors, famous throughout Katanga. Could he cheat death? Would he die? The vast crowd held its breath in awestricken suspense as the rope was placed around Kimba's neck and the knot snugged down. A wave of cold fear ran through the mob. It could be felt. Not a sound could be heard. The trap door banged open and Kimba dropped—only to hang there twitching, squirming, but very much alive. A roar of disbelief rose in crescendo as Kimba was cut down and the rope placed around his neck again. Once more the trap door flew open and again Kimba dropped—and again he was seen to be alive.

Panic surged through the crowd. Kimba was a witch; they knew it . . . they had to get out of his presence at once. The terrified people surged backward and forward, kicking, shoving, and trampling each other in their panic to escape the scene. In the mêlée, dozens were crushed to death. The third time the rope did its grisly work.

And what of Mobutu's other erstwhile enemies? What of Pierre Mulele, the man who led the rebel movement in Kwilu in 1964? His end was tragedy writ large. In 1968, Mulele was living quietly in Brazzaville, the capital of the Congo Republic, separated from Kinshasa by the mile-wide Zaire River. Mobutu declared an amnesty for all former rebels and sent envoys to encourage Mulele to return home. Persuaded by a written guarantee that would ensure his safety, Mobutu's word of honour, and the presence of the presidential yacht sent especially to escort him home, Mulele decided to return. Accompanied by Justin Bomboko, the Zaire foreign minister, Mulele returned to Kinshasa with pomp and circumstance. At the glittering reception held that night in his honour at Camp Kongolo, the army barracks, it really did seem as though all had been forgiven and forgotten.

But this was very far from being true. I quote Jules Chomé, the Belgian communist author of *L'Ascension de Mobutu*, a book which caused a serious diplomatic rift between Belgium and Zaire when it was first published in Brussels: "During the night the soldiers who had just come to fete him, arrested him, beat him up, tortured him, and killed him on the orders of Mobutu. It was pretended after his death that he had been tried and convicted in camera by a military court and that he was shot immediately after sentence." My eye rested on the words "tortured him." If you are at all squeamish don't read on. If not, here are the hideous details. While Mulele was still alive, his eyes were gouged out, his genitals were ripped off, and his limbs were amputated one by one.

The Popular Movement of the Revolution was founded in 1967, and in 1970 Mobutu pronounced it the only political party in the Congo. Then he had himself elected president, unopposed. He ruled by decree through a Council of Ministers and began by nationalising some major industries. He diminished the power of the Catholic Church but allowed missionaries to remain, possibly because he had been educated by the Christian Brothers mission at Lisala himself. He did away with all Christian names—Mobutu now became Sese Seko Nkuku Ngbendu wa za Banga, officially translated as "the all-powerful warrior who, because of his endurance and inflexible will to win, will go from conquest to conquest leaving fire in his wake." (Personally I preferred the mellifluous Joseph Désiré.) He expelled certain foreigners, confiscating their businesses and giving them to local aspirants, although so much chaos ensued that much of this edict had to be rescinded. When the student body in Kinshasa was rash enough to demonstrate against the one-party state, they were conscripted into the army as private soldiers, never to be heard from again.

Next, Mobutu encouraged a return to African authenticity. He renamed the country Zaire, which was the original name of the Congo River. He abolished colonial place names, so that Leopoldville became Kinshasa, Stanleyville became Kisangani, and Elizabethville became Lubumbashi. He tried to develop some unity among the Congo's diverse ethnic groups, an almost impossible task given the fact that the country was populated by more than 200 independent tribes. Flemish was removed from school curriculum, and French became the official language. At the same time, he encouraged the use of indigenous languages, the main ones being Lingala, Swahili, Kikongo, and Tshiluba.

Despite much turmoil and confusion, Mobutu's Congo became, to some extent, a bulwark against the spread of communism in Central Africa, a matter of considerable importance to the United States in the Cold War against the Soviet Union. In the early 1960s, Chou En-lai, the prime minister of China, had visited the Sudan, Kenya, and Tanzania, a tour that caused some trepidation in diplomatic circles at that time. Probably with a view to counteracting this Chinese initiative, the United States established a CIA office in Kinshasa, headed by the redoubtable and highly efficient Larry Devlin. Shortly afterwards, Mobutu—guided, without a doubt, by the United States diplomatic mission in Kinshasa—declared his support for Holden Roberto's anti-communist party in neighboring Angola, the National Front for the Liberation of Angola (FNLA). Mobutu encouraged the FNLA to use the Bas-Congo as a base from which to fight the Cuban mercenaries sent to Angola by Fidel Castro in support of the communist candidate, Augustino Neto.

In 1976, partly as a result of the dramatic fall in the price of copper, the country's chief export, and partly due to lack of know-how and corruption on a heroic scale, the economy of the Congo slid into a fatal decline. Once more, the United States, which had supported Zaire financially over the years, mainly because of its anti-communist potential, came to the rescue.

In the face of earth-shaking difficulties, President Mobutu proved himself capable of holding Zaire together. A lesser man would have disappeared long since under the welter of administrative inefficiency and corruption. He traveled extensively and was on excellent terms with many world leaders, chief among these being President Ronald Reagan of the United States. He was adequately rewarded for his Herculean labours, you may be sure. In the early 1980s, he was reckoned by *Forbes* magazine to be one of the five richest men in the world. It was rumoured that he had appropriated billions of dollars in Western aid and revenue generated by his country's mineral wealth.

Without doubt, Mobutu amassed a vast personal fortune, believed to have peaked at $4 billion in the mid-1980s. Tales of reckless extravagance emanated from Kinshasa with startling frequency. Some had undoubted style, such as the one about the

Boeing 747 specially requisitioned from Sabena one Saturday morning to take his beautiful young wife and 12 ladies of the Mobutu household from Kinshasa to Brussels for a three-hour shopping spree. *Tiens!* Even so, he never forgot his humble beginnings and took great delight in creating a prosperous town at Gbadolite, north of Lisala where he was born. Meanwhile, this potentially wealthy country, plagued with corruption and mismanagement, continued its disastrous economic decline.

Regrettably, over the years the Zaire National Army failed to improve. Certainly it in no way distinguished itself in its engagements with the Katangese rebels in 1977 and 1978. According to U.S. intelligence reports quoted by President Jimmy Carter, the rebels who invaded Katanga in March 1977 had been recruited and armed by the Soviet Union and trained by Cuban mercenaries. The Zaire army offered them little resistance. Ultimately, Mobutu appealed to the Moroccans to expel the invaders. The next invasion in April 1978 came via northwestern Zambia and seized Kolwezi itself. This time the Belgians and French mounted an operation to rescue their nationals, 120 of whom had already been slaughtered by the invaders in horrifying circumstances.

Mobutu crushed political dissent ruthlessly and on occasion ordered the execution of rivals he regarded as threats to his régime. He consolidated power by sharing his country's wealth with his political allies, a system which came to be known elsewhere as kleptocracy. By the 1980s, he was in an unassailable position as the lifelong president of the Congo. It is a truism that power corrupts, and truer still that absolute power corrupts absolutely. And so it was going to be with Mobutu.

\* \* \* \* \*

About two years after I had left the Congo I was summoned to Kinshasa to see the General, as I always called him. First, at a special parade at his general headquarters, I was presented with a decoration—the type you wear around your neck—L'Ordre de Zaire, Officer class. Then, at an audience with Mobutu, still attended by his faithful aide-de-camp, Baron Powis de Tenbossche, he asked me what I thought he should do with the French and Belgian mercenaries still serving as part of his army. My advice was unequivocal: send them home. Mercenary soldiers are by definition assault troops. In the role of garrison troops they are inevitably an expensive nuisance; their inaction causes trouble. The General seemed to concur and took my advice, but only in part. He sent 5 Commando home, but retained 6 Commando, the unit of French and Belgian mercenaries stationed in Stanleyville. It was a decision he lived to regret.

We went on to discuss another matter. Since my departure from the Congo, the province of Orientale had remained devastated, its economy ground to a halt. The vast palm oil and coffee plantations that had taken decades of hard work to cultivate had been abandoned. Lianas and weeds were suffocating the trees, which very soon would die from lack of attention. I asked the General if I might make a suggestion. "Yes," he said, "but give me solutions—not problems!" I outlined a scheme for bringing to Zaire men who would reorganise the economy of Orientale, men who could speak French or Swahili, men who would restore confidence to the local population and get everything moving again. Not mercenary soldiers but motivated civilians, probably middle-aged, preferably married men with their families. For security purposes, I suggested supporting them with a small mobile force of mercenary soldiers who could put down any banditry at short notice. I enthused. The General liked it. Turning to Powis he said, *"Jean, donnez-lui tous ce qu'il veut. Arrangez-ca"*—"John, give him everything he wants. Arrange it." I could hardly believe my ears. But somewhere between that bold decision and its execution, some little men from South Africa got in and destroyed the dream. The beautiful plantations in Orientale were devastated.

I kept in touch loosely with the General over the years, and one day I was delighted to hear on the BBC Foreign Service that he had been invited to visit the United Kingdom as the guest of Her Majesty, Queen Elizabeth. At that time, November 1972 or thereabouts, I was sailing my 100-ton Baltic trader in the Mediterranean with my family as crew. We moored for a few days at the yacht club in Palma de Mallorca. I telephoned the Congolese ambassador in London and asked him if it would be possible for me to meet President Mobutu during his visit. He suggested that if I came across to London immediately, he would do his best to arrange it.

I took up a position on the sidewalk along the Mall, a few hundred yards from the gates of Buckingham Palace. I was part of a large crowd lining the route down which the Queen of England and her squadron of Household Cavalry would pass. In due course the cavalcade rode by, and I saw Mobutu and Her Majesty sitting side by side in the Queen's open carriage, the Queen waving to the crowd of onlookers on either side. The General looked happy. I was thrilled. I began to wonder if, like Alexander the Great, he would weep when he had no more worlds to conquer.

A few days later I received an invitation to a ball that Mobutu was giving in Claridges Hotel. I was one of five local people who would be presented to the president. We paraded in a reception room on the first floor. In due course, Mobutu arrived. He walked slowly towards us supported by two tall men, one on either side. I was shocked. The General looked terribly ill. When he came opposite me, he recognised me at once, smiled, and greeted me in a soft voice, "Allo Mark!" He had never been able to pronounce my Christian name. He said he was "so 'appy to see me," asked how I was, said he remembered me well, and so forth. That was a thrill in itself and gave me great pleasure. He moved on and then returned to the privacy of his room, while I joined the other 600 guests in the banqueting room. I never saw him again. I had only known him in the days when he saved his country from disaster at the hands of communist rebels, and I shall always remember and admire him for that. Years later I learned that he was suffering from cancer of the prostate gland; it had first attacked him in 1962.

By the late 1980s the Cold War was diminishing, and Mobutu became less important to his Western allies. In 1990, the United States Congress, alarmed at corruption and human rights abuses in the Congo, cut direct aid to the Mobutu régime. His political heyday was over. Throughout the early and mid-1990s, despite rising opposition and looming economic disaster, Mobutu clung to power. Ultimately, as the result of domestic and international pressure for reform, he announced the creation of a multiparty system for Zaire.

XII          *Congo Mercenary*

In late 1996, a rebellion broke out in the Kivu province of Zaire, overwhelming the country's underfunded and poorly disciplined army. Led by veteran guerrilla fighter Laurent Desiré Kabila—yes, the very same gentleman whom I had fought at Baraka in 1965—and supported now by Angola and Rwanda, the movement turned into an anti-Mobutu rebellion. At that very moment Mobutu was obliged to leave Zaire urgently to undergo desperately needed medical treatment in France and Switzerland. It was not an excuse; Mobutu was never short of courage. On his return to Kinshasa in March 1997, he found the rebels had captured most of eastern Zaire and were advancing rapidly on the capital.

Days before Kabila's capture of Kinshasa in May 1997, Mobutu relinquished power and fled the country. Having ruled the Congo for nearly 32 years, he died in exile in Rabat, Morocco, in September 1997.

—Mike Hoare, 2008

# CONTENTS

# ILLUSTRATIONS

1 A training session led by Mike Hoare in Kamina, Katanga province, 1964

2 The 5 Commando letterhead in 1966

3 A 5 Commando jeep with additional decoration

4 The beachhead at Baraka, 1965

5 Injured 5 Commando men being medevacked by chopper, 1965

6 Sgt Tim Dreyer and the chopper pilot Bob Houcke at Albertville airport

7 A T28 in Isiro in the north-east of the Congo

8 Mike Hoare and the wounded John Peters supervising the evacuation of the wounded after the battle of Baraka in September 1965

9 Injured 5 Commando volunteer being flown out of Baraka to Albertville, end of 1965

10 The dropping zone (DZ) in Albertville

## FACSIMILIES

## MAPS

# ABBREVIATIONS USED IN THE TEXT

ABAKO   Alliance des Bakongo. One of the main political parties in the Congo.

A.N.C.   Armée Nationale Congolaise—the Congolese National Army.

B.A.K.A.   The Kamina Base. Contraction of Bas Kamina.

B.I.A.S.   Belgian International Air Services.

C.B.S.   Columbia Broadcasting System of America.

C.F.L.   The Railway Company in Katanga—Compagnie des Chemins de Fer du Congo Supérieur aux Grands Lacs Africains.

C.I.C.R.   Comité Internationale Croix Rouge—the International Committee of the Red Cross.

C.-in-C.   Commander-in-Chief.

C-47   A cargo-carrying aircraft similar to the D.C.-3.

D.S.   Directing Staff.

D.C.-3   The Dakota, a two-engined passenger-carrying plane built by the Douglas Aircraft Corporation of America.

D.C.-4   The Skymaster, a four-engined passenger-carrying plane built by the Douglas Aircraft Corporation of America.

F.A.T.A.C.   Force Aerienne Tactical. The Congolese tactical airforce.

F.N.   Fabrique Nationale. The Belgian F.A.L. rifle which is standard equipment for N.A.T.O. forces. Fires single shots and automatic. ·762 cartridge. Twenty-round magazine.

FORCE PUBLIQUE   Congolese army until Independence when it became the A.N.C.

G.H.Q   General Headquarters.

G.R.C.9   American Army radio transmitter-receiver, normal range about twelve miles.

KM   Kilometre. About three-fifths of a mile.

LEO   Leopoldville—now Kinshasa.

M.N.C.   Mouvement National Congolais. One of the main political parties in the Congo.

N.A.T.O.   North Atlantic Treaty Organisation.

N.B.C.   National Broadcasting Co. of America.

N.C.O.   Non-commissioned officer.

O.A.U.   Organisation for African Unity, founded 1963.
O.C.A.M.   Organisation Commune Africaine et Malgache, a group of French-speaking countries in Africa.
O Group   Orders Group.
P.R.C.10   American Army radio transmitter-receiver, normal range about five miles.
P.S.P.   Pressed steel planking.
Q.G.-A.N.C.   Quartier General Armée Nationale Congolaise. Headquarters of the Congolese National Army.
R.A.M.C.   Royal Army Medical Corps.
RIVE GAUCHE   Left bank of the Congo River at Stanleyville.
R.P.C.   Republique Populaire du Congo, the Popular Republic of the Congo.
R.S.M.   Regimental Sergeant Major.
S.A.F.N.   Semi-automatic F.N. rifle.
S.S.B.   Single side band radio transmitter-receiver capable of very long range.
STAN   Stanleyville.
VOL.   Volunteer.

*To those who did not come back*

# PREFACE

Early in 1964 a minor communist-inspired revolt took place in the Kwilu Province of the Congo. The event seemed of little importance at the time and went largely unheeded, but it was in fact the first clap of thunder to presage the coming storm. Within a matter of five months the minor revolt became a major uprising and involved more than half the Congo's 14 million inhabitants in armed conflict and ranged over two-thirds of its one million square miles of territory. Before the rebellion had run its course it caused the death of many thousands of innocent Congolese and Europeans and finally it staged a tragedy in the full glare of world publicity which for sheer unparalleled savagery has few equals in history.

The communist character of the rebellion was evident from the very beginning. The centre of operations was at Stanleyville, the stronghold of Antoine Gizenga, the political and spiritual heir to Patrice Lumumba. Ghana and Guinea were both actively supporting the rebel cause and the Soviet bloc, which had previously upheld Gizenga's claim to be the head of the only legal governement in the Congo, was subsidising the rebel movement.

A full year had passed since Mr. Moise Tshombe had been ousted as President of the independent State of Katanga and he was now in voluntary exile in Spain. The United Nations forces in the Congo, financially and morally bankrupt from their "peace keeping" efforts in Katanga, were in no position to undertake any new adventure in the field and were making ready to depart.

Notwithstanding the events of the recent past and the bitterness and rancour which they had engendered in Congolese politics, in the face of the national catastrophe President Kasavubu invited Mr. Tshombe to return from Spain to become Prime Minister of the Congo with a mandate to form a coalition government and suppress the rebellion with all speed.

This unexpected step took the world completely by surprise but served once again to prove that anything can happen in the

Congo and frequently does. Mr. Tshombe's first move on his return to power was to try and reconcile the parties to the conflict but when this failed he was quick to appreciate the real and sinister nature of the uprising and saw it clearly for what it was—an all out attempt by the Communist Bloc to seize power in the Congo, overthrow law and order and establish a communist presence in the heart of Africa.

The initiative was with the rebels and mounting success was theirs. The National Army, bewitched and demoralised, retreated on all fronts and in many cases deserted lock stock and barrel to the enemy. Faced with this extraordinary dilemma Mr. Tshombe decided on extraordinary measures. His immediate resolve was to hire white mercenary troops to assist the Congolese National Army put down the rebellion before it was too late.

Whilst it was an intensely practical solution to the problem and many will say the only one open to him, it was one which brought down on his head a torrent of abuse from members of the Communist Bloc and O.A.U., none of whom, however, were able to offer any assistance other than the formation of a Committee of Conciliation which proved moribund from the start.

This book tells the story of the events of the next eighteen months and the adventures which befell 5 Commando A.N.C., the unit of white mercenary soldiers which fought through four campaigns in the Congo to suppress the rebellion. It is very much the personal story of that unit and for that reason makes little mention of the Congolese National Army.

Mercenary soldiering is what one makes it. For my part I wanted only the adventure and the fulfilment of command, but in the event I found myself taking a substantial part in the political life of the Congo and the shaping of the future of that great and magnificent country. If this experience has taught me anything it is that the battle for Africa is now on, and that the newly independent African states are ill equipped physically and ideologically to fight it. Who knows but that the mercenary soldier—if he measures up to the high standard required—may yet prove to be the only real and positive check to the communist invasion of Africa which has now begun?

I make no apologies for being a mercenary soldier. Quite the reverse. I am proud to have led 5 Commando. I am proud to have fought shoulder to shoulder with the toughest and bravest band of men it has ever been my honour to command. I am proud that they stood when all else failed. And I have two regrets. The first is that it should have cost us so dearly in men killed and seriously wounded. The second is that I never quite realised my ambition—to erase the image of *les affreux* and replace it with a standard of discipline and soldierly behaviour which would have entitled 5 Commando to be called worthy successors of the noblest mercenary soldiers who ever offered their swords for reward and their hearts for an ideal— the "Wild Geese" of the eighteenth century.

M.H.

Kloof,
South Africa

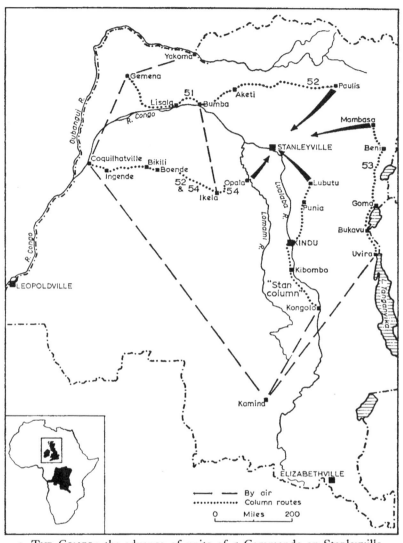

1. THE CONGO: the advance of units of 5 Commando on Stanleyville.
5 Commando assembled at the Kamina base and then moved as follows:

*51 Commando*—by air to Gemena via Coquilhatville; then to Bumba. By air rejoined "Stan Column" at Kindu.

*52 Commando*—by air to Coquilhatville; then to Ikela. By air to Bumba; relieved 51 Commando and continued to Paulis.

*53 Commando*—by air to Uvira; then to Mambasa.

*54 Commando*—by air to Coquilhatville; then with 52 Commando to Ikela; on their own to Opala.

*"Stan Column"* (55, 56 and 57 Commandos and H.Q.)—by air to Kongolo; then to Stanleyville (joined by 51 Commando at Kindu).

# 1

## A CALL TO ARMS

The Sabena Boeing touched down at Ndjili right on time, making a perfect landing in the statutory two languages—French and Flemish. I had arrived in the République Democratique du Congo, the ex-Belgian Congo. The hot Congo night bounced up off the tarmac to greet me, and only me. Nobody else alighted from the Brussels-bound Boeing, for Leopoldville in July 1964 was far from being a tourist attraction.

I was met at the gate by Gerry Puren who manouevred me through the formalities with an astonishing flow of bad but effective French. He addressed all Congolese officials as "Chef" or "Monsieur le Directeur". Gerry knew his Congo. He had not changed much in the three years since I had last seen him and he was now a good-looking forty, tall and well dressed with a confident air which exactly matched his bow tie and cheroot.

I had flown up from my home in Durban as quickly as possible in response to his urgent telegram and I was most anxious to know what it was all about. On the way to the Memling Hotel Gerry brought me up to date with the latest situation in the Congo. Events during the last six months had gone from bad to worse, armed rebellion had broken out, the rebel advance had swept across the country at an alarming speed and at no point had it been checked. The United Nations troops had left at the end of June and Mr. Moise Tshombe had been invited back to the Congo to be the new Prime Minister to see if he could sort out the mess. This much I knew already.

Gerry went on to explain that during the last fourteen months he had been very close to Mr. Tshombe and had acted as courier for him on a number of occasions and as a result of this close association he felt that he knew what might now be in the Prime Minister's mind. In fact he had anticipated that Mr. Tshombe might require white mercenary troops and he had taken it upon himself to alert over two hundred men in Johannesburg who had declared themselves ready to fight anywhere and anytime. I was the Commander designate and he was to be Commander Air Operations!

I could not help admiring his nerve and the confidence which he placed in his own judgement but to me, at that moment, it all looked highly improbable. We arrived at the Memling Hotel to be met by Madame Puren, Alastair Wicks and a small group of pilots whom Puren had brought up from South Africa with him. The only one I knew was Alastair whom I had not seen since our adventures in Katanga in 1961 when we had formed a loose but lasting friendship. I was happy to see that the years between had done nothing to mar his handsome features, perhaps another grey hair or two, but he was still the same debonair charmer with the same well modulated voice and Harrow accent, and the same impeccable manners. He was to be my second in command. As an executive officer in Rhodesian Air Services he was more in touch with Congolese events than I and had seen quite a lot of Gerry in his comings and goings to Europe; but we shared the opinion that our arrival in Leopoldville was at the best premature and, at the worst, a not unpleasant waste of time. We retired for the night after some joyful drinks, confident in the knowledge that on the morrow Gerry would be summoned to the presence and our exact role in the future of the Congo made known to us.

Of all the lasting benefits which the Belgians bequeathed to the colony which they administered so ably for fifty-two years, the city of Leopoldville is perhaps the most glittering, beautiful and enduring. Four years of Congolese misrule had certainly tarnished its classic features, but on the whole it was still a city to astonish the Western eye, set as it is in the heart of darkest Africa. Avenue Albert, now renamed Boulevard Trente-Juin, remains an architectural masterpiece—an avenue over one hundred yards wide and two miles long; and the stately homes gracing the banks of the Congo are still a major domestic glory, now enjoyed by the Congolese. The Belgians, unlike the British in Africa, planned their colonial cities with a broad and generous hand and every village and town in which the Belgian presence was manifest is a lasting tribute to their administration. Future generations of Congolese will come to look upon the Belgian town makers in the same way as the English still look upon the ancient Roman road makers of Britain.

It was my first visit to Leopoldville and I was distressed at the filth and garbage lying on the sidewalks, the absence of everyday household merchandise in the shops, and the flourishing black market in Congolese francs. The official rate of exchange was 150 francs to the dollar, but dollars were selling at 350 quite openly. The Government had taken a bold step in devaluing the currency once already since Independence, but this had only checked the slide down the slippery slope to insolvency.

The political scene was confused and uncertain. Cyrille Adoulla, the previous Prime Minister, an able and hard-working politician with a solid background in the Trades Union movement, had done his best to lead the country along the road to a viable economy, but despite a benevolent American interest had failed to do so. The Congo was suffering from a malaise compounded of inertia and inexperience. A general feeling of insecurity was abroad and large numbers of thinking Congolese now realised with dismay that the scaffolding had been pulled away from the building before it was ready to stand on its own foundations. Confidence had fled the country. Hundreds of thousands of villagers, unable to continue their normal agricultural occupations for want of territorial administration, had migrated to the big cities to batten on their more prosperous city cousins. The communes were swollen to bursting point. Unemployment rapidly reached dangerous proportions, and all the ingredients of national unrest were in the pot ready for stirring.

This was the moment chosen by Pierre Mulele, the ex-Minister of National Education and Fine Arts to descend on the stage of Congolese politics like a fiery demon in a children's pantomime. Mulele, a Peking trained agitator, selected the heavily populated area of Kwilu in the Leopoldville Province for his first efforts at fomenting trouble. Vast numbers of Congolese, disillusioned by the small fruits of independence and bitterly disappointed by the lack of improvement in their personal fortunes, improvements which Lumumba had promised them went hand-in-hand with Independence, were ripe recruits for the skilled communist agitator.

Mulele, a rabble rouser in the tradition of his former leader, Patrice Lumumba, was quick to appreciate the potential force at his command and began to spread the doctrine of Communism throughout the land. Soon stories reached Leopoldville bearing the unmistakable imprint of Chinese Communist techniques. They began with the killing of the "chefs coutumiers", the village chiefs, notables and "intelligentsia", the literate few who held clerical posts and on whom the administration depended; then the familiar and nauseating catalogue of crimes involving the destruction of schools, hospitals and missions; and in the end the complete and final overthrow of law and order.

The militant force at Mulele's disposal was, as always in the Congo, the *jeunesse*, youths of from twelve to twenty who had broken away from parental control or the restraining influence of their tribal chiefs, to flock for adventure to Mulele's banner. Mulele, clever psychologist that he was, now seized on two of the most potent weapons available to the African demagogue of today— witchcraft and superstition. It seems hard for the Western mind to appreciate that witchcraft and superstition have roots deep in the subconscious mentality of all Africans, educated or otherwise, and that a large proportion of their everyday life is governed by the witch-doctor and his mumbo-jumbo, but that this is so is an indisputable fact. Numerous cases are on record where a Congolese has retired to his hut, fit and healthy a few minutes before, only to die in a matter of hours because his witch-doctor has pronounced this to be his inescapable fate.

As an extension of this belief Mulele introduced a new doctrine to his followers. Believers in him had only to shout the magic words *"Mai* Mulele" and their enemies and worst fears would be overcome. In battle, after taking the *dawa*—a specially prepared medicine—they would be immune to all danger, bullets would turn to water or pass through them harmlessly,[1] and they would be invincible. Having taken the *dawa* they would immediately be possessed of superhuman powers; for instance, they had only to "throw their eyes" on their enemy to render him helpless and impotent for ever. The *Mai*, literally "water", would be dispensed by his witch-doctors. The medicament was, in fact, nothing but water and was administered from small glass phials. This, together with

---

[1] The belief that witch-doctors are able to make bullets pass through one's body is fairly widespread in the Congo. Old Congo hands tell me that it is probably based on the fact that whenever the Force Publique or the Police were called out to quell a major disturbance they invariably fired off blank cartridges.

liberal doses of marijuana, rendered the recipient insensible to pain and totally incapable of intelligent action.

In this drugged state the followers of Mulele firmly believed in their invincibility and their immunity from all harm. The immunity the *dawa* gave existed only in their half-crazed minds, but their centuries' old beliefs in witchcraft were sufficient to convince them that they could go into battle against machine guns and all the weapons of modern warfare and emerge unscathed and victorious merely by screaming "*Mai* Mulele".

The losses they inevitably suffered were explained away by the witch-doctors with a show of elementary psychology. The soldiers had failed to observe the strict rules laid down in the taking of the *dawa* they declared. They had been told never to leave the track, never to look upon a white man, not to lie down or eat anything, and to return without fail after four hours. These rules must be obeyed, they explained, if the *dawa* was to be effective.

Whilst the effect of this doctrine would be negligible on white soldiers the effect it produced on the Congolese of the A.N.C.— the Armée Nationale Congolaise, the National Army—was nothing short of catastrophic. The mere announcement that "les Mulele-istes" were on their way, or worse still, the sight of them standing drugged, hands outstretched, throwing their eyes in their direction, was sufficient to reduce entire garrisons to a state of instant panic and headlong flight, in which they frequently abandoned their arms and equipment to the advancing rebels.

By means of this fantastic ritual Mulele gathered around him many thousands of followers to form the hub of the Congolese rebellion. These were to be responsible for the killing of many thousands of innocent and peace-loving Congolese villagers, ordinary men and women, whose dearest wish was only to be left to till their fields in the manner of their fathers for centuries before them.

But the cancer spread. Without warning the Maniema district of the Kivu Province in the eastern Congo, long the epicentre of political unrest and the hard core of Patrice Lumumba's M.N.C. party, erupted into flame. The sword of rebellion was carried on high, dripping with blood, into neighbouring Bukavu and Albert-ville. The hideous events and the atrocities of Kwilu repeated them-selves. With no responsible leaders to formulate demands or aims, nobody to control the mobs of insurgents killing, raping and looting, the situation grew progressively worse.

Mr. Tshombe, who had now returned to the Congo from his self-imposed exile in Spain, tried heroically to bring all dissident parties to the conference table in his efforts to form a "Government of Reconciliation". In this he was hampered by inability to identify the leaders of the revolt, but he made successful tours of Kwilu, Stanleyville and the Kivu province, the centres of unrest. The tours resulted in standing ovations for the popular diplomat—but all to no avail. Secretly the Communist-backed "National Committee of Liberation", headed by its President, ex-bank clerk, Gaston Soumiallot, had decided to weld the separate insurgent movements into a homogeneous uprising to give it a national character and impetus. Their avowed intention was to set up an Independent State of Oriental and Kivu which would espouse the Communist cause and be run on the Chinese pattern. Those that were not in favour of the change must be put to death.

The mass slaughter of Congolese villagers began. Thousands were executed and thousands more fled the towns and villages for the safety of the bush. The rural economy, such as it was, collapsed under the strain and territorial administration ground to a halt for the want of clerks and officials. Step by step law and order gave way to tyranny, murder, and pillage until the country held by the rebels was reduced to a state of anarchy. Out of this condition, communist doctrine declares a new and more equitable order will arise, but meanwhile untold havoc reigned throughout the territory, bringing in its wake misery and suffering, the like of which had not been seen in the Congo since before the coming of Stanley.

In Orientale Province, the most heavily populated province in the Congo, Christopher Gbenye[1] and Thomas Kanza,[2] two hitherto well respected politicians, both of whom had been Ministers in the first Congolese Parliament, threw in their lot with Antoine Gizenga, the heir of Patrice Lumumba, and Gaston Soumiallot. Together they formed the first Executive Council of the "Republique Populaire du Congo".

[1] Christopher Gbenye was born in 1927 in the Bas-Uele district of Orientale Province. He was a leading light in Lumbumba's M.N.C. party and was appointed Minister of the Interior in the first Congolese Parliament. He was dismissed at the same time as Lumumba in September 1960 and returned to Stanleyville. He was again appointed Minister of the Interior in Adoulla's Government.
[2] Thomas Kanza was born in 1933 and was the first Congolese to graduate from a university—Louvain in Belgium in 1956. He represented the Congo at the United Nations in New York until the fall of Lumumba. He was chargé d'affaires in London for the Adoulla Government in 1962. He has written a number of books and pamphlets.

In addition to the forces of "Muleleism" set in motion in the Kwilu, the new Council were quick to take advantage of another serious cause for unrest. For months past the National Army had been indulging themselves in brutal and licentious behaviour at the expense of the civilian population. Feelings were running high against the A.N.C. and the Council of the Popular Republic rode the crest of their wave of mounting indignation. Now that they were faced with a chance to rid themselves of their oppressors the people came out strongly in favour of the new régime.

With the weight of public opinion manifestly behind them the Executive Council brushed aside Mr. Tshombe's entreaties for talks in Leopoldville and decided to unleash their forces "of liberation". On the fifth day of August, 1964, they struck. Unheralded, a column of sixty motor vehicles descended on Stanleyville from nearby Wanie Rukulu, led by a handful of prancing witch-doctors, waving palm leaves before them and chanting incantations. The population was spellbound. The thousand strong garrison of the city, terrified by the sight of the witch-doctors in their full regalia and the rag-tag army of rebels dressed in monkey skin caps and feathers, fled in disarray, flinging their arms into the Congo River as they went.

Within twenty-four hours the Stanleyville Airport had been taken over by the rebels, the city was closed to all comers and nobody was allowed to enter or leave, including the staffs of the various consulates. The city was firmly in the hands of the new Popular Government. For the next one hundred and ten days government was at the whim of a handful of semi-educated megalomaniacs, drunk with power, uncertain of their aims and incapable of maintaining the slightest vestige of discipline within their ranks.

Nicholas Olenga, an ex-railways booking clerk with no military training whatsoever was promoted to the rank of General and given command of the "Popular Army of Liberation", whilst Soumiallot was to govern the eastern part of the new Republic with his seat at Albertville.

From the average villager's point of view it was indeed a "Popular Republic". At one stroke he seemed to have rid himself of the hated National Army in favour of a more benevolent régime. The soldiers of the Popular Army of Liberation, calling themselves "Simbas", lions, were in the beginning the very model of good behaviour, but history was shortly to record that the last stage would be worse than the first. Finally the rebel Government and the Popular Army indulged in excesses which far outdid their predecessors in every facet of vandalism and extortion.

The flames of rebellion, fanned by the strong wind of success, ran riot across the country. To the west the rebels marched on Coquilhatville, in the north-west towards Gemena, and in the south they had already captured Albertville and Manono. One half of the Congo was now in rebel hands.

This was the alarming scene which confronted Mr. Tshombe and his hoped for Government of Reconciliation in the middle of August, 1964. Tshombe, the astute diplomat, was now pitchforked into the middle of a seething cauldron of revolt after nearly sixteen months abstention from Congolese politics. Nothing abashed, he confidently announced his determination to bring peace and unity to the Congo before the end of September.

Mr. Tshombe did not see Gerry the next day, or the next, or the next. I was perfectly aware that he was occupied with affairs of state which would have daunted the stoutest heart, but as the situation grew steadily worse my conviction grew steadily stronger that he would be forced to use a tool other than the National Army to quell the rebellion.

This conviction finally blossomed into a firm belief that the employment of white mercenary troops was the only logical course open to him. The A.N.C. had proved a dismal and shameful failure and the half-hearted offers of assistance from Ghana and other members of the O.A.U. would have done nothing to stem the flood of insurrection, even if accepted.

But would the Prime Minister take this step? To employ white men to fight his own countrymen, rebels though they might be, seemed to many at the time to be an impossible solution. The realists saw it as inevitable and the only way; the idealists shuddered at the prospect and anticipated the wrath to come of the O.A.U. and the censure of the Afro-Asian bloc at the United Nations. Day by day the situation deteriorated and speculation as to how Mr. Tshombe would rescue the Congo from the threshold of anarchy became the main topic of conversation in Leopoldville.

We were incredibly bored. Day followed day and still we waited. Endless trips to Gerry's room revealed nothing. "Be patient", was his counsel, "I know the old man, I know how his mind works; one of these days he will send for us and the game will be on". Patience and loyalty to Tshombe were Gerry's long suit and probably his most marketable asset at that moment. His days in Katanga when he stayed right to the bitter end in charge of the tiny Katangese Air Force, withdrawing them finally to Angola, were a reminder of the depths of his attachment to Mr. Tshombe.

Nevertheless, we were worried. Gerry seemed to have no contacts with the Prime Minister that were worth while and he infuriated us all by ringing up Tshombe's house-keeper for information.

"Yes," she said, "the Prime Minister is dining tonight with Mr. Mennen Williams. He has just sent out for an American flag."

Alastair and I were right—our arrival was indeed premature.

The rest was not doing us any harm and gave us plenty of time to look around. The Memling itself is a sober establishment and would probably rate four stars by European standards. The very walls shriek respectability. In fact, there is a notice by each lift warning the would-be larker that that sort of thing would not be tolerated in the rooms after nine at night. Reasonable hours, I thought. Certainly all the time we were there, there was no hint of impropriety.

Each evening at about 10 p.m., just before turning in, we witnessed an entertaining ritual. The Congolese ladies of the town would saunter in to the Memling Bar to see what was cooking. They were a collection of the most remarkable dolls I have ever seen. They were exceptionally well-dressed; overdressed, I suppose would be a more accurate description. Some had on gold lamé knee-length dresses which must have cost a fortune, whilst others wore tight satin jobs, cut deliberately to accentuate the goods. One usually wore a full-length silver gown imprudently décolleté which imperilled her treasures every time she bent down. The creations were stunning and would have induced instant thrombosis in any Paris couturier. In a word, they were the sort of dress every man likes to see on a woman—providing she is not his wife.

The gals themselves were young and good-looking. Black beehive wigs and superb carriage completed the picture. They stayed together as an unselfconscious clique, sometimes attracting a customer, but most times not, but always filling the bar with gaiety and raucous laughter. Conversation, the unknown art, was carried on at the top of their voices, the whisper being unknown to the African female. "Divertissement" was how Alastair described it all and nick-named them "les Parisiennes".

One evening an Italian professor, a gay bird who was known to be a bit of a lady killer could deny himself the pleasure no longer and dated, if that is the *mot juste*, one of the Parisiennes, much to the amusement of onlookers lingering around the reception desk. The immediate negotiations over, he escorted Mam'selle gallantly to the lift ignoring the written remonstrance against this type of behaviour and failing to notice the sign which said "Lift out of order". All eyes were on the lift. After an agonising minute he emerged with what aplomb was left to him and tried another lift with more success. The management bloodhounds were on him in a trice and what might have been an interesting tête-à-tête ended briefly to the great amusement of all in the foyer.

The Congolese girls of Leopoldville of the "Parisienne" type are exceptional in every respect. They are completely westernised in their dress and manners and altogether charming. They are well turned out, polite and well acquainted with the social graces. In fact, they are the exact equivalent of the courtesan of Marie Antoinette's day. They fill a much needed want in this respect. Many of the Congolese politicians have advanced so speedily that their wives are still in the mud-hut stage and are totally incapable of behaving in public according to western standards, and the sight of a table laid with an array of knives and forks is known to send them into panic. Not so the courtesan. She has studied this situation. I was not surprised then to learn that these girls are greatly in demand by the recently arrived and that formal invitations to official functions even made provision for this fact, by acknowledging that they will be welcome as guests in default of a wife.

At long last the call came. A ministerial Chevrolet drew up at the Memling and we were whisked away to see the Prime Minister at his official residence at Kalina. The meeting lasted no more than five minutes. Could we bring a large number of mercenary troops to the Congo in a hurry? Gerry answered confidently that we could. Mr. Tshombe then settled out of his private resources Gerry's arrears for two years—the gesture was almost medieval—and we were ushered out to get on with it.

It was the first time I had seen Mr. Tshombe in action. The ease with which he took decisions of the first magnitude impressed me forcibly. I was to see him do it many times in the future and it served only to reinforce my opinion of him as a statesman in the world class.

Gerry now announced that I was "Supremo" and withdrew with tremendous enthusiasm to his own task of raising a T6 Harvard squadron and began at once—that day in fact—with a mission to strafe a rebel group somewhere in the Kwilu area. My first task was to send Alastair back to Johannesburg to organise the recruitment of men and my second to ask for an audience that evening with the "National Security Council"—the Prime Minister, Minister of Interior, Mr. Munongo, Minister of Security, Mr. Nendaka, and the Commander-in-Chief, General Mobutu. My main purpose was to obtain a written directive as to my duties and to confirm the terms of the contract under which we would serve.

Julia Puren, who represented her husband, was my sponsor. We waited in the main waiting room for the General and Victor Nendaka. Tshombe and Munongo were already within. Nendaka arrived wearing a cloth cap similar to those worn by continental goalkeepers, and choker. Mobutu arrived in a sports shirt and flannels. Julia introduced me. She described my career in a few well chosen words, referred to my previous service in Burma and Katanga and ended by saying that I was a good soldier and a fine officer. Mr. Munongo nodded vigorously and said he could see by looking at me that that was true. I took to Mr. Munongo immediately.

Mr. Tshombe called for refreshments and began by explaining that the Government had agreed that white mercenary troops were now needed to help the National Army put down the rebellion which was in danger of overwhelming the country. It had been agreed with Belgian Foreign Minister, Paul Henri Spaak, after some consultation with Averell Harriman of the U.S. State Department, that Belgium would increase its aid to the Congo by a further two hundred technical advisers, making four hundred in all, and that the United States would increase its shipments of trucks, aeroplanes and radio equipment to help the National Army. These two Powers, he added, were not averse to the Congo's employment of mercenary troops, in the circumstances, providing they were neither Belgian nor American.

He enlarged on the situation whilst I examined him closely. He was a young 45, glowing with good health and confidence. His voice, which is the most arresting thing about him, is deeply resonant and persuasive. His eyes are the eyes of Africa—sad and appealing, with an expression that speaks of the suffering of Africans down through the ages. I had met him before, but I felt once again the extraordinary magnetism of his personality. No one to my knowledge has been able to explain his subtle ability to command loyalty in both white and black men, but that such a loyalty exists, I had ample evidence. Puren was an example. Alastair was another.

His enemies amongst his own people have described him as a European with a black skin, but I know him now to be the exceptional man who is able to understand the African and the European mind at one and the same time. In the long days ahead I grew to admire his quiet courage and outstanding diplomacy more and more, until I thought he might be the greatest hope the West has in Africa, the bridge, the Bailey bridge, between African and European.

Drinks arrived, amongst them some Simba, the beer of Katanga, without which the Prime Minister never travels. Mr. Munongo surprised me by uncorking a bottle of Coca-Cola nonchalantly with his teeth and then drinking from the bottle. Godefroid Munongo, the faithful lieutenant of Mr. Tshombe, is a man to be reckoned with. He is conscious of his great forebears and a worthy descendant of his famous grandfather the great M'siri, Ruler of Katanga, Chief of the Bayeke, the fiercest tribe in the Congo. He had never forgotten that his grandfather's head was displayed by the Belgians in a paraffin tin and his hatred for them is undisguised. He gave the impression that he would prefer an all-Congolese Congo, but he was prepared to accept that for the time being Europeans were necessary. Fair enough.

I never ever met Mr. Munongo when he was not wearing his gold-rimmed dark glasses and these, coupled with a very low speaking voice, gave him a somewhat sinister aspect. I was told that he made a fetish of being scrupulously honest, even to the extent of not using his ministerial car at night or on private business. A refreshing change from many of his compatriots to whom office merely represented a welcome extension to their private bank accounts.

Mr. Tshombe ended, and Major-General Mobutu, the Commander-in-Chief of the Armée Nationale Congolaise, then took a sheet of paper and at my request began to write down exactly what it was he wanted me to do. There was some discussion first as to the priority to be accorded certain operations, but finally there was general agreement that Albertville was to be the first objective and Stanleyville the next. Victor Nendaka, the Minister of Security, cast a dissenting vote in favour of Stanleyville first. I heard subsequently that he had large business interests there, but perhaps I am being too hard on his strategic appreciation.

The General wrote out his directive in a painstaking hand and showed it to the Prime Minister and then passed it to me. I have kept it ever since as I regard it as an historic document. I read it quickly and was astonished at the size of the mercenary force to be employed. The directive (facsimile overleaf) read:

1. A company of 200 men must arrive *immediately* at Kamina: MISSION—Retake Manono, Albertville, Fizi, Uvira.
2. 300 volunteers should be formed into six platoons for the six mobile groups now in creation.
3. 500 volunteers in company with elements of the A.N.C. must retake Stanleyville *immediately*.

Signed: Commander-in-Chief, A.N.C.

J. D. Mobutu

Major-General.

I tried to draw the General on the terms of the directive, but as he was anything but forthcoming I was forced to leave it at that. I asked if there were to be any Belgians in the overall command and I was assured that, in accordance with the Spaak-Harriman agreement, there were definitely no plans for the employment of Belgians in this operation. To make doubly sure on this point, I then asked for an assurance that I would have absolute autonomy in the execution of their directive and, again, that no Belgians would be placed above me. This assurance was readily given.

The General seemed a little reticent throughout and I sensed then that he resented my presence, not, I felt sure for myself, but for what I represented—a foreign element called in to do the job the A.N.C. had shown themselves incapable of doing. The General was proud of his army and hated to admit that its fighting qualities were practically non-existent. I could see that our relationship would have to be handled tactfully.

Major-General Joseph Désiré Mobutu was thirty-three years old. He had served in the Force Publique for seven years and had left the army with the rank of Sergeant—the highest rank available to him. He then took up journalism, worked for the well-known

1) La Cie de 200 hommes qui doivent immédiatement arriver où l'ancien

Mission : Reprise de { Baudoin Albertville Fizi Vira

2/ 300 volontaires soit 6 pelotons pour les 6 groupes mobiles en création

3/ 200 volontaires qui doivent en compagnie des éléments A.N.C reprendre Stanleyville immédiatement

Le Commandant en Chef A.N.C

J.J. Mobutu
Général - Major

General Mobutu's directive to the author

Belgian journalist, Pierre Davisterre, and later edited the newspaper, Actualités Africaines. He was a member of the Mouvement National Congolais (Lumumba) and first came to political prominence on his appointment as Secretary to the Presidency in the first Congolese Parliament. Ten days after Independence he was made Chief of Staff of the Congolese Army with the rank of Colonel. On 14th September 1960, the world first took cognisance of Colonel Mobutu as the "strong man" of the Congo, when he caused Lumumba to be placed under house arrest, suspended President Kasavubu[1] from his office and expelled the Russian and Czechoslovakian diplomats from the Congo at twenty-four hours' notice. These actions stamped him as a fearless leader and one, above all, who had the real interests of the Congolese at heart.

I was concerned at the large size of the proposed force and asked bluntly if the A.N.C. was able to arm and equip my one thousand men on arrival. The General asked me if I had not heard of Kamina and assured me that everything we should need was already there. It all seemed too good to be true. There was only one last hurdle to be cleared and that was agreement on the terms of the contract. With the devaluation in the Congolese franc I was anxious that we should not sign up to fight for a seemingly large sum of Congolese francs, which would turn out to be a disappointingly small sum in hard currency. The basis I had in mind was that a private soldier, unmarried, should be able to earn a basic pay of not less than £140 per month, at least half payable in sterling. This would enable a man to live well in the Congo and save virtually the whole of his "transferred" amount so that at the end of his contract he would have a reasonable nest egg. After considerable argument as to the "index"—the multiplier by means of which our basic wages were to be augmented to compensate for the rise in the cost of living and the devaluation of the currency since independence— we finally agreed that the Katanga contract would serve as the basis of the new contract and the present index of 4·69 I agreed was satisfactory. So that there should be no doubt in anybody's mind on the morrow I asked the Prime Minister to record this little thing on paper.

[1] Joseph Kasavubu was born in 1917 in the Bas-Kongo. He is generally regarded as the father of Congolese politics and became President of the ABAKO Party in 1956. In 1958 he became Mayor of one of the African communes in Leopoldville and was recognised as the leader of the Congolese Independence Movement in 1959. He was the first President of the Congo and remained Head of State until the military *coup* by General Mobutu in November 1965.

Taking a pen he drafted the agreement himself, prompted by Victor Nendaka who had some legal training and helpfully suggested the French equivalent of "the party of the second part, etc." whenever he thought it made the contract sound more legal. Finally, this was typed and signed and stamped and a copy handed to me.

I exchanged a few words with Mr. Nendaka to whom I instinctively took a great liking—perhaps it was the cloth cap—and got Julia to outline his background to me. Astute was the word which described him in a nutshell. Somehow he had managed to hold office in every Government in the Congo since Independence and remain a power in the land. Certain it was that he was greatly feared as Minister of Security, but it was his mischievous air and lively eye that took my fancy.

Mr. Tshombe then escorted me to the gate in a friendly fashion, stopping in the garden in the full glare of the flood-lights to assure me of his personal backing wherever I should need it. It was unthinkable he said, that this country, the rich and beautiful Congo, should be held to ransom by a bunch of gangsters. Shaking my hand with a great show of emotion and sincerity he said, "Au revoir, Major, we count on you. The Congo counts on you. You are our man of destiny."

# 2

## THE FIRST STEPS

"Any fit young man looking for employment with a
difference at a salary well in excess of £100 per month
should telephone 838-5203 during business hours.
Employment initially offered for six months.
Immediate start."

A rash of advertisements in the "Situations Vacant" column of
newspapers in Johannesburg and Salisbury carried the news that
recruiting was about to begin. In Johannesburg Alastair appointed
an old school chum of his, Patrick O'Malley, as Recruiting Officer
and flew up to Salisbury to open an office there himself. I had
impressed upon Alastair the Congolese viewpoint with regard to
recruitment, the keynote of which was speed with security. Publicity was to be eschewed at all costs. It was fundamental that we
should recruit the right type of man and in my view the right type
was young, fit and with a sense of adventure. Military experience
was desirable, but not absolutely essential. I would give them the
training I knew would be required for fighting in the Congo, a very
different thing from Europe, and a far cry from the barrack square
background which most volunteers would have anyway. As far as
actual combat experience was concerned I was not very hopeful—
in any case World War II was nineteen years ago and those with
experience of fighting in it would be a bit long in the tooth for the
Congo.

It was a fairly loose mandate and I was under no illusions about
the difficulties. Both recruiting officers then set to work with commendable zest to perform what was in fact an impossible task—
to recruit one thousand men without a ripple of publicity. Patrick
O'Malley was a man with considerable background, the son of a

C

former British Ambassador to Portugal and a top-line broadcaster in South Africa. He was extremely well known as a radio personality, even though his career as an announcer had ended summarily in a *cause célèbre*, some matter involving fisticuffs and a civil servant. His war record as a fighter pilot had been scintillating and during the Battle of Britain he had limped back to Manston Aerodrome on many an occasion to deposit the remains of his Spitfire on the tarmac. I admired O'Malley in a number of ways, not the least being the manner in which he had fought off alcoholism with the aid of his strong Catholic conviction.

He began his task with a zeal matched only by his flair for attracting publicity, an unfortunate adjunct in the circumstances. Reports soon reached Quartier-General in Leopoldville about his efforts and the culminating moment came a little later when I was asked to explain to General Mobutu a five-column photograph showing O'Malley holding his head in his hands and reputedly saying to the Johannesburg press corps—"Leave me alone, chaps, I'm trying to fight a war!"

In Salisbury Alastair was more discreet, but again I found it impossible to explain away to the C.-in-C. reports of his television appearances. A blanket of secrecy over the whole thing, we all appreciated, was desirable, but in the circumstances quite impossible. It was news and as such the press saw their duty and advantage in publishing it. I protested to the General that the job could not be done without some publicity and left it at that.

The news when it broke rang round the world evoking every response from surprise to resentment. In South Africa the English-speaking press came out strongly against the use of South African mercenaries for reasons which were not readily apparent, but were probably based on traditional opposition to the Nationalist Government. At a later stage they took great delight in publishing everything that would show the mercenary effort in a bad light and rushed into print the lurid and inaccurate tales of "returned heroes" who had been found below the standard required for fighting in the Congo. But more of that later.

Throughout the world, reaction to Mr. Tshombe's startling move was hostile and unfavourable. As anticipated, the members of the O.A.U. were indignant, angry and insulted that the Congolese Prime Minister should have the temerity to call in white troops to put his house in order without reference to them. They completely ignored the fact that their piddling and inefficient armies were quite incapable of looking after themselves, let alone embarking on a foreign adventure. Hatred for Mr. Tshombe and his bold edict mounted through the length and breadth of Africa.

In America *Time* Magazine declared on 4th September:

"Throughout most of Africa, both mercenary and Tshombe were about the dirtiest words on the list. Hiring troops from hated white-supremacist countries will just about finish whatever chances Tshombe may have had of ever getting along with other black African nations."

This was an accurate summary of the situation, but the world was unaware that it was merely by chance and not by design that mercenary troops were recruited in "white supremacist countries". As far as Tshombe and Mobutu were concerned they were indifferent as to where the mercenaries came from so long as they came, and came quickly. The choice of countries followed automatically from Tshombe's reliance upon Gerry Puren as the prime mover in the mercenary market; Gerry was a South African; South Africans had been used before in the Katangese Forces. Thus it came about that South Africans were recruited, but it would be wrong to say that Tshombe specifically asked for men from Southern Africa or from anywhere else for that matter. Had it been a decision for me I would most certainly have advised in favour of recruitment in the United Kingdom, unpopular step though it would surely have been with Her Majesty's Government. Perhaps by this means some of the stark realities of the African scene, as depicted in the Congo during the next eighteen months, would have been brought home to the people of Britain by dint of personal contacts.

However, the fat was in the fire, Tshombe stuck to his guns nothing daunted, confident that the world would see his action to be what it was—the lesser of two evils and a positive step towards arresting anarchy in the Congo. His tremendous faith in my ability to recruit, organise, train and lead a unit of mercenary troops in support of the National Army until all rebel resistance was crushed caused me a moment or two of sleeplessness, but I took courage in his confidence and busied myself with the tasks of preparation. Recruitment continued unabated and in less than three weeks O'Malley and Wicks between them had signed on over one thousand men ready to fight as mercenary soldiers in the Congo in the unit to be known as 5 Commando.

My first task was to get to Kamina and to get there in a hurry. Before setting out from Leopoldville, however, I decided as a matter of courtesy to call on the British and American Embassies "to polish my marble" as it were, and to learn, if possible, what their official attitude was to the mercenary force now being raised and Congolese politics generally.

I began with the British Embassy. The Military Attaché, Lieut.-Colonel Kirk, achieved the difficult task of being chary and enthusiastic at the same time, whilst leaving me in no doubt that the hiring of mercenary troops was a ghastly error, old chap, political suicide for Mr. Tshombe, and something H.M.G. would not like to be mixed up in. I was introduced to various other members of the staff and left with the distinct impression that I must buy myself a bell forthwith to ring out the warning "unclean".

Further down the road I asked to see the U.S. Military Attaché. It was like going from an old ladies' home to a gymnasium. Colonel Knut Raudstein, tall, wiry, capable and amusing, sat me in a deep leather armchair and proceeded unashamedly to wring me dry of any information I possessed before tackling lesser topics. I steered the conversation back carefully to the purpose of my visit and an hour later I was completely *au fait* with the Congolese scene, the official U.S. State Department view of mercenary troops, and how matters stood between Goldwater and President Johnson.

Briefly, we were bad news. The Colonel made it abundantly clear to me that the employment of white mercenary troops to fight black men, regardless of the apparent necessity, was something which did not have the approval of the United States Government. In maintaining this attitude I sensed that the Americans were in something of a dilemma. It could be argued on the one hand that the use of mercenaries would help to achieve a stable and unified Congo. To that extent we should be acceptable, *faute de mieux*, the end justifying the means. On the other hand Washington must for ever, it seems, justify its African policy to that one-tenth of its population which is Negro, and the notion of white mercenaries fighting black men with the tacit approval of the U.S. Government was not one that would prove popular at home.

As a result we could expect no assistance whatsoever from them other than that which had been promised to the Congo as a whole under the terms of the general agreement between Harriman and Spaak. Their attitude was clear, concise and correct, but at the same time friendly. What I liked about the American officials in the U.S. Embassy in Leopoldville was that they were always able to maintain their formal policy yet at the same time remain helpful and charming on a purely personal level.

If I was in any doubts about the U.S. official policy towards the Congolese Government headed by Mr. Tshombe these were swept away by the bald statement that U.S. policy in the Congo had not changed one iota since Independence—it remained what it had always been, namely, that a strong and unified Congo was its own best insurance against Communism and economic ills.

If I was concerned that their attitude towards Mr. Tshombe, the new and unexpected Prime Minister, might be influenced by past relationships my fears were put at rest. Despite the fact that it was barely two years since the United States had put its weight behind the United Nations to topple the Independent State of Katanga and Mr. Tshombe with it, their policy today was to assist the head of the Congolese Government as much and as fully as possible to achieve their common aim—a unified and stable Congo. Personalities did not enter into it.

It was an example of big thinking and the loan of four C-130 aircraft concrete evidence of their willingness to help. Mr. Tshombe for his part, as I knew, was more than prepared to forget the past in his efforts to create a new order in the Congo and he accepted eagerly and with gratitude such aid as the Americans could give him. *Entente cordiale.*

The Congo is a vast country and getting my body from one place to another was for me a never ending problem. At this time there was virtually no civilian air traffic; Air Congo was operating at a fraction of its capacity, nine-tenths of the Congo airfields being in the hands of the rebels. Road and river transport was unthinkable where it existed and from a military viewpoint was ruled out if only on the grounds of its slowness. Leopoldville to Albertville, for instance, is over a thousand miles and the terrain sluiced from top to bottom with a hundred rivers making transportation difficult at the best of times and in the rainy season almost impossible. Normal transport from Matadi, the port of Leopoldville, to Elisabethville would take up to thirty days, necessitating as it did a river journey from Leo to Port-Francqui and a rail journey from there on.

I decided to ask the Americans for a ride on one of their C-130s

to Kamina, no other transport being available for the 650-mile
hop. With much reluctance they agreed to carry me this once, but
warned that future requests would have to receive the approval of
the U.S. Ambassador. My argument that we were members of the
Armée Nationale Congolaise failed to impress them and gave me
some indication of the peculiar position we were to occupy in the
scheme of things. Individually it seemed we were to be social out-
casts; as a unit, an acute embarrassment to everybody, including
our employers. I resolved there and then to alter that image as soon
as I could. In the event it took me twelve months to do it.

It was my first flight in a C-130. The mighty four-engined turbo-
prop aircraft is undoubtedly the greatest aeroplane in the world
to-day, a masterpiece of engineering, surprisingly beautiful in its
ugliness. The crews of the C-130s were the most efficient and carefully chosen airmen I had ever met; someone back in Florida set a
very high standard. A plane which costs £750,000 would be placed
in the hands of six exceptional men, one imagined, but that the
standard never varied was something which greatly impressed
everybody. I came into contact with dozens of C130 crews during
the next eighteen months and frequently remarked that they were
the finest ambassadors the United States could have, representing
as they did discipline, technical know-how and the very substance
of great power.

I arrived at Kamina to be met by Major Blume of the Belgian
Air Force. The Belgians had established an air transport unit at
Kamina which they called FATAC and it consisted chiefly of some
eight or nine C-47 aircraft in support of the army. The use of the
unit was restricted rigidly to logistical support and it was forbidden
to take part in actual operations. Very few of the Belgians seemed to
resent this limitation on their activity.

My curiosity as to the state of readiness of Kamina for the incoming drafts was hard to conceal. Half fearing, but already
knowing the answer, I asked Blume if everything was ready for the
reception of my one thousand troops. He stopped dead in his tracks,
a look of exaggerated horror on his face.

"A thousand men! *Nom de Dieu!*" he said, his voice rising
crescendo, "You must be kidding. Do you know what we have here
to defend ourselves with—one pistol!"

*Ca c'est le Congo.* Of course I would have been astounded if
everything had in fact been ready.

Alan Blume was a popular, efficient, and easy-going Belgian Air Force officer, who had fought as a fighter pilot in the Battle of Britain with the Royal Air Force. His keen sense of humour and unflustered approach to our early problems, some of them alarming —how to feed three hundred men with no food and twenty sets of eating irons for instance—attracted me to him at once, but it was his basic wish to help and his fearlessness in action which won my unceasing admiration.

Blume took me to his Ops Room to outline the tactical position of the Albertville front. He traced the forward position of "own troops" on the large wall map. Colonel Kakuji with a battalion group of A.N.C. were surrounding Kongolo and their axis of advance was Kongolo-Nyunzu-Albertville. Kakuji was having reasonable success, but the A.N.C. were dragging their feet and it was doubtful if they would move on in the next few days. At Baudouinville at the southern end of Lake Tanganyika another battalion column commanded by Lieut-Colonel Bangala had run up against severe enemy resistance and his advance along the line Kapona-Albertville had been halted. This unit was showing even less desire to engage the enemy. Small groups of the rebels had infiltrated to a point eighty miles north-east of Kamina, but they had outrun their initial impetus and would soon peter out.

After consultation with Blume I decided to get to 4 Group Headquarters at Elizabethville immediately to see what could be done for the incoming drafts. I was met at the airport by the Belgian Vice-Consul, Monsieur Guillot, and the Supply Officer, G 4,[1] from 4 Group H.Q., Commandant Cochaux.

Guillot was an energetic little man, dedicated to his nationals and he lost no time in telling me that the situation in Albertville was *très grave* and that their latest news was that a large number of Belgian civilians, priests and others would most certainly be killed by Soumiallot if something was not done quickly. He deplored the slowness of the advance of the A.N.C. and begged me to act now. I agreed to come to the Consulate in the morning where I would be shown maps of Albertville and the approach routes.

Commandant Cochaux was a career officer on whom the success of 4 Group Headquarters clearly rested. He was painstaking and

---

[1] The A.N.C. has adopted the American Army system which divides army headquarters into four main groups: G 1, Personnel; G 2, Intelligence; G 3, Operations; G 4, Supply. The letter G denotes an Army Headquarters. All subordinate headquarters take the letter S.

thorough and genuinely pleased to help. He was the second Belgian regular officer who had demonstrated to me that day that there need be no animosity between "regulars" and "irregulars". My heart was uplifted at the prospect of happy co-operation with the Belgians, but owing to a series of misunderstandings it was a prospect destined to early failure. Cochaux suggested that it would be politic to call on the Officer Commanding 4 Group without any further delay, so we drove round to pay my respects to Major-General Louis Bobozo. Bobozo was put out at not having been informed by G.H.Q. of the latest moves and this gave him an opportunity to air his pet grievances, which were that he was a soldier and they (Leopoldville) were all politicians, and secondly, who had been the senior Congolese in the Force Publique at the time of Independence? Tell him that! He had, Sergeant-Major Bobozo—why, therefore, was he relegated to the command of a Group, when he should be directing things at the very hub? I nodded tactful agreement and tut-tutted in the right places. Now, what could he do for me? My sense of diplomacy warned me not to pursue things after this peroration and I requested permission to retire and to see him again the next day.

I spent the evening chez Cochaux and withdrew at a respectable hour, dog tired, to the Katanga Hotel to be lulled to sleep by a ten-piece band making the night air hideous with their stampings and blowings. It was the first time I had seen the "Surf" danced by Congolese gentlemen without the assistance of ladies and I was forced to admit that they made a graceful job of it.

During the night—the time when I do such thinking and planning as I am capable of—I conceived the idea that a quick victory for Mr. Tshombe was paramount. Somewhere he must demonstrate to the Congolese people that the tide of rebel successes had turned. Albertville was the obvious choice for such an action and with two columns already on their way I developed the idea that a large-scale raiding party—say a hundred men furnished by my unit—would start the ball rolling in the right direction and show the A.N.C that we meant business.

I discussed this with Cochaux in the morning and with Guillot at the Consulate later on. They were both enthusiastic and pointed out that such a move would have the added advantage of goading the A.N.C. into action, if only to save face. I looked at the maps. An advance by road was the obvious, but Cochaux warned that to supply me with transport of any sort was quite out of the question. This narrowed things down to the Lake. From Moba, the port of Baudouinville, to Albertville is a distance of 100 miles. I decided to make a personal recce of Moba as soon as I could.

It appeared after my talk with Cochaux that the prospect of equipping one thousand men from 4 Group arsenal was negligible and he advised me to drop the idea in favour of one hundred sets of everything for my raiding party. This, he thought, stood some chance. We went back to Bobozo who was in a poor mood. Definitely not, was his decisive answer. Nothing was going to leave Camp Massart in the direction of Kamina and that was final. If Leo could think up these schemes, Leo could provide. I decided on a long shot. Mr. Tshombe had told me to use his name to support any reasonable scheme of mine. I did so now, telling the General firmly that I would have to signal Mr. Tshombe at once. I felt like Wingate bearding the generals in G.H.Q. Delhi and threatening them with his hot line to Mr. Churchill. It worked. Grudgingly, and after tedious argument, I was authorised to draw one hundred sets of everything from Camp Massart. He promised to do everything he could for the balance of the force which would arrive shortly.

I went down to the Post Office still bullet scarred from the events of 1961—and sent off a signal to Alastair and O'Malley asking them to let me have without fail on the first draft one hundred men ready for combat in the course of the next few days.

The difficulties of keeping in touch with Salisbury, Johannesburg and Leopoldville without any form of personal wireless communication were insuperable. I decided to seek the aid of a friend of mine in Elizabethville who ran an establishment adjoining the Post Office known as The Kleen Shop. I rapped on the counter. A large moustache came round the corner of an inner sanctum, followed by a large nose, a booming voice and a hearty manner. It was the irrepressible Latz sparking on all cylinders and not looking an hour older since I last saw him in the dark days of the Katanga mêlée.

In a few moments we had arranged that he would transmit and receive all messages for the south and relay them to me at Kamina via the Belgian Consulate transmitter and by so doing solved my biggest problem in one stroke. It was the start of a long and pleasant association during which Latz, much misunderstood at times, did his best for 5 Commando, frequently without reward or recognition. His dual occupation as a reporter for Associated Press was not always easy to reconcile with his duties as Liaison Officer 5 Commando, which he later became, but he managed it to everybody's satisfaction.

I returned to Kamina and put the idea of a waterborne attack on Albertville to Blume. We had the same mind on tactics—carry the battle to the enemy if you feel superior. Personal reconnaissance was essential and he arranged a plane to take me to Kamipini the following day. Kamipini is the closest strip to Moba and is situated on a ranch owned by Monsieur Demagh, to whom Blume gave me an introduction. As I was still without uniform, Blume offered to lend me his barathea Service Dress, less its badges, and it fitted beautifully. Unfortunately it gave rise to Walter Mitty illusions in my mind and I thought it wiser to decline it with thanks.

Kamipini is a narrow grass strip on which a C-47 can land with some difficulty. At either end a steep ravine makes careless landings unprofitable. The Belgian crew who were greatly experienced put me down without any difficulty, introduced me to Mr. Demagh and confirmed our rendezvous for the next day. Mr. Demagh, a thickset, red-haired, jovial type, is typical of the hard-headed, no nonsense, Belgian farmers one meets in the Congo; they are the men who make the wheels go round and the sort that does not disappear at the first sign of trouble. Unfortunately there are not enough Demaghs. He had a son, aged eighteen, like unto him and between them they ran the farm and kept everything in the area in touch with reality.

Demagh outlined the rebel position. They had only just been ousted from Baudouinville and gangs of them were still roaming the country terrorising the civilians, destroying missions and hospitals. The main body of resistance was at Lusaka half-way to Kapona. He offered to drive me to Moba, but warned me that there was nothing there, no boats, no Europeans, nothing, just a shell of a place, burnt out and looted.

I decided to go, nevertheless, and called at the Mission in Baudouinville on the way to get first-hand information from the front. Two priests were the only occupants. One was hobbling around on crutches and Demagh informed me that he had recently been hamstrung by one of his own ex-pupils, a rebel aged fourteen. A slash from a panga behind the knees had done it. The priest apparently bore no ill feeling towards his attacker and accepted it all with a philosophical air, tinged with melancholy. The other priest was a mine of information about Albertville and he sat down to give me chapter and verse. He knew that there were only a handful of rebels there and they were badly armed. *Jeunesse* mostly, he said. One forward lad, aged twelve, had been given the rank of Sergeant-Major as a reward for his outstanding brutality. In addition to this he had terrorised the entire civilian population and had chalked up a number of rapings to his discredit. (In the Congo puberty arrives much earlier than in Europe.) I made a note that I would like to meet Sergeant-Major Rapist, aged twelve. Perhaps a small operation might cure him of his extravagant behaviour.

The priests and Demagh were able to give me first-hand information about the uprising. There was no doubt in their minds that the civilian population were not behind it. They were suffering at the hands of the *jeunesse* who, for the most part, were strangers to the district, the bulk of whom had come from the Maniema, in particular from Kindu. A number of local opportunists had jumped on the band wagon when the rebels succeeded in taking Albertville, but like most of the ordinary civilians they would side with whatever force was in power; anything for a quiet life. But this rebellion differed from the tribal disputes of recent years inasmuch as courts had been set up in Albertville which condemned dozens of people to death daily for petty crimes—failure to carry a M.N.C. Lumumba card, failure to agree with the new régime.To be well dressed or to be able to read and write were an invitation to attend the daily tribunal. Daily executions took place in the main street, the Avenue Storms, when the victims were stood against the bricked-up windows of the mission church to face a firing squad. Their bodies were carted away unceremoniously in wheelbarrows to be dumped in the fast-flowing Lukuga. The bullet-pocked walls are there to this day, a grim reminder of senseless tyranny.

We motored down the steep escarpment to Moba and found it all exactly as Demagh had said. No boats, no people, just meaningless destruction.

Back once more in Leopoldville I took my plan straight to the General. Without hesitation he approved it and gave orders for the maximum co-operation to be given to me in its execution.

I called on Colonel Logeiste, the head of the Belgian Technical Assistance in the Congo. Guy Logeiste had served most of his career with the Force Publique and had just spent two years as Resident in Ruanda, representing the Belgian Government. He was greatly respected as an able administrator and as one who knew the Congo and its problems. He promised to do everything in his power, which was considerable, to get me all the equipment I needed and he was as good as his word. Only on the question of boats were we stumped and if it had not been for a chance conversation I might never have known that sixteen glass-fibre assault boats and engines had recently arrived at the Army stores. I mentioned this to Colonel Logeiste and the last problem was solved.

I visited Mr. Tshombe at his home at Binza to give him a brief interim report on how things were going. I was alarmed at the lack of normal security precautions at his home, which was exactly opposite Brazzaville and he promised to do something about it.

I asked him if he knew that the world was saying he had committed political suicide by hiring us to assist the A.N.C. He replied:

"My dear Major, I am here in the heart of the Congo, a Congolese, and I see the problem one thousand times clearer than all my African critics think they see it. I am confident that the course of history will show that I am right. If, in doing what I consider to be in the best interests of the Congo and the Congolese people, I write finis to my political career, I still say posterity will vindicate my actions."

It was a tense moment and the light of his conviction and sincerity shone out of his eyes. He had taken the big decision and from that moment never wavered or faltered until its successful conclusion.

I waited impatiently on the tarmac at Kamina for the two D.C.-4s which would bring the first hundred men from Johannesburg. The first one arrived, its red tailplane glistening in the sun. Thirty-eight men disembarked. There was no second plane.

Disheartened I began to wonder if the raid was worth while with such a small force and decided that if only from a morale building point of view and for its effect on the A.N.C. it was still a proposition.

I paraded the draft and gave them a talk in which I said that I needed men for immediate action and that anybody that did not feel able to take part in it must say so then. Nine men withdrew straight away on the grounds that they had not signed a contract and they did not wish to take the risk of being killed or wounded without it. It came as a bit of a shock to many of them that this was a shooting war where a man could get himself killed. It all looked so different in Johannesburg.

I gave them half an hour's drill myself. I reckon on being able to spot a soldier after ten minutes' drill quicker than in any other way. It was a chastening experience. The twenty-nine were mostly foreigners and some could hardly speak English, but about a dozen stood out as old soldiers. Of these I selected four, three to be officers and one as an N.C.O. I had an eye to the future and this operation would be invaluable as training for what was to come. The lieutenants were Kirton, Bridge and Mueller, and the sergeant a hard case Scot named Grant.

Pat Kirton was a handsome young South African, the very picture of a soldier, who had been through the Military Academy at Pretoria. He was a natural leader, it turned out, but wanting something in severity. He took most of the English-speaking under his wing.

Eric Bridge had recently been in the Royal Marine Commando and I was in no doubt of his ability to lead a small group in a raid. He had a slight stutter and a mild manner, both of which evaporated in the face of action. He carried a light air of authority with him and I was happy to have a man with his experience.

Siegfried Mueller was forty-two and as Prussian as a *Pickelhaube*. He had a marked guttural accent and had been a Sergeant in the Wehrmacht during the last war. His Iron Cross impressed me and the others. His gentle voice and temperate manner were rather at variance with what the Iron Cross stood for, but I hoped for the best. His outlook was mature and balanced. I noticed that he had brought a typewriter with him, to my mind a sign of some experience in soldiering—a typewriter and a radio are as essential to the commander of to-day as a pistol. He took over most of the foreigners in the group and began by asking permission to wear his Iron Cross. This I gave readily, and I don't think I ever saw him again but it was pinned to his breast. Rumour had it that he had another for his pyjamas, but I cannot vouch for it.

Grant I remembered from his service in Katanga. He had been an N.C.O. in the Black Watch, which was sufficient military recommendation for me, and had the Military Medal. He was a hard man with an inbred love of fighting for itself, a cause was superfluous. He warmed to the idea of immediate action. He believed that discipline could be best maintained by the use of his fists and demonstrated the theory with some effect. Despite his tough exterior, he was completely devoted to his mother, a fine woman of whom he often spoke and who had attended to his Calvinistic upbringing with a firm hand. I made a mental note that what the world could do with was more Mrs. Grants.

I briefed the men on the operation and issued their uniforms, equipment and arms. Bobozo had sent us the SETME F.N. rifle— the Spanish equivalent of the Belgian weapon—and we spent some time familiarising ourselves with it. The civilians became soldiers—in appearance anyway. The rest of the equipment was checked over. Assault boats were readied, outboards unpacked and cleaned, and drums of petrol mixed with oil to the right proportions.

If the men were short on training they were long on spirit and every one of them looked forward with enthusiasm to the adventure of action. War and adventure, however, are not always the same thing, and this sad fact we came to discover for ourselves in the course of the next few days.

I finalised my general plan with Blume. It was simple enough. Fly down to Kamipini in three flights the next day, motor to Moba, and set sail for Albertville under cover of darkness. Two and a half days later we would attack the airfield which lay by the water's edge. Once this was captured, Blume would fly in reinforcements and we would rescue the white hostages in the Albertville gaol. Meanwhile we hoped the A.N.C. columns would be striking Albertville from the west and the south simultaneously. It was a reasonable plan in the light of our information. I was convinced then, as I was to be in every action we ever fought in the Congo, bar one, that the enemy were greatly overrated, and I was certain that they would run at the sight of a well-armed and determined group of white men.

That night we worked late making final checks on our arms and ammunition. The only item of equipment which had failed to arrive in time were the wireless sets. This in itself was practically a fatal blow, but notwithstanding I gave the order for the first flight to take-off for Kamipini at dawn the next day.

"By the way," said Major Blume as we parted for the night, "what are you calling the operation?"

I thought for a moment. The piece of jewellery much worn by Victorian gentlemen and graced by the Prince Consort's name leapt to my mind.

"Operation Watch-chain," I replied.

# 3

## OPERATION WATCH-CHAIN

The advance party took off at dawn. Lieutenant Bridge was to get down to Moba as soon as possible and keep the men and the equipment under cover until the whole part assembled later in the day. Secrecy was essential. As soon as it was dark we would load the boats, test the engines, and set sail for Albertville one hundred miles up the lake.

The lake is of fresh water, four hundred miles long and fifty miles wide at its widest point. In places it is over three thousand feet deep. By day it is fanned by a steady north-east wind, but storms over the lake can raise enormous seas and a few years ago one of the lake steamers capsized and sank. By night the lake is normally mirror calm and remains so until about nine in the morning when there is a slight off-shore wind.

When I arrived at Moba late that night the lake was on its best behaviour, calm as a millpond, reflecting a three-quarter moon. I hurried along the sandy street down to the small beach, anxious to get cracking before too much of the night was lost. It was almost midnight. The men rose to their feet and gathered around their section leaders. The atmosphere was tense and I sensed that something was wrong.

"They don't want to go, sir," said Lieutenant Kirton, flatly.

"Why not?" I flashed.

"It's that Belgian. He's been filling the men with stories of the lake and how rough it gets. He reckons we will all drown."

"Have you tried out the boats?"

"No, sir. In any case there are only three left. One was badly damaged on the way down here."

I examined the damaged boat. Someone had deliberately put a

hole in its bottom, and I assumed it was all part of a plan to frustrate the raid. Obviously the trouble-maker was behind it all so I determined to deal with him at once. He walked over to me, hands in pockets, avoiding my gaze which spoke volumes of fury. He stated his case in a surly manner, but the substance of it was that he knew the lake very well, he had lived in Katanga all his life, and he could assure me that as soon as the wind got up we would all drown, he was certain of it. He had no intention of getting into any boat that night and that was that. He shrugged his shoulders and folded his arms, saying, "You go if you want to, but I'm staying here." He cooked his goose by adding, "And most of the men will stay with me."

I imagine there comes a moment like this in every commander's life when his authority is challenged and everything stands or falls on his instant reaction. In a flash I whipped out my heavy Browning 9 mm. pistol and clouted him on the side of the head. He collapsed like a pricked balloon. There was no fight in him, no guts either.

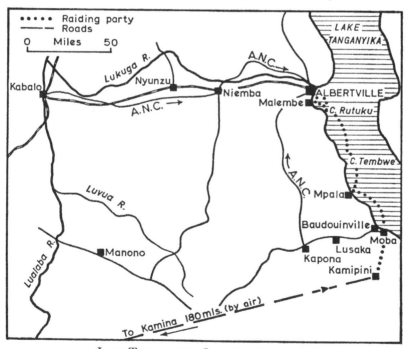

2. LAKE TANGANYIKA: Operation Watch-Chain

D

It was all over in a second, but it was a watershed in my life. The leadership of mercenary troops by force of personality alone demands a hardness of character and a conviction in one's own invicibility which I did not possess. I was obliged to assume those qualities then and there. It was a case-hardening I did not regret; without it I could never have done my duty or lived through the horrors which were to be my lot.

I spoke to the men.

"Now listen to me," I said. It was the first mutiny I had ever handled, but it was not to be the last.

"We are going to raid Albertville from the lake in support of two A.N.C. columns and I am going to lead you. Anybody who refuses to go can take three paces forward."

Nobody moved.

I detached six of the weak-kneed who had no stomach for the fight and divided the rest of the party into three boats which were then loaded up and tested. Bernard Kohlert, a young German mechanic tinkered with the outboards and got them running smoothly, while I checked the boat-loads. Only the flares were missing, lost inexplicably on the way down.

We pushed off at 00.30 hours.

We kept one hundred yards apart in line ahead right through the night. The steady progress gave the men confidence and at five in the morning we found a suitable landing place to lie up for the day.

About midday our look-out sighted a small motor boat speeding towards us. Everybody stood-to. As it drew nearer we could see a white man in the bows holding up aloft a large wooden cross, his white robes flowing in the breeze. The men lowered their rifles and some waded into the surf to steady the prow of the boat as the priest came ashore.

He was from the Mpala Mission which lay just north of us. He had received a radio message in Flemish over the Albertville C.F.L. net an hour ago telling him that Soumiallot had issued an order to kill the sixty white priests in the Gaol within the next forty-eight hours. He had reported it to Elizabethville and they had asked him to intercept us with instructions to abandon our original plan and go straight to the Gaol. "Forget the airfield, Major," he begged me earnestly, "For pity's sake, we must hurry."

It put me in an awkward position. I hated changing my plan at this late stage, particularly as I had a rendezvous with Major Blume on the airfield in two days' time. If I changed my plan now and went instead for the gaol, I would miss Blume and my only means of communication with Kamina Base would be lost. On the other hand I could hardly ignore the priest's message.

Much against my better judgement I decided to forget the aerodrome plan and to make an all-out effort to save the priests.

The second night went badly for us and two hours before dawn we were limping along with one good outboard still running, two out of order and everybody paddling. Just as dawn broke we made for the beach and grounded the boats around the corner of a headland in the cover of some clumps of mangrove. We did not know it then, but we had landed on Cape Rutuku, fifteen miles south-west of Albertville. It was deathly quiet and nothing could be heard but the surge of the surf on the beach and the call of a sand-piper. The men were exhausted and flopped out on the ground whilst Eric and I made a reconnaissance. We could just make out Albertville in the distance, glinting in the first rays of the morning sun.

On my return to the boats our sentry, who had been standing "properly at ease", sprang to attention and presented arms—the formal salute for a Field Officer. "Great Grief", I thought, "now I've seen everything." I gave him the rough edge of my tongue.

"Where the hell do you think you are?" I asked, "Buckingham Palace? Take cover, you idiot, and use your eyes and your ears. Lie in that bush there where you can see without being seen."

It was a nice time to be teaching elementary soldiering.

I gave out the plan with a bit of a pep talk. Confidence was at a low ebb, the men were tired after two rough nights and very few of them were fit. I explained the tactical position and that in my view we had nothing to worry about, twenty-two F.N.s had a fire power nothing in Albertville could stand against. The men had plenty of courage and we set out to march the twenty kilometres with great determination.

Siegfried led with two scouts well forward and orders to inspan as many civilians as he could to carry our heavy baggage. At nine I called a halt and went down the column to see how the men were faring. One man lay on the ground sobbing his heart out. I prodded him with a bayonet.

"What the devil's the matter with you?" I demanded. Sympathy at a time like this, even if warranted, is fatal.

"Please, sir, let me go back. I should never have come. I had a row . . . with my fiancée . . . ."

"Too late to think about that now," I told him curtly. "Fall in with the others."

He worked himself into hysterics.

"You're mad, Major, you're mad. We're all going to be killed. I know we are," he screamed, terror-stricken, until Grant put a fist in his mouth. Blood trickled down his chin as he fell in.

We arrived at a lakeside village called Malembe at noon and as the men were beaten I called a halt for a swim and a rest. We were all sleeping soundly in the shade of a mango tree by the water's edge when a knot of villagers ran up with panic in their faces to warn me that the Simbas were upon us. We scrambled into our equipment and stood-to. Through my glasses I could see a group of rebels making their way down the hill which overlooked Malembe, about seven hundred yards away. There was something odd about the way they were walking, swaying from side to side as though staggering under an unseen weight.

I gave out my orders.

"Mueller, get back on the track and stop them outflanking us. Eric, take a section along the beach and spread out. Remainder stay here with me."

Then they were on us. They broke into three groups, dodging from hut to hut, until they appeared again in the open less than a hundred yards away. Single shots sizzled into the tree above.

I could see now they were all hopped up and mad with *dawa*. "*Mai* Mulele, *Mai* Mulele," they screamed with blood-curdling yells, firing their Mausers and brandishing their pangas and long knives. "*Mai* Mulele," they screamed louder as they came for us.

"This is it, boys," I shouted, "Wait for it, wait for it."

I raised my F.N. rifle and fired the first shot of the battle. All hell was let loose as my men poured out a fantastic volume of fire, most of it inaccurate, so that the enemy came on with every appearance of being immune from the bullets. Where a rebel was hit he advanced regardless, eyes staring, and in some cases hands held out before him. One or two stopped in their tracks to "throw their eyes" on us.

A Hollander named Van der Hoek, a seasoned hand, picked them off one by one, and in less than fifteen minutes it was all over.

Three of the rebels were flying for their lives up the hill and the rest, twenty-eight in all, lay dead in the sand.

Bridge and I examined them. They were *Jeunesse* all right, most of them between sixteen and twenty. I wondered if the Sergeant-Major was among them. They wore scraps of uniform and monkey-skin caps and feathers, which made them look grotesque in death. Apart from a few Mausers, they were pitifully armed with home-made weapons.

One of the *Jeunesse* was a pale-skinned mulatto and another wore the badges of rank of a Commandant and had 30,000 francs in his blood-soaked wallet. Bridge turned another over who was still alive, just, but horribly wounded.

"*Mai . . . Mai* Mulele . . . *Mai . . . Mai*", he gasped. His eyes had the hurt look of a wounded buck. A merciful bullet put him out of his agony.

In a corner of the battlefield Claude Chanu, a massive Frenchman, was still battling it out with a rebel in the long grass. Another burst and the rebel rolled out on to the path with half his head blown off.

It was the first time I had seen the damage caused by an F.N. bullet. A wound from an F.N. usually spelt death, particularly if the bullet hit a bone in the body. Many of the wounded bled very little, and Eric said he had seen this before in Kenya during the Mau Mau business. The dope tended to congeal the blood and stop its flow.

The village headman asked for permission to dispose of the bodies, and with a whoop of joy several hundred villagers, women and children included, raced across the sand to loot the clothing and pitiful belongings of the dead rebels. It was a barbaric sight and a nauseating show of revenge. The headman told us that since the arrival of the "Popular Army" no-one was safe. Several of his people had been killed for no reason other than that they could read and write and the village had been forced to feed the rebels and to give them blankets and clothing. He hoped we were going to stay in Albertville, he added wistfully.

I asked him to point out the road to Albertville. It went inland at this point and was over thirty kilometres long. A shorter track went along the foot of the cliffs, but he strongly advised against that one. The rebels used it as a stronghold.

It was three in the afternoon and too late for any further marching.

I impounded two large fishing boats with guides and decided to attack Albertville from the water.


It was a pitch black night.

At seven we cast off the tow lines from our one good outboard and guided by the black fishing boats, paddled in towards shore without a sound. I was convinced we would be able to land unobserved, then could make our way up to the church and round the back of it to the Gaol and free the priests.

Thirty yards from the beach a red light flashed from the hill in front of us. It was a recognition signal, but we ignored it and drew closer in. Pat Kirton's boat grounded, and a second later pandemonium broke out. Two machine guns opened up on either side of us yellow tongues of flame stabbing the night. Mausers joined in up the hill.

"Don't fire, don't fire," I cautioned my boat, "it will only give our position away," but it was too late. Somebody in Kirton's boat opened up an automatic and the enemy got our range. Bullets whistled all around us as we lay flat in the bottom of our boat, scared to death.

"Back, boys, back!" I shouted. "We're in the ——."

We pulled off the beach unhurt. It was a miracle no-one was hit.

Five minutes later a bright moon came up, silhouetting us for all the world to see. There was nothing for it but to try again somewhere else. The coastline is seven miles long at Albertville and I was damn sure they could not be holding it all.

I looked around for the guides in the fishing boats. They had vanished; so that put an end to that.

We had withdrawn in the night and now held an impregnable stronghold on the beach south of Malembe. We were dug in on the perimeter with alternative positions in depth, and could have staved off the Brigade of Guards. We knew at once that we had a superb defensive position—we began to wish the enemy would attack!

The Albertville Aerodrome was thirty kilometres across the bay and during the morning we saw Major Blume make three low circuits in a C-47 looking for us. It was a daring feat and needed courage. Later he told me that three bullets had entered his cockpit just missing the co-pilot. If only we had not lost our flares we could have signalled to him, but there went our last contact with Base.

Fires were doused after the evening meal and orders given for the night. Any movement outside the perimeter is enemy movement. Fire when you see a target. Don't give your position away unnecessarily.

At three in the morning I jumped up to the sound of a burst of F.N. fire followed by screams of pain.

"Mr. Kirton's compliments, sir, trouble on his sector."

I ran back with the runner to Pat's position. On the water's edge, back lit by the moon, I could see a dug-out canoe piled high with bundles of clothing. Three figures lay half in and half out of the water. A small boy and a girl lay dead in their own blood, monstrous wounds in their chests, their mother alongside them, her intestines bulging out on to the sand.

"Get Evans, quick," I ordered Pat. Evans was our medic, a good lad, greatly experienced. He ran up with his bag and gave the woman a shot of morphine, but there was nothing he could do except ease her death. She died a few minutes later.

"Who fired?" I asked.

"I did, sir." A man stepped forward. "I saw the canoe land in the dark and I thought we were about to be attacked. Your orders were . . ."

I stopped him. It was not his fault. If there must be blame then it was mine. I realised I would have to live with that knowledge for the rest of my life.

Although I knew that our very presence was a thorn in the side of the enemy who would not know where we might strike next, I felt that the role was too passive for us and decided to do something more constructive to help the two A.N.C. columns now converging on the town.

My immediate need was supply to enable us to move more freely, and I sent Kirton back to the Mission at Mpala to radio to Blume at Kamina for an air-drop of essential items. After the drop we would motor across the bay to attack the airfield and hold it until Kakuji and Bangala entered the town lower down.

Two days passed and still there was no sign of the air-drop. Half-way to Mpala Kirton's engine had broken down and he had decided to march. As he approached the mangrove-covered beach a small aircraft flew low over him and dropped a message. It was John Latz who had been wondering how we were doing and had chartered an aircraft in Elizabethville to see for himself. Unfortunately, seeing Kirton and his men apparently in difficulty in the swamps, he jumped to the conclusion that the whole group were bogged down in the mangrove and had lost their way. On his return to Elizabethville he informed the Press accordingly. The story was embroidered further by others, that we had used paraffin in our engines instead of petrol—the French for paraffin being "petrol".

These erroneous stories were to do the unit generally and me personally an incredible amount of harm in Leopoldville as I shall recount shortly.

On the third day I decided to strike at the airfield, petrol or no petrol, even if we had to paddle the whole way across the bay. The skippers of the fishing boats told me there would be no trouble landing anywhere on a frontage of two thousand yards, all of which ran parallel with the aerodrome.

I estimated it would take twelve hours solid paddling to get there, so we left our stronghold at three in the afternoon, two fishing boats forward and two assault boats following. It was heavy going, but at two in the morning we were almost opposite the yellow lights of the Filtisaf factory. Another hour and we were standing off the beach behind which we should find the aerodrome. It was deadly still as the four boats gathered for final orders. Eric went in to make a recce of the beach with one fishing boat. It needed guts and everybody admired his quiet courage, as he pushed off alone for the beach. Ten minutes later he signalled back with a torch— O.K. to land.

Eric and I doubled across the sand on to a concrete road. Some telephone wires went north through the bush and I felt certain they would lead to the Control Tower. Grant and I set off with a small recce party to follow them up, our boots ringing on the concrete road. It ended in a cluster of houses but no tower. We crept forward silently to examine them closely. Incredible as it seemed, this was the aerodrome—and it was deserted! Piles of petrol drums were strewn over the runway and there was a big dump of them to one side. A control tower just did not exist for some reason. Grant and I hurried back to the main party with the good news.

I was forming the intention of occupying the airfield until Mueller mentioned to me that a recce party he had sent down the road reported a house with a bright light in it and the sound of voices. We set off to investigate.

Mueller stood in the dense bush on the path leading to the house with his men under a large mango tree. Eric went forward alone to investigate the noise and the light. The main party stayed with me at the entrance and covered the road. As Bridge reached the door a sentry challenged him. He answered in Swahili, but it was too late. The sentry fired a shot and someone flung a spear striking Eric in the face. The shot alerted the Simbas inside the building, who now began to scream "*Mai* Mulele, *Mai* Mulele" in panic-stricken voices. It was an unnerving animal sound, over and over again. At the same time men began to pour out of the building on all sides. Shooting began and Bridge was wounded, whilst for a few seconds thousands of rounds were fired on both sides.

"I've had it, sir," said Bridge, as I laid him on the ground and stripped off his shirt. There was so much blood on him that I could not find the wound in the dark. Although he was clutching his stomach the wound was actually just above his elbow where his main artery had been severed, and blood was also gushing from a hole in his face. We got a tourniquet on to him quickly and two men helped him back to the boats.

Meanwhile the enemy had withdrawn into the house, as Mueller crawled over to my position with the bad news. "I've got two killed," he said, "Nestler and Kohlert."

We were a mile from the boats.

"Siegfried," I ordered, "take a party back to bring up the boats. We'll hold them off here until you arrive when we can evacuate the dead."

He went off leaving me with five men. We fired on the enemy intermittently, changing our positions immediately, half guessing that the enemy were regrouping for a counter-attack. Later I found it was the Filtisaf clinic which the rebels were using that night, having evacuated the Albertville aerodrome. The men inside were the airfield garrison. A few minutes later the full fury of their counter-attack began with mad shouts and screams to give themselves courage. I was forced to withdraw down the road. Covering the retreat myself we made the beach just as a mad horde of rebels chanting "*Mai* Mulele, *Mai* Mulele," rushed upon us. I emptied my F.N. magazine into the dense mob and dashed for the beach. One of my men opened fire on me but missed.

We pushed off the beach pursued by desultory fire just as the first rays of light were showing across the lake. Grant and seven men were in my boat, Mueller had Bridge and the balance with him. At nine that morning I could see that we were in for a rough passage. Already the wind was strong and soon the surface of the lake was whipped up into advancing white horses, which threatened to capsize us. We tacked across the direction of the waves which were about three feet high and sufficient to sink us if we broached-to. The glass-fibre assault boat is merely a shell and has no built-in flotation, so we bailed for life and paddled on orders, first one side, then the other to keep afloat.

It was a grim and frightening day and at the end of it we arrived north of Malembe utterly fatigued, mentally exhausted and thoroughly demoralised. At eleven that night Grant and I were the only two still paddling. We nosed the boat into the doubtful cover of some mangrove, posted a sentry (who promptly fell asleep) and slept soundly.

Meanwhile the other boat was skippered by Claude Chanu, an experienced sailor, and those in the boat owed their lives to his superb seamanship and tremendous strength. Lieutenant Bridge was propped up in the bows of the boat, deadly white from loss of blood, his tourniquet being eased from time to time. It was touch and go whether he would last the day as he had lost so much blood, but he was made of stern stuff and he survived. The spear may have been poisoned for it paralysed his left side for months to come.

Early next morning I ordered the withdrawal to Mpala and we made the long journey in two days paddling once more all the way. After dark on the evening of the second day a guide in a canoe led us up the estuary to the Catholic mission, yelling all the time to the Katangese troops on the north back not to shoot, that we were friends.

On the stroke of midnight we banged loudly on the massive doors of the mission. The noise echoed through the ancient building, and after some time an old priest, wiping the sleep from his eyes. showed us to some beds by the light of a candle.

It was the oldest mission in the Congo, said the aged priest, and had been built by Captain Storms in 1875. He showed us round with pride, pointing out the high red brick wall which encircled the whole mission and had embrasures let into the top of it for use against the Arab slavers of old. The church itself was within the wall and had often been used as sanctuary in its chequered history. I went in alone. The cold stone floors, well worn benches and primitive paintings bore silent witness to the generations of worshippers it had known. It was indeed a sanctuary. I knelt to give thanks to God for delivering us out of the last few days of hell. The anguish of the battle, bloodshed and death dissolved in the holy calm of the church.

Father van Loco, the old priest in charge of the mission was standing in in the doorway watching me. His long life had been spent in the devoted service of his Order and serenity shone in the goodness of his face.

"You are troubled, my son?" he asked.

"No more, Father," I replied.

Albertville fell to Kakuji the next day and I flew in there on my way back to Kamina, which I was now anxious to reach as soon as possible.

General Bobozo, all smiles, arrived at almost the same time and we had a long talk. The contrast in our appearance was startling—he in his resplendent uniform, marred only by outrageous hockey boots, and me in the blood-stained uniform of an A.N.C. private, which had not left my back for ten days.

The conscientious Belgian Vice-Consul, Monsier Guillot, was there, attending to his nationals, hundreds of whom were being evacuated. I asked him about the fate of the priests. Most of them had been saved, but many had been killed by the Simbas in a last orgy of blood lust before they abandoned the town. I apologised for my failure.

A few hours later a F.A.T.A.C. plane took me to Kamina. My real task was now about to begin.

# 4

## THEIR MERCENARY CALLING

The lessons of the Albertville raid weighed heavily on my mind. There was a great gulf fixed between the standard of training required for fighting in the Congo and the standard of my recruits, if the first draft was a fair example. Not that there was a whit wrong with their spirit. This had been magnificent, but it had been an error to try them so highly so soon. I reproached myself bitterly for the loss of Nestler and Kohlert and I determined to wring every advantage I could from the operation for the benefit of those to come. At the top of the list in letters large and bold stood the one word—training. The Commander-in-Chief was firmly convinced that the men we were bringing to the Congo were fully trained soldiers and ready for combat. For my part, I was equally convinced that no man henceforth would see battle until he had received a thorough basic training. The decision coloured all my plans for the future.

The Kamina Base, or Bas Kamina, or B.A.K.A., as it is generally known was a military marvel set in the heart of Africa. It had been erected at a fantastic cost by the Belgians with the understanding that a large proportion of the expense would be borne by the N.A.T.O. alliance, for whom it would provide a strategic base. Its paved runways were capable of taking the heaviest planes and long enough even for Boeing Jet air-liners. Its housing complex was built to maintain a garrison of roughly two divisions—say 30,000 soldiers, and included a complete air training school and the usual complement of cinemas, post offices, swimming baths, married quarters and so on. In brief, it was a garrison town built deep in the African bush.

If the men of my force now gathering at Kamina Base had any

illusions as to its grandeur, these were to be rudely shattered. The skeleton existed, but the flesh had been eaten away during the four years of Independence. Congolese troops and civilians had overrun its previous magnificence and every house and establishment was in a state of utter disrepair. There was no water; the pump house had long since ceased to function. There was no electricity, no bulbs and no wiring. This had been torn down and looted. There was no plumbing. Excreta littered the floors of nearly every dwelling. The whole place was a hideous monument to neglect and a sizeable threat to the health of the men about to arrive.

On my arrival at Kamina I found that Lieutenant Mackintosh had worked miracles of improvisation. Latrines had been dug in the grounds, water was stored in assault boats, and cooking was carried out over an open wood fire near the men's mess, which was just a bare hall, innocent of tables or chairs. Every man had a blanket and some had camp beds, but that was the full extent of the provision made for the influx of one thousand men.

Mackintosh informed me that the men were on the point of mutiny at the outrageous conditions and that our strength was then just over five hundred with more on the way. I ordered an immediate parade on the football field outside the "College" and prepared to address the men. A large figure approached me and introduced himself as my Regimental Sergeant-Major, Jack Carton-Barber. His manner was in the best tradition of British Army R.S.M.s and with his six-foot-six and 230 pounds' build certainly looked the part.

I watched from a window as the men "got fell in" and a glimmer of hope surged through me as I noticed a dozen or more competent N.C.O.s chivvying the men into position. I made the men call out their names as I came to them, a trick which I learnt many years ago and which helps me to fix name and face in my memory. Here and there was a familiar face from Katanga '61, but on the whole they were a very mixed bag. There were nineteen different nationalities represented but the bulk of the men were South Africans and Rhodesians.

I gathered them around me in a half circle and "put them in the picture". I explained the political position and what we were called in to do. I told them that apart from putting down the rebellion, they had an opportunity to change the face of the Congo and to alter

the course of history; that it was a great and worth-while task that
confronted us. At the same time, I pointed out, we were helping
to keep at bay the very real threat of communist infiltration into
the Congo, and that, in doing this, those of them that were
South Africans and Rhodesians were helping to protect their own
homes.

I then explained how I intended to organise the unit into commandos of forty men with two officers to a unit, with three sergeants
in each, and bade them be of good cheer that the rough conditions
of the moment were only temporary and things would improve.
Those that did not think they could take it could go home. I said
that the Congo would soon separate the men from the boys.

"What about our pay?" shouted one from the back. "And our
contracts?" shouted another. I explained the basis of our contract
with Tshombe and my belief that all this was being worked out in
Leo and that if it was not forthcoming soon, I would make a special
trip to see what was happening. I assured them that we would not
fight unless we were paid—"No ticket, no laundry," was my exact
expression which raised a laugh. I did not tell them that I was as
much in the dark as they were about the arming and equipping of
the force, but I resolved to get to Leo just as soon as I could to
sort things out at the highest level. I signalled Alastair that evening
to cease recruiting and to report to Kamina forthwith and to hold
up any further drafts at Johannesburg until the dust had settled.

I interviewed all the aspirant officers and N.C.O.s and selected
about twenty Sergeants who would have the rank equivalent to
"adjudant" in the A.N.C. Adjudant, or *sous-officier*, is a nebulous
rank to my way of thinking, and I decided that the back-bone of the
unit would be made up of sergeants, British Army style.

At the end of the evening I found that, apart from young Wilson,
who was a Sandhurst man, and Jeremy Spencer, an ex-Coldstream
Guardsman, I found not one man suitable for appointment as an
officer. I realised that I was setting my sights too high and tried
again. This time I came up with about six.

Spencer was a tall, gangly young Englishman, very much my
idea of officer material, and within weeks he was to prove himself
to be a magnificent leader, loved by his men whom he led with a
grip of iron tempered with great understanding. Gary Wilson was
a godsend in the circumstances and I separated a command of forty
men for him at once and called them 51 Commando. He set to

enthusiastically to make up a unit with two Sergeants, Parkinson from Lancashire, and Wepener from Rhodesia, both hard nuts who would brook no nonsense.

Organisation of the camp was priority for me and I turned my attention at once to the Men's Mess. A volunteer named Darby de Jaeger, a man of about fifty, was coping with the feeding of five hundred men three times a day on an open wood fire, assisted by a small fatigue party and a dozen Congolese labourers, with a minimum of fuss and maximum of difficulty. I was lost in admiration.

"That's nothing," he said, "I used to feed 25,000 men in the Med during the war and had 150 cooks under me!" I was sure it was well within his ability and I made him a sergeant on the spot and a sergeant-major a few days later.

"By the way, sir," he said, "there are no official rations being issued and I have been buying the stuff on credit in Kaminaville, using your name. Is that O.K.?"

"Certainly," I agreed, "how much am I in for now?"

"Only eleven million francs," he laughed. I laughed too, but not quite so heartily.

The general situation was chaotic and after receiving no response from Leo to my signals, I decided to go there to sort it out for myself and render my report on the Albertville action. Before going I organised the main departments and felt greatly relieved when Alastair arrived and took over the administration, such as it was.

Army Headquarters in Leopoldville is situated four miles from the centre of the town on a prominent hill overlooking the Congo river and exactly opposite Brazzaville. The building has five stories and the lift has not worked for years. The people I wanted always seemed to be on the fourth and fifth floors.

Colonel Logeiste, who I was now regarding as an old friend, introduced me to the main personalities in the Belgian Technical Assistance, who were Colonel Bouzin of the Belgian Air Force and Colonel Marlier of the Army. Bouzin was a dapper forty-five, the complete staff officer with every fact at his elegant fingertips. He was extremely helpful, but our paths crossed seldom, except on those occasions when I was begging a lift around the Congo. Colonel Marlier was my idea of a fighting man and spent most of his time actively encouraging the A.N.C. to fight and, as a result, was

in the field more than in his office. I was sorry when he left the
Congo a few weeks later at the end of his term; he was a man one
could talk to.

I sought audience with the General urgently to attend to the
problems arising out of the contracts, or lack of them, and the pay.
I was brushed aside and told to see Colonel Vanderwalle. I regis-
tered astonishment. Who was he? Who, indeed!

During my absence fighting the good fight I had been decisively
outflanked. Gone were the promises of absolute autonomy, gone
were the assurances of an independent command, gone was the
"Mobutu plan" to conquer the enemy. In their place was the
Colonel Vanderwalle, a veritable "eminence grise". Not for nothing
had he been called the Richelieu of Katanga. The Colonel was a
Spaak man and had been military adviser to the Belgian Consulate
in Elizabethville in 1961. Prior to that he had a distinguished
record in the Congo as Head of Security. I observed on entering
his door that he was also "B.E.M."—a graduate of the Belgian
Staff College. He was a man of about fifty-five, grey-haired, short,
thickset and disagreeable. In civilian clothes he looked like a retired
successful grocer. I could see no military bearing in him whatsoever. He gave me a penetrating glare, as if weighing me up and
finding me wanting. The feelings were mutual. On this unfortunate
note we began a barbed and extraordinary association. He was
angry and he made no bones about it.

"Who are these madmen in Johannesburg and what do they
think they are doing sending hundreds of men to Kamina, which
is totally unprepared to receive them? Stop it at once!"

He sent for a Signals Officer and dictated a telegram to the South
African Government, advising them that he would accept no
more men from South Africa and recruitment must stop at once.

He disposed of a number of other illusions that I may have been
suffering from and then advised me that regardless of what might
have been the case two weeks ago, he, Vanderwalle, was now in
supreme command of the situation as the chief adviser to the
C.-in-C. and the whole thing was going to be run his way. Those
that didn't like it, looking at me, could go home. I thought of my
comfortable existence in Durban and my wife and my yacht and
mentally wrote out a resignation.

When the trauma subsided I produced my report on Operation
Watch-chain.

"I have no time to read reports by people who get lost in the swamps and use paraffin in their engines instead of petrol," he said, relegating the lengthy report to a position one step away from the waste-paper basket, its obvious destination.

But now it was my turn. If he was to be Supremo, he could take over the nightmare that was Kamina. I handed it to him in all its glory, detail by detail. He made careful notes. He sent for his staff officers. He spoke to the General. He told Mr. Tshombe. He telephoned everybody. He determined it would not beat him.

It was then that I realised that Vanderwalle, prickly pear though he might appear to be, was in fact solid gold right through. Here was a master mind struggling with the incredible inefficiency of the Congolese, a perfectionist plagued with the idiocy of the half-trained Congolese officers who were making a sham and a pretence of running the Army. I heard later that not a single record had been kept at G.H.Q.-A.N.C. from the moment the Belgians left. That Mobutu was able to reconstruct the entire army into a workable and reasonably efficient machine in the space of the next fifteen months speaks volumes for his administrative ability. But let me not anticipate.

I explained to the Colonel that Pay was problem number one and proper equipment number two. He assured me, gruffly, that he would attend to everything in due course, but he was under the impression pay was the responsibility of the Purens. This was so, but with his responsibilities as a squadron-leader, Gerry was plainly unable to cope with it.

"Return to Kamina," said the Colonel, "and in a few days I will arrive myself with a complete Belgian staff."

I withdrew making a thoughtful reappraisal of the Colonel. I cannot say I liked him at that moment, but I certainly admired him sufficiently to hope that perhaps one day we might come to be friends.

Small men are always relieved when big men take over. I went back to my room at the Memling that night feeling mighty relieved and mighty small.

When one goes into the market for soldiers what is the response likely to be? Is there a reserve of would-be soldiers lying dormant in the community at any one time waiting for just such an opportunity as this? And what type of men are they likely to be supposing there

E

is? These were some of the interesting questions exercising my mind on my return to Kamina and to which I was now about to get the answers.

The general standard was alarmingly low. There was too high a proportion of alcoholics, drunks, booze artists, bums and layabouts, who were finding it difficult to get a job anywhere else and thought this was a heaven-sent opportunity to make some easy money. In addition, I discovered to my horror, that there was a fair sprinkling of dagga-smokers and dope addicts, many of whom were beyond recall. Perhaps, the greatest surprise of all, and it was to remain so right through the three six-month contracts we served, was the incidence of homosexuals. Of all places to find these highly sensitive and usually very intelligent gentry I would have thought a mercenary outfit to have been the last.

I then began a cleansing operation to rid the unit of the dead wood and those who would never ever make soldiers. Soldiering is an honoured profession and calls for the highest qualities in both mind and body and I would be a miracle man if I would undertake to produce reasonably trained men out of such material. I decided the chaff must go and go quickly. I left the door open to a large number who, after hearing what was in front of them, eagerly accepted the passage home; but many had to be informed that 5 Commando was to be a fighting unit and would see action soon and sustain casualties, before they got the message.

Gradually we settled down and the numbers were thinned to just over three hundred men. An amusing by-product of the thinning-out proccess was the eagerness with which the South African papers seized upon the returned heroes and printed their fantastic stories without very much concern for the truth. Naturally, a man who has been found unfit to serve for some reason will try to save face and the usual excuses were lack of pay, frightful conditions, poor food, and no organisation—most of which the Sunday papers devoured whole. That, I personally did not mind because basically a lot of it was true. We all have to live, and that sort of story is quite palatable on a Sunday morning when you have nothing else to do but read tosh. But the ones which staggered me were the reports of action. We were still training, we had not been committed to battle, there was no fighting anywhere near us, but that did not stop the publication of a few choice "battle" stories.

One that really brought belly laughs to 5 Commando was a

returnee who had in fact seen a little action at Bikili—and a little had been enough. In bold headlines the Sunday papers printed his startling story—"I strangled a Chinese officer with my bare hands!" As that represents the ultimate in inaccurate reportage I will now draw a veil over the remainder of our press, good, bad and indifferent.

I regretted, however, that the image of the mercenary force being projected as a result of this sort of thing was somewhat distorted and not at all surprised, if somewhat amused, when I was sent a cutting from the London *Daily Mail* from Bernard Levin's column which recorded his observations on

> the chocolate cream soldiers of Salisbury and Johannesburg, gaily enlisting one week to kill a few munts, and getting the hell out the next when the munts in question decided to do a bit of killing on their own account.
> "The food," said one such disappointed warrior, "was terrible."
> "There was," pointed out a second would-be saviour of the Congo, "no beer."
> "We were," declared yet another intrepid irregular, "getting hacked to pieces."
> To be physically attacked by the enemy while one is thirsty merely because there is a war on must be a disconcerting experience, and one can sympathise with those who decided after a few days of such dreadful conditions, that they would be better off with the Natives back home, who knew their place, than tangling with upstart Balubas who think nothing of chucking assegais at a fellow merely because he is trying to shoot them.

The ones that were left were good material and included a number of ex-regulars who stood out head and shoulders above the rest, a good assortment of genuine adventurers (a dying breed), youngsters, who did not know what to do with themselves and thought they would "give this a bash," and quite a few undergraduates and professional men who really did not know why they volunteered and whom I did not embarrass by asking in case they might ask me the same question. In addition, there were a dozen or more introverts who had come to find themselves or prove something or other, I forgot what it was and it didn't really interest me. Most of them found themselves all right—right back where they started from in Johannesburg. I often reflected in the Congo that the character of man was being steadily eroded by too much amateur pursuit of psychology. The perfectly sane and mentally healthy chap often ended up with every symptom in the book as a result of his half-understood reading.

If there was any single common motive for enlisting as a mercenary soldier then it was plainly the desire to make big money quickly, all risks accepted. Much as I would like to say that we were motivated by anti-communist sentiments I am unable, in truth, to say so. Here and there, there may have been an idealist whose actions were governed by these principles, as there were also some who came for the adventure and not basically the reward, but by and large we were there for one reason only—money. Having accepted the mercenary calling the only principle I insisted upon was a reasonable standard of personal behaviour.

If there were more than five per cent of us who had carefully considered the moral implications of fighting for money I would have been surprised. On the other hand, if any intelligent man really sits down to examine the whole problem of war he can only arrive at one answer—fighting is futile. The logical corollary ought to be that every man should refuse to fight, we should all in conscience be pacifists and there should be no war. But do five per cent of us think this way?

I am a great believer in impressing one's personality on one's men by frequent talks. All soldiers like the conspiratorial air of being huddled together to hear the latest moves, but more particularly they appreciate the "oneness" which meetings of this type usually foster. We had the added advantage of being already somewhat apart, as it was, shunned by the Belgians and the Congolese alike (but for different reasons) and feared by all. "If Hoare loses control of that lot, God help us," was the general feeling around Kamina and Kaminaville.

We came together as a unit very quickly now that the dross had been burnt off and the men responded enthusiastically to my demand for a unit at regular army standards. Not for us the dubious title "les Affreux" (the frightful ones) which the Belgian mercenaries of Katanga days rejoiced in. Not for us the sloppy dress and three days' growth of beard almost mandatory for a Belgian mercenary. Not for us the indecent short shorts and socks rolled down schoolgirl fashion. With us to be unshaven was a crime. "Fancy dress" was my enemy, and a decent soldierly appearance my foremost demand.

The men were as keen as mustard. More can be done with a

volunteer soldier than a conscript and in a twentieth of the time, an encouraging fact which came to my rescue many times in the future. But even the most basic and elementary training requires some equipment, uniform and transport. None of these were forthcoming. Uniform and small arms were the responsibility of the Belgians we were told—they would provide. Day followed day and nothing arrived despite our strongest protestations. Finally, three weeks after mustering the unit we were able to issue every man with one uniform. I paraded the men for a short route march so that we could drink in the heady scene—everybody clothed as he ought to be for the first time. It was a Sunday morning and half the men were convinced I was going to march them to church. As we moved off Alastair murmured to me, "And this day shall be known as the First Sunday in Tenue."

Much used semi-automatic F.N. rifles were issued to the men at my insistence, although these were originally destined for the A.N.C. A rifle is better than no rifle, as Churchill remarked when he accepted half a million out-dated rifles from the Americans during the war for distribution to the Home Guard.

Training began in earnest and far too soon four Commandos were ordered off by Mobutu to defend various parts of the Congo and check the rebel threat to Gemena, Bukavu and Coquilhatville.

Some days later, part of the Belgian staff arrived, and our role was now made known to us—we were to be the spearhead for the column which was to attack Stanleyville. The select little group duly inspected our establishment, clucked sympathetically at our difficulties and withdrew to decent, well furnished little dwellings. Alastair and I meanwhile were sharing an unfurnished house and basking in the comfort of a drawing-room furnished sumptuously with one mattress and a bare electric light bulb.

I recall those early days in Kamina with particular venom; long days beginning at five in the morning and ending at ten at night, when my greatest ambition was to weld a little unit together that we could be proud of and to see it properly armed, trained and equipped. A modest enough objective I would have thought. The going was rough, but I was buoyed up at every turn by my second in command, Alastair Wicks, a never-failing source of strength and encouragement and good humour even in the blackest times. Alastair's character was complementary to mine. Where I was

; and rash, he was calm and calculating; where I was for dashing the Belgians on the nose, he was a restraining influence, counselling reason and patience. I look back on our evening drop of whisky taken each night on the mattress as being our best moments at Kamina, ugly, miserable and degrading place that it was.

The battle for equipment was on. On my arrival at Kamina I had been pleasantly surprised to find amongst the N.C.O.s a weather-beaten face that I had cause to know quite well—Tom Harrison. Tom was a hornery Australian who had sailed single-handed across the Indian Ocean into Durban on his 25-foot yacht, *Sundowner*. He had berthed her alongside mine and we had become good friends despite his having tried, unsuccessfully, to seduce my pretty female cook away from my crew. There was no question of any moral turpitude, but sea-going cooks, pretty ones at that, are a very rare commodity! He was a tough baby and I was momentarily concerned about our previous friendship; I believe that a commander has no friends. I need not have worried. From that first moment to when I finally waved him good-bye many months later, he never addressed me except as "Sir," and his behaviour was an example of correctitude.

Tom was duly appointed quartermaster to the unit. As such he had to attend the Belgians who were running the ordnance depot and he and they got on together like two pieces of sandpaper. Finally, I was asked to remove him for the sake of co-operation. It seems that they objected to being called "Bloody Belgians," a term which I tried to explain to them was really only one of endearment. Perhaps the Belgians were unaware that Tom might even have applied the great Australian adjective to them, but of this they did not complain. Tom then went into a Commando as its leading Sergeant and figures prominently in this narrative. I can confidently state now that without Harrison there would have been no Stanleyville column and the whole massive effort would have ground ignominiously to a halt at the first river crossing, at which we were to discover the real worth of this extraordinary Aussie.

But co-operation was vital at this stage and his successor was an equally attractive character, an Italian named Gino Tozzi. Gino was handsome and smooth, spoke several languages, understood what life was all about, beginning with beautiful women and ending with machine guns, and soon had the Belgians eating out of his hand. The unit got its share of equipment. If Gino engaged in a little sleight of hand for our advantage, I did not care, he was feeding us royally and the stores were filling to capacity.

In those early days I leaned heavily on my R.S.M. Jack Carton-Barber was a pleasant, even-tempered man, loud-voiced and soft-hearted—a not unusual mixture in big men. He loved a bit of show and was never happier than when he was marching at the head of the column on a route march, the regulation number of paces behind his C.O., showing the flag. He was unaccountably popular with the men, but more so with the little group of Americans who were servicing aircraft at Kamina. To them he was a figure out of a story-book with his enormous build and his pace stick, striking fear into a man's heart at two hundred yards.

The Belgian Staff, headed by Colonel Vanderwalle, now paid us the long awaited formal visit. The Colonel seated himself in my chair, unzipped a document case and selected some papers from a bulging file. These he carefully smoothed down, removing a pin and squaring up the edges of the documents meticulously. His actions told me more about the man than reading his private mail. He loved paper. He introduced the members of his staff, two of whom I had met before. Commandant Liegeois and Commandant Grailly were old-timers from Katanga days and had a noble record in the Force Publique. I was happy to see them and they remembered Alastair and me. A young Captain, rejoicing in the name of Closset, was to be their S 3. He had deemed it fit to remove every vestige of hair from his head before arrival in the Congo and the general effect was something between Yul Brynner and a recently released convict. He was a singularly humourless but efficient man, obviously happy at the posting which would give him an opportunity of trying out at first hand what he had learnt at the École Militaire in Belgium, an establishment of which he was a proud graduate.

Their corporate attitude was hostile. Furthermore, they were frightened. Would we co-operate, was plainly the unspoken question on all their minds. Nothing is quite so preposterous in the military sphere as a staff with no troops to command. A Gilbertian situation! Mobutu had obviously warned them that Hoare had been promised autonomy of action and might prove to be recalcitrant. But they need never have worried. I had given the whole thing a lot of thought and was convinced that, in the circumstances, a Belgian run show was the right and proper thing and I was determined to co-operate with Vanderwalle to the best of my ability. As for their apparent animosity towards us, I felt that this was not unreasonable in the circumstances. How would we like it, I said to Alastair, if the Indians had brought in Belgian mercenaries to help them clean up India after the British had left? We would have regarded them as intruders in what was after all a British sphere of influence.

Then again, mercenaries were an unknown quantity and from the look of us they might have been excused some momentary misgivings. We certainly looked a rough bunch.

They outlined the shape of things to come, promised to do all they could to ease our administrative problem, which we trotted out once again, took another conducted tour of the barracks, and departed, promising they would now take over the pay problem which had finally become too much for the Purens and which once more was threatening to strangle the whole effort.

An intensive training programme continued, physical fitness being the keynote, and we practically lived on the rifle range firing a generous allocation of ammunition. One of my young recruits amused me one day when I heard him exclaim to an old sweat who had missed the target completely, "Garn, you couldn't hit a cow's arse with a banjo!"

My main concern was in the training of officers and N.C.O.s and I ran a number of sand-table exercises and T.E.W.T.s (tactical exercises without troops) which were popular and illuminating. The D.S. solution was always energetically challenged, a good sign in itself, and I felt that day by day we were getting to grips with the real problems of soldiering in the Congo and shuffling off preconceived notions. There is no book on the Congo, I told them; we must write one ourselves.

Colonel Vanderwalle then set about raising 5 Brigade Mecanisée, which would comprise ourselves as the strike force and two ponderous columns of Congolese infantry to be called Lima One and Lima Two. The "mecanisée" part of the Brigade was not very much in evidence at that time, but the Colonel had been working on the problem and had assembled over two hundred new vehicles at Kongolo in northern Katanga; Kongolo was to be the start point for the advance on Kindu and Stanleyville.

In due course an O Group was called by Vanderwalle at which we were treated to a military discourse which can only be fairly described as brilliant. He spoke to the commanders concerned in the operation for about an hour and a half never once referring to a note and never once forgetting his facts or his figures. It was a "tour de force." We were in the presence of a military genius.

"Any questions?" asked the Colonel with one of his rare, but flashing smiles. I raised my hand. "What about air?"

Stationed in the Congo at that time was a small number of B–26 twin-engined light bombers and about ten T–28 single-engined fighter planes, both models being obsolete in modern air forces. They were piloted by anti-Castro Cubans and formed the nucleus of an excellent little air arm which was to give us the closest air support. The Colonel had not forgotten the air; he had plans for them which would form part of subsequent and more detailed orders.

Excitement now electrified our camp and all that remained was an issue of brand new rifles and machine guns which arrived direct from Brussels. These were given out to the men on the evening of 29th October 1964, almost two months to the day since we had arrived, amongst scenes of great joy.

I held a final briefing in the canteen that night, which had gone dry by design, and after outlining what was to be expected of every man in the unit, I ran through my Rules for Battle (which I reproduce at Appendix IV for those who may be interested). Rule One was simply "Pray God Daily", a simple injunction which would stand us all in good stead during the four campaigns to come.

A subdued and thoughtful commando went early to bed for on the morrow they would begin the adventure of their lives, an adventure during which they would release almost two thousand Belgians from inhuman imprisonment and liberate hundreds of thousands of Congolese villagers, the innocent victims of a ruthless, degrading and barbaric régime; an adventure in which they would cover over six hundred miles of rugged terrain; an adventure which would stamp them for ever as a courageous little band of men—a far cry from their popular image as callous and bloodthirsty killers.

I left the canteen to the inharmonious strains of "For he's a jolly good fellow," somewhat affecting, and took a night-cap with my officers in our Mess. Captain Latz ventured to remark, "If I may say so, sir, you've made a unit and they will fight behind you to a man."

Coming from John Latz, who had known the brotherhood of the Parachute Regiment and the ennobling effect of Arnhem on what remained of his battalion, I was indeed profoundly moved and gratified.

# 5

## STEMMING THE TIDE

At the beginning of September 1964, almost one-half of the Congo was in rebel hands. The only reverses the Popular Government had suffered so far were the loss of Albertville and the repulse at Bukavu. Flushed with success, the Popular Army of Liberation had swept westwards across the country with the speed and ferocity of a grass fire. The coming of the Simbas struck terror into the hearts of the Congolese villagers and whole garrisons of the A.N.C. capitulated without firing a shot. In a number of cases, all that was necessary was a telephone call, warning that the Simbas were on their way!

In Leopoldville, the vast civilian population, swollen to three times its normal size, grew uneasy at the approach of the rebel army. Hour by hour reports reached the Commander-in-Chief at his headquarters in Leo Deux of the rebel advance.

"Where is the General at twelve o'clock every day?" a cruel joke asked at the time.

"Waiting for the B.B.C. to tell him where the rebels have got to!" was the answer.

One day the B.B.C. told him the rebels were threatening Gemena, his own home town, and that further south another column had reached Ingende, sixty miles from Coquilhatville. It was high time the National Army acted.

The General's only reserve was 5 Commando, now in formation at Kamina, as yet unequipped and untrained. Nevertheless, I was ordered to send forty men immediately to Gemena to support the hard pressed A.N.C. I formed 51 Commando at once and under 2nd Lieutenant Gary Wilson they took off for Leopoldville with a flourish, regardless of the fact that they had absolutely no training, and many of them were still dressed in civilian clothes. On arrival at Ndjili, the urgency of the situation was impressed upon them as they were armed, clothed, equipped and despatched up north within the space of a few hours.

Wilson decided not to wait for the enemy to attack Gemena and, with a bold show of initiative, pushed down to meet them at Lisala. With a company of A.N.C. under command, he stormed into the large riverside town to do battle with over one thousand rebels, many of them armed with machine guns and bazookas. It was a walk-over. Wilson's men went through the Simbas like a scythe through grass, leaving one hundred and sixty dead in the streets. One man in 51 Commando was slightly wounded, when a bullet parted his hair.

The news of the victory was received with great joy in Leopold-ville and cheered in Kamina by the men of 5 Commando. But more important still, we were able to draw some weighty conclusions from the battle. Wilson had demonstrated conclusively that the enemy were greatly overrated. Secondly, the A.N.C. would fight if properly led, and lastly, the mercenaries looked like the answer to the military problem.

51 Commando consolidated their grip on Lisala and within a few days Air Congo was flying in again and the civilian administration returned to pick up the broken threads. Patrols continued daily to push the enemy back towards Bumba and on one of these, Volunteer Young was killed in a severe ambush, two others being wounded.

Wilson reported that given sufficient support and reinforcements, he saw no reason why he should not continue his advance towards Bumba and then along the axis Bumba-Aketi. If the Lisala garrison was anything to judge the enemy by, said Wilson, the rebels would be the least of his troubles. I agreed that he should be given the opportunity to exploit his success and took the matter up with H.Q. at Leo. The suggestion had a mild reception, for reasons which became apparent later on.

51 Commando entered Bumba shortly before the end of October, with little difficulty. Unfortunately, some of Wilson's men fell into bad odour here over an allegation of looting and, although this was never proved, it was sufficient to warrant their removal to Kamina, where they arrived shortly after the main column left for Kongolo.

Coquilhatville is the capital of Equator Province and stands a few miles north of the Equator at the confluence of two great rivers, the

Congo and Busira. The town is beautifully laid out, with a background of lush green equatorial forest, from which it has been hard won. Enormous evergreen trees stand with their roots in shallow water the year round, their thick foliage shutting out the merciless sun,

The roads running to the east are engineering marvels, hundreds of miles of causeway built up ten feet above the surrounding swamp with deep ditches on both sides and impenetrable jungle beyond. The terrain is a soldier's nightmare There is no scope for manoeuvre on roads such as these and a determined enemy could hold up an advancing column indefinitely.

The enemy were now at Ingende, sixty miles to the east of Coquilhatville along such a road, and the whole population of the town made ready to decamp. 52 Commando under Siegfried Mueller, now a Captain, was rushed up to protect the town. The threat to Coquilhatville petered out and Mueller advanced on Ingende. After 52 Commando had cleared the enemy, they pressed on eastwards towards Boende, two hundred miles further on and the centre of rebel resistance in the Cuvette Centrale.

The town of Boende lies on the south bank of the River Tshuapa. With tremendous drive, but little in the way of reconnaissance, 52 Commando arrived on the north bank facing Boende. The enemy promptly opened up on the column with machine guns and mortars and raked it from top to bottom, killing one of our men and wounding another. There was no cover on the narrow causeway and the men were pinned down until nightfall, when they withdrew to Bikili, a village twenty miles to their rear.

Two days later a strong enemy force attacked Bikili from both ends of the village. Lieutenant Ben Louw ran back to protect the rear with a section of men and fired on the rebels, who were advancing up the main street in numbers, screaming "*Mai* Mulele." His machine gun crew made short work of them, but a burst of enemy fire hit Volunteer Nel, the machine gunner, and killed him outright. The rebels withdrew, leaving over one hundred dead on the ground.

During the night the enemy regrouped and encircled the Bikili garrison, who now appealed urgently for help.

In the extreme north-western corner of the Congo the rebels were having it all their own way. The Popular Army of Liberation had now reached the outskirts of Yakomo on the Uele River and were poised, ready to attack. 54 Commando, under 2nd Lieutenant Forsbrey were flown up to assist the A.N.C. They started their career with a jolt, when their aircraft ran off the runway and turned over, but fortunately nobody was hurt.

At Yakomo they were just in time to repel the enemy, who withdrew in disorder, taking with them a civilian prisoner, an American, whose name was destined to ring around the world—Dr. Paul Carlson.

As soon as the battle of Yakomo was over, 54 were sent south to aid 52 at Bikili. Siegfried Mueller now took upon himself the duties of Force Commander and despatched 54 on arrival to a position ten miles south of Bikili on the river, established his headquarters in a large plantation house and concentrated 52 Commando at Bikili with the A.N.C. Together with a Belgian Army adviser, he busied himself with the plan for an attack on Boende, using 52 as a left hook, down the road they had previously used, and 54 as a right hook, along the river in boats, to strike the enemy in the rear.

Feelings were running high in 52 Commando on a number of scores and I decided to visit the units in the north as soon as I could.

I arrived in Leopoldville much worried by the turn of events. I had not been made privy at this stage to the Vanderwalle plan for the capture of Stanleyville, for reasons best known to the Belgians, and it seemed to me that Army Headquarters had no settled policy, other than to react violently to enemy attacks as and when they occurred, using my unit, which was badly in need of training, for the purpose.

If this policy was to continue, the final result must be the total fragmentation of 5 Commando into seven or eight small units, all fighting along different axes and with little or no co-ordination. In addition, and not the least disturbing aspect of the splitting up process, was the fact that the independent units would be commanded by junior officers who were, for the most part, untrained, untried and as yet an unknown quantity, as far as their ability to carry the heavy responsibility of command was concerned.

The idea of 5 Commando distributed over the face of the Congo in penny packets filled me with alarm. I saw the unit very clearly as being the salvation of the Congo, providing it was used in conjunction with the A.N.C. as a cohesive striking force. I decided to see Mr. Tshombe at once.

I explained to the Prime Minister, somewhat forcibly, that 5 Commando was being frittered away wantonly and that the mercenaries—his most powerful weapon against insurrection, the weapon which he had forged in the political fires of O.A.U. with so much fret—was doomed to disintegration, unless the present policy was reconsidered. He was worried and promised to talk to the General about it.

At the same time, I presented Mr. Tshombe with a plan to give him Stanleyville by the end of October. The plan was simple. 5 Commando should be concentrated forthwith at Lisala, with orders to advance on Stan via the axis Aketi-Buta-Banalia, as a highly mobile and armour-tipped column, supported by air. As each town fell, it must be garrisoned by troops of the A.N.C., who would be flown in. Belgian mercenaries, who were now arriving in the Congo in large numbers, would accompany the A.N.C. and would be used as military police. Finally, Belgian Technical Assistance would provide men to administer the captured towns, as we went forward.

The Prime Minister nodded his approval. He was attracted to the idea of a quick capture of Stanleyville and he could see that, although the plan would be heavy on air transport, it would be light on road transport and had the element of speed about it. He liked it in principle, he added, but he was not a military man and he was loath to interfere with the Commander-in-Chief, whom he trusted implicitly in these matters. He would discuss it with him, however, and he felt sure the General would give it a sympathetic hearing.

As it was now getting quite dark, Mr. Tshombe switched on his desk lamp. Nothing happened. He tried the room lights, with the same result. I tried a standard lamp in one corner. Still no light.

"*Ça c'est le Congo!*" said Mr. Tshombe with a broad grin.

That evening I was introduced to Ferdinand Calistrat, a naturalised Spaniard, Roumanian by birth. He had served with the Spanish Foreign Legion in romantic sounding places like Rio Muni and Ifni and wanted to join 5 Commando. Furthermore, he had been world record holder of the hop, skip and jump for some years—he proved it with some well creased records—and was just the man to take over the training of my men in P.T. and unarmed combat. He had not one word of English at this interview, but a few days later he had mastered the fundamentals of the English language and could swear convincingly at my horrible men in Kamina. He was a personal friend of Mr. Tshombe, having been his physical fitness instructor in Madrid and, as such, I felt he could be of great value to us. He proved his worth almost at once. That evening he conducted me on a tour of the Leopoldville nightclubs!

Leopoldville night spots cater principally for the Congolese. They do not pander to the tourist. Consequently they are less inhibited, and the tourist feels daringly conscious that he is lifting the veil a little on real African life. Noise is the chief deterrent in these places, as the average Congolese cannot believe he is being entertained unless his eardrums are on the point of bursting. Conversation is quite impossible and there is no alternative but to relax and give oneself over to the sensual rhythm of a noisy band.

Most nightclubs have floor shows of great length, but these lack something in versatility. African ritual dancing is the usual offering. Large gentlemen wearing very little beat out the time on giant drums whilst well-proportioned maidens, similarly undressed, stamp out the dance without a fault, executing tricky little routines which would win the admiration of any Broadway producer.

Somewhere along the line, we were joined by an American journalist, a handsome man, Harvard, spoke good French, and was obviously one who had taken pains to study the Congolese, particularly the women. We found ourselves in a dive called "Oui Fifi." No sooner were we seated than we were "lapped" by a pair of startling dolls.

"This one," said the American, grabbing an armful of heaving breast which appeared to be in some danger of escaping, "was Miss Leo, 1964!" I could believe it.

"Er, how do you do?" I said, feeling it was perhaps a little inadequate to the occasion. It is not every day that I am introduced to a beauty queen. My wife sees to that. I engaged her mate in conversation, strong heady stuff such as "Nice place you've got here" and, "Do you come here often?" etc. By the time I had covered the high cost of drinking, my gusher ran dry. The party of the second part who was runner-up to Miss Leo, 1964, obviously regarded me as Champion Bore, 1964, and took off abruptly for more obvious pickings.

Before the party broke up, the American astonished us all by dragging out his wallet and, for no reason other than admiration for Miss Leo, 1964, presented her with 25,000 francs. A King's ransom!

I concluded on my way home that I did not understand Americans, but could not help admiring the spontaneous gallantry of the thing, rash though it might look in the cold light of tomorrow.

I arrived in Coquihatville the next day, minus one of my escort who had deserted in Leopoldville the night before. I could not have timed my visit better. At the local army headquarters, a great argument was going on as to who should be issued with a newly arrived Unimog armoured car. As it was most needed by 52 Commando, I promptly issued it to them and drove off in it myself with Volunteer Paul Mills for Ingende.

My first action at Bikili was to expel a group of foreign journalists, who had attached themselves to Captain Mueller's headquarters. It was in the interests of certain European newspapers to depict the mercenaries as bloodthirsty killers and two Germans had been at great pains to produce photographs, purporting to show numbers of *Jeunesse* killed by 52 Commando in cold blood.

52 Commando had been a very unsettled unit and had a long list of troubles, to which I listened patiently in an effort to sort out some of their gripes. The time had come, apparently, for a change in personnel and I now appointed Lieutenant Ben Louw as O.C. 52 Commando and left Siegfried to complete the planning of his operation to capture Boende, after which he was to return to Kamina, to take over the Base from De Jaeger. Captain Mueller had commanded 52 Commando in a somewhat detached manner, which did not have my approval. I have always held very strong views about the relationship between a leader and his men and the remarks which follow are not intended to be a criticism of Mueller's handling of his command so much as a reflection of my views.

At platoon, company and battalion level, I am convinced that a commanding officer must live in the pocket of his men. He must know them intimately, their troubles, their fears, their weaknesses, their strengths, their hopes, their backgrounds, better even than their own families know them. Thus only will he feel his command. Consequently he must share their day to day life, but without being familiar to the point where his men will cease to respect him. Leadership in these circumstances is a difficult task, but success begins with "nearness." A remote leader at this level is an absurdity.

I paid my last respects at the grave of "Utah" Nel and hurried on down to the river to see Lieutenant Forsbrey and 54 Commando. His unit were living on a barge in the river and looked like soldiers.

F

A few days later Mueller's attack went in on Boende exactly as planned and he had the satisfaction of seeing the town fall without a casualty.

52 Commando were now transferred up north to replace 51 Commando at Bumba and 54 pressed on down the road towards Ikela. Back at Kamina the main column was about to leave for Stan.

The town of Bukavu, the largest on the eastern Congo border, stands at the southern end of magnificent Lake Kivu, a ruby in an azure setting. Towards the end of August the Popular Army of Liberation, flushed with its easy success at Stanleyville, marched on Bukavu. Their main object was to consolidate their eastern flank, before opening operations in the west and sweeping on to Leopoldville. The attack was made in the traditional Simba style with thousands of drug-crazed soldiers chanting *"Mai* Mulele" descending on the town *en masse*. The A.N.C., rallied by Lieut.-Colonel Leonard Mulamba, beat off the attack and inflicted an enormous number of casualties on the enemy.

The victory was of the first importance in that it marked a striking change in the morale of the National Army who, for the very first time, had stood their ground and fought back with success. In addition, it heralded the arrival of a truly great Congolese soldier, who had proved himself more than a match for the rebels. As soon as the battle was over, Mulamba set about erecting impregnable defences for Bukavu and began to tighten up on the discipline of his troops, who were sorely in need of it.

Bukavu was held and the rebels' plans for the quick domination of the eastern border of the Congo decisively thwarted. But counter-attack threatened. In addition, the road running south to Uvira, the port at the northern end of Lake Tanganyika, was in the hands of the rebels, who also controlled the whole of the Ruzizi Valley leading to it. Reinforcements for Bukavu were urgently needed. The Commander-in-Chief once more looked to his strategic reserve and on 23rd September I was ordered to despatch yet another Commando into immediate action.

53 Commando was made up of some of the best material we had at Kamina. They had had the advantage of some training, not by any means sufficient, but they were already a unit with a considerable unit spirit, which had been fostered by their commander, Jack Maiden, and their second-in-command, 2nd Lieutenant George

Schroeder. Jack was a South African from Durban and a mature and level-headed chap with a wealth of experience under his capacious belt. Schroeder was an ex-professional soldier, who had been in the South African Defence Force, and was later described by Jack as "a military machine." I saw the troops emplane at Kamina with pride. They were the best yet, and their shining record during the next few months brought nothing but credit to 5 Commando.

No sooner had they landed in Bukavu, than the expected enemy counter-attack came in at Kabare, a town about twenty kilometres north. 53 Commando went into action for the first time and the result was decisive—the enemy were soundly beaten and never came again to menace Bukavu. During the action, however, there had been some hand to hand fighting, in which Volunteer Lotz was seriously wounded by a spear in his side, a wound which paralysed him for the next fourteen months.

After this early success, Lieut.-Colonel Mulamba sent the unit to clear the Ruzizi Valley and to capture Uvira, which they did in double quick time for the loss of one Belgian guide, killed at Uvira. This town was garrisoned by the A.N.C. and 53 Commando recalled to Bukavu to spearhead a column which was to move northwards to capture Lubero and Butembo. The Simbas had massed in Butembo and Maiden's plan of attack to take the town was to split his unit into two parts, one part led by George Schroeder, which would attack from the rear, and the other part, which he led himself, to attack frontally. George Schroeder's column ran straight into a mass of about three thousand rebels and dealt out fantastic damage, until the Simbas broke and fled, leaving hundreds dead behind them. Butembo fell to 53 Commando on 28th October for the loss of Volunteer Howard-Willis, a brave and popular youngster who had shown great courage and spirit in the attack.

The unit was now ordered to consolidate its position in Butembo and to await orders for a further move forward, in concert with the Stanleyville column, which was to leave Kongolo three days later.

# 6

## VERS KINDU

A chartered D.C. 4 ferried us into Kongolo during a day of thunderstorms. 5 Brigade Meca was taking shape and all around Kongolo there was the buzz of excitement and busy preparation. A bridging unit was practising at the river, my men were firing on the rifle range, and signallers were tapping out practice messages for the real thing which was to begin the next day.

The column rolled out of Kongolo on the morning of the 1st November bound for Samba, an important railhead one hundred kilometres north on the road to Kindu. 5 Commando was the strike force and led the column, preceded by some armour. Behind us trailed a long column of Congolese infantry and engineers.

We were organised into three commandos, 55, 56 and 57, with a small headquarters containing a signals section which travelled in a "tentacle"—a Dodge truck fitted with radio gear. I rode in a signal jeep driven by the R.S.M. and the commandos travelled in jeeps and new five-ton trucks, piled high with everything from boxes of ammunition to cooking pots. All units were self contained.

The armour comprised two Ferret scout cars and three Scania Vabis, Swedish armoured cars left behind by the United Nations in 1963. They looked like giant bath tubs and they were just as effective. The pathfinder was a Frenchman named De la Michelle— "Frenchy" to everybody—who sported a bushy R.A.F. moustache and a manner which left you in no doubt that he would fire first and ask questions later. He had guts of iron, but I did not envy him his task.

5 Commando was to do the actual fighting under my command, but the column itself was commanded by a Belgian regular officer, Lieut.-Colonel Liegeois. He was short, fat and unsoldierly-looking

and was never to be seen without a cigarette drooping from one corner of his mouth. He wore a floppy green beret pulled well down one side of his face, the traditional headgear of his famous regiment, the Chasseurs Ardennais. He had a worried look most of the time, but his eyes were happy and smiling. He had a soft voice which went with his mild nature, but in action he was bold and completely fearless. Liegeois led without fuss, shunned publicity and was quiet and efficient. He was extremely popular with all of us in 5 Commando and we were happy to serve under him and voted him the best active service officer in the Congo—bar none. (We were all genuinely distressed when disaster overtook him some weeks later.)

Column warfare from an infantryman's point of view is most unsatisfactory. The Congo is so big that the enemy can only hold certain key positions and his line of communication cannot be guarded along its entire length. One of the main principles, therefore, in this type of warfare is to recognise which points the enemy will defend and to get to them quickly. A nice balance has to be struck between going too fast and too slow. Too slow and the enemy knows you are coming and prepares; too fast and you fall into his ambush. On arrival at the defended position you are faced with a choice of tactics—to go in using the traditional approach to contact on foot with scouts, etc., or to make a motorised dash for it, hoping you will overwhelm the enemy by surprise. Liegeois always preferred the latter system and at the beginning it worried the life out of me.

Liegeois had spent most of his service in the Force Publique and he knew that a sudden show of force would scare the rebels and that nine times out of ten they would run. He placed all his trust in speed, superior fire power and determination. I learnt steadily from him and in the three campaigns to follow, in which I had overall command, I employed his tactics with success, adding more traditional methods whenever I felt the situation warranted it.

Samba was my first experience of this type of advance. Without any reconnaissance, air, fire support, or warning, the column swarmed into Samba, overcame a very slight resistance and seized the main tactical features all within an hour!

I sent Spencer off with his commando to the Lualaba to patrol to the river's edge and to seize the ferry if possible. He ran into two ambushes on the way, but fought his way out of both, inflicting heavy casualties on the enemy, and got to the river in time to see the ferry disappearing over to the other side, which was Kasongo. His unit were the first to be blooded and their tails were up.

I put 57 Commando in defence of the railway station. The commander was Captain Ian Gordon, probably the hardest man I have known in my life. He was about thirty-five, short-sighted, generously moustached and strongly built. He spoke quietly in short clipped sentences and there was no small talk in him. His background was Winchester and the Rifle Brigade, his manners were impeccable, and he was the nearest thing to the perfect fighting man—mercenary if you will—that I was to meet in the Congo. An order was an order and would be carried out regardless, even if it risked the destruction of himself and his unit. He was fearless, bold and utterly ruthless. He attracted the same type around him. His unit built up, in a very short space of time, a reputation for rugged and successful fighting. His men were proud to be in 57 Commando and considered themselves the "élite".

He had as his right hand a sergeant named John Peters. Peters was a Yorkshireman from Leeds, a professional soldier with a background in the Special Air Services. Right from the beginning he had worked hard on 57 Commando, fostering the unit spirit so important in small warfare, begging, borrowing and stealing equipment and reserve rations, and training the men to a standard almost as high as the S.A.S. He was a compact man of about five foot eight with the build of a welter-weight boxer, which he had been in his earlier days. He had nerves of steel and a soldier's conscience which recognises only the order and the exigencies of the moment, backed up by a deadly efficiency in all weapons and every facet of soldiering. He was tough and untameable, as a Belgian volunteer had discovered when he made the foolish mistake of claiming Peter's camp bed for his own at Kongolo, an error which led to a knife wound for him and a severe reprimand for Peters. I hammered Peters frequently in our early days, but he always came up smiling. It would take more than me to extinguish the look of sheer devilry in his twinkling green eyes.

One of Ian's men, Roets, was from Kenya and could speak Swahili like a Congolese, even to the inflections of voice. He called up enemy-held Kibombo two hundred kilometres away and began to talk to the rebel operator, on the telephone. We learnt that reinforcements were on the way including two bus loads of infantry and heavy weapons. Furthermore, a train was due to leave for Samba that afternoon! We lay in wait for it that evening, but they must have been warned somewhere along the line for they did not turn up. The other information turned out to be accurate enough as we found out later.

The incident was typical of war in the Congo and I was reminded that the rebels had often used the telephone to frighten off the A.N.C. when they advanced in August. A phone call to say they were on their way was usually enough to ensure instant evacuation.

Right from the start we had the inestimable advantage of air. If the enemy had had aircraft against us, the result might have been very different. I was always very conscious of this powerful weapon and gave it into the special care of Commandant Wicks, who had much experience as an Air Liaison Officer in the last war and was himself a pilot. The main role for aircraft was to recce the road ahead. The T-28, slow and cumbrous as it is, is the ideal plane for this purpose.

Their first task was to let us know the condition of a major bridge on our route, the concrete three span affair over the Lubufu. Back came the answer—all O.K. Our track went through thick jungle, much of it already invading the road where it had not been used for the last three months. In other places it met overhead, shutting out the light and keeping the track damp and dark. We arrived at the bridge only to find it had been completely destroyed. The approach had been washed away for a distance of over fifty yards and the river was running deep and fast with steep banks. The enemy had decided not to defend it. A section of 55 Commando swam the torrent and put out a screen on the other side until we could get the rest of their unit across in assault boats.

Adjudant Fernet of the Belgian Army quietly and efficiently brought up his bridging unit and their heavy material from the back of the column and in less than four hours erected a pontoon capable of taking our heavy vehicles across one at a time. The Congolese sappers were as efficient as any I had seen; engineering and signalling were two branches of soldiering at which they were particularly good. Fernet rigged up arc lamps and his men worked through the night. By four in the morning we were all across.

Next morning the B.B.C. carried two interesting items of news. Lyndon B. Johnson had been elected President of the United

States in a landslide victory! Ben Bella of Algeria had promised men and equipment to the Congolese rebels! I preferred the former item.

Tension mounted as we approached Kibombo late that afternoon. We rushed the barrier and got into the town without trouble, the enemy withdrawing into the bush and along the railway line to fire on us wildly and high.

One of my patrols reported back after a few minutes that a band of rebels had just murdered three European prisoners at the other end of the town. I went up to investigate. In a small bare room filled with the smell of cordite I saw a sight fit to chill one's marrow. Two of them had been shot dead within the last few minutes, but the third, an older man, was still living. The right side of his face had been completely blown away by the blast of a shotgun fired at point blank range. Mercifully he died quite soon without regaining consciousness.

It was the first of a long, long line of atrocities which I was going to have to witness and the senseless act of savagery filled me with revulsion.

Kibombo was deserted and as it held no tactical advantages for us Liegeois decided not to dally, but to go hard for Kindu and to try to take it by surprise. He reasoned that if we travelled all night we could be at Kindu early in the morning and perhaps catch the rebels with their pants down. Communications were bad and they might think we were still in the Kibombo area. The idea of a night march through enemy-held territory with the possibility of ambush every mile of the way gave me pause. Added to that the men were hungry and tired, but the advantages were obvious. The commando leaders accepted the plan with mixed feelings.

We snatched a meal of sorts and rolled out of Kibombo just before dusk. When dark fell all lights in the column were blazing and the enemy must have thought a thousand trucks were descending on them. Just as we entered a long, deep cutting with bushy overhanging banks, I said to the R.S.M., "I don't like the look of this, Jack. God help us if the enemy . . ." The words were hardly out of my mouth when the air was rent with the savage chatter of heavy machine guns. Men dived out of their trucks blindly to take cover. Tracer bullets whistled over the top of the column and apprehension gripped me in the stomach. If the enemy were on the tops of the banks, we were in for a hell of a time. I went forward to look for myself. Our leading armoured car was face to face with three enemy armoured cars, evil-looking mock-up affairs, and the gunners were slogging it out toe to toe. Fortunately, they were at the top of a rise and the bullets were passing a few feet over us.

"Bazooka, sir?", enquired a soft voice behind me in the dark. It was Captain Gordon.

"No, I don't think so, Ian", I said. "You'll never get there alive."

"I think I can manage it from the cover of that third armoured car," he went on. "Let me try it anyway. It will give them something to think about."

"O.K.," I said, reluctantly, "give it a bash. Watch yourself."

He knelt in the sand and undid a white clinical looking box which contained the two halves of the rocket launcher, an eye shield and one rocket. He and Sherriff crawled slowly forward until they were within range behind our third armoured car. Everything would depend on speed in coming into action. Ian knelt by the rear fender, levelled the contraption, waited for Sherriff to tap him on the head to signify the rocket was loaded and ready to go, and then, a click, a flash and . . . WHAM! A brilliant flash of yellow light lit up the tunnel of the track as an almighty bang reverberated down the length of the column and the front of the leading enemy armoured car flew into a thousand pieces.

The crews of the other two cars, panic-stricken, tried to bale out, but all were caught in the merciless fire from Frenchy's machine gun. In his excitement Frenchy fired a complete belt of 250 rounds!

The bodies of the dead were strewn on the track ahead of us, but nobody got out to remove them and the column continued after its fright "vers Kindu", each vehicle bumping over the bodies in turn until they were reduced to a squashy pulp.

The rearguard to our column dismantled the enemy ·50 Browning machine guns and blew up the remains of the armoured cars and we were once again on our way. This time we put all our lights out and crept along at ten miles an hour, not quite so confident, and antici-pating trouble at every bend and cutting. It was nerve-wracking and at three in the morning we were relieved when Liegeois called a halt. We slept on the track, dead beat and out to the world, guarded by a handful of sentries.

At dawn we were up again, coffee appeared miraculously and the light chatter of relief filled the air. The daylight loosened tongues and everybody related his personal experience of the night before.

Ralph Hider, the orderly-room Sergeant, had been driving Alastair in the tentacle when the firing first broke out. "This is it," they both yelled, opening their side doors and leaping for the bush, grabbing at their rifles lying between them at the same time. In their panic they put their hands through each other's slings so that when they pulled apart, they engaged in a maddening tug-of-war, convinced that any second they would be filled full of lead! Sergeant Hider, who, as the unit funny-man, acted every inch of the fat part and had us in fits of laughter. His morale building virtues were incalculable.

It was six in the morning and we were one hundred kilometres from Kindu. The column rolled on.

Kindu is a large town on the banks of the Lualaba River. The river rises in the highlands of Katanga where it is called the Luapula, becomes the Lualaba at Kongolo, and finally the Congo when it reaches Stanleyville. The town is spread out on both banks of the river, but mainly on the west bank and supports about 150,000 people. Kindu is the heart of the Maniema district of the Kivu province and was the core of the biggest political party in the Congo, the Mouvement National Congolais Lumumba. The people were fanatical in their belief in Lumumba. They had set up the headquarters of the A.P.L., Armée Populaire de Liberation, and the local rebel government in Kindu.

Kindu had been world news once before. In 1962 eleven members of the Italian Air Force, attached to the United Nations in the Congo, had landed at Kindu. Congolese troops had arrested them for no reason and hacked them to pieces with pangas in an orgy of sheer blood lust. Parts of the bodies were then distributed around Kindu and the soldiers were proud to have their photographs taken, showing them eating the flesh. The men were under the command of a Colonel Pacassa. None of the culprits was ever brought to trial and when the rebellion broke out, Pacassa and his entire battalion deserted to the rebel cause. The Italians in my unit had good cause to remember Kindu.

For three months now no official word had reached the outside world of what was happening in Kindu, but from time to time news leaked out of the mass murders of Congolese intellectuals, chiefs, and notables, which were taking place before the Lumumba monument in the centre of the town. Every day a new line of prisoners would be paraded before the monument, goaded and jeered at by the populace. A young boy of about fourteen had installed himself as the chief executioner, and took fiendish delight in running up and down the line hacking his panga at a defenceless man here, or savagely attacking a woman there, lopping off a hand or a foot as it took his fancy. The crowd would encourage him in his excesses, until maddened with his own power he would give the order to fire, when a dozen or more Simbas would open up at point-blank range, sometimes killing, sometimes wounding the men and women selected for death that day. The bodies of the prisoners were then flung into the Lualaba, dead or alive.

The European and Asiatic population of Kindu had been reduced to two hundred and twenty and these were now securely guarded in their houses by Simba warriors. They had been warned that morning that they were all due for execution at four in the afternoon and the young sadist had boasted openly of the manner in which he intended to carry out the death sentences, and more luridly of what he would do to the white women before death. To die after that, he bragged, would be their most fervent prayer. The rebels had heard of the advance of "les Americains," as they called us, and General Olenga had decided to get the hostages out of the way before we arrived.

Fifty kilometres from Kindu we hit two bus loads of Simbas in a village. We got most of them before they melted into the bush and one who was badly wounded told us that they were reinforcements for Kibombo and they had no idea we were so near to Kindu. This was heartening.

Two kilometres from Kindu the column halted and our air reported feverish activity in the town, particularly at the southern entrance where they thought they could see a road block. Excitement became intense right through the column and every man checked his weapons for the final assault. Alastair asked the air to strafe and rocket the road block as hard as they could right up until the moment we appeared—we would accept the risks of very close support—and then to transfer their attention to the town itself; they were to rocket the landing stage and as we entered the town proper, they were to make dry runs to keep the enemy heads down. The Cubans repeated their instructions, anxious to make no error.

"Is that affirmative, Johnny?"

"That's affirmative, Bravo," said Alastair and the battle was on. The column accelerated for the dash into Kindu. The warplanes came screaming down from 5,000 feet, each blasting off its eight Browning ·50 machine guns in a terrifying cruuuump! Now two Bravos came out of the sun and loosed off their rockets in a silent swoosh to explode on the target with a sonorous didoom! The column was getting nearer and nearer and still the air kept at it.

"Tell them to hold it," I screamed at Alastair over my radio as empty cartridge cases rained down on us from above and pieces of rocket shrapnel whizzed dangerously by—this was close support all right, too close. We crashed into the southern entrance of Kindu and swept past the road block dealing with the defenders like lightning. The column careered along madly, travelling too fast for control, all guns blazing. The enemy had fled into the bush and was keeping up a sporadic fire on our flanks as we sped through.

We halted at the entrance to the town. Commando leaders dashed to my side for orders. I rattled them off. "Jeremy, seize the landing stage and grab the ferry—don't let it get away. Ian, attack the rail-way station and clear the wharf. Ferdy, (Captain Calistrat) you stay here and watch our rear." His face fell. A few yards away a Ford truck, blazing furiously, exploded with a bang, the flames scorching my clothing.

Now for the final assault on Kindu.

"But, sir, what about us?" Alfredo Proetti and a number of Italians were part of 55 Commando, the unit I had detailed to stay behind. They had been waiting for this day.

"Ferdy," I shouted, "attach the Italians to Jerry."

With a broad grin they ran to the leading trucks and were off in a flash, revenge in their grasp.

It was obvious that we had taken the enemy by surprise and we must hit hard. We crashed into the main street, firing everything as we went.

The leading armoured cars got to the ferry, swivelled their turrets and began firing on the enemy. They were thick on the ground and holding it and the surrounding buildings in great strength. 56 Commando flung themselves off their trucks and went into action, advancing deftly from cover to cover. Dozens of rebel soldiers were crowding the *bac* in their panic to get away. The engine had cut and the helpless ferry drifted slowly downstream, a sitting target for our guns. They were cornered. The slaughter was sickening and blood coloured the surface of the Lualaba. Spencer blew his whistle and stopped the firing, calling on the enemy to surrender. It was all over. Under a tree my Italians were unloading their weapons, grim faced and determined. Proetti blew down the barrel of his 9 mm. Browning. Honour had been satisfied.

57 Commando secured the railway and Peters led his men in a dash to the water's edge from where they engaged the enemy on the ferry as it drifted by. One by one they dropped off into the river, surfaced for a brief moment, showed an arm or leg and were gone. Very few got away.

The Congolese infantry in our rear now fanned out and went through the town digging out the rebels and clearing the streets, house by house. Kindu had fallen, but we had lost the ferry, some said with General Olenga clinging to it as it whirled away downstream. His Mercedes Benz was at the landing stage and he had been about to cross, so it was not improbable. We searched the car for papers.

It was three in the afternoon when we set about releasing the European prisoners. They had been saved in the nick of time. Their gratitude was overwhelming, as they kissed my men on both cheeks, continental fashion, with tears and laughter and much choking back of emotions.

All that remained was to find the aerodrome and capture it. I gave this task to Jeremy Spencer, but went with him in case he needed further troops. It was just dark as we arrived and the new air control tower shone white in the half light. 56 Commando dismounted some distance from the entrance and led by Spencer deployed in a long line and advanced to the attack, bayonets fixed.

"Come on now, you chaps," said Jeremy, "spread out a bit, don't bunch up like that, there's good fellows," and then, pointing his swagger stick at the tower, shouted "Get in!" Led by Jeremy, they charged across the tarmac. The enemy up and fled at the sight of them, leaving three dead on the verandah. Spencer had taken the airfield.

I reported back to Liegeois, who was busy composing signals to Leopoldville with one hand and holding off the overwhelming gratitude of the Belgians with the other. It was a great victory for him, but even in his moment of triumph he found time to apologise to me that he had not been able to give us good quarters for the night.

A bottle of champagne was sent up to my H.Q. by some Greeks and we sat around a low table to drink it in the soft light of a candle. Ralph Hider poured it out with due ceremony, but before we could drink we were all sound asleep, including Ralph. And for those of us who know Ralph, the story takes some believing.

I inspected the prisoners by the ferry at dawn the next morning. A rope had been tied round their necks, all save one man who was sitting on the ground, leaning up against a tree.

"Get up," shouted the R.S.M., prodding him with his bayonet. He rose with some difficulty to reveal a great red gash where his left hip should have been. It had been shattered by an F.N. bullet. The wound would have been sufficient to kill an ordinary man.

"Rank?" I asked.

"Major," he said, with a natural dignity and a fearless courage, looking me straight in the eyes. The black Caractacus won my admiration.

"Separate this man, R.S.M." I said, "and see that he is treated as an officer." He was later sent to Leo for treatment, but I believe that it might have been better for him had he died in Kindu.

The Lualaba at this point is nearly a mile wide and Kindu is the terminus for river traffic. The river runs at four knots and is subject to strange currents and sand bars. Tied up alongside were a number of barges and tugs, some as big as two hundred tons. Tom Harrison reported that he could get one of them going if he had sufficient batteries, and was confident that he could navigate it across the river, which was no worse than the waters around New Guinea which he knew.

"Right then, Tom." I said, "you are now in command of all ships and river crossings. Get yourself a crew and report to me when you are ready to make the first trip."

"O.K., sir," said Tom, "just one thing, though. Will it be O.K. to wear me yachting cap?"

The rules about "fancy dress" were stretched to permit this and ever after Tom wore his yachting cap whenever we were engaged on river work.

I was then given the task of capturing the other bank of the Lualaba. If we could get across in Tom's tug, we could bring back another ferry which was anchored on the other side and which was specially designed to carry vehicles. The ferry was vital in the scheme of things. I gave the task to Ian Gordon, but prepared the support plan myself. It was traditional. Air would soften up the defended positions and our 81-mm. mortars would give support almost until we got across. Meanwhile, our heavy machine guns would take on the snipers and others who were infesting the island in the middle of the river. It was such a pretty set-piece affair that I invited Colonel Liegeois and his staff to occupy deck-chairs on the stoep of my H.Q., which overlooked the river so that they could view the battle blow by blow. Tea was served at 10.45 hours and battle was to commence at 11.00 with the arrival of the air. This, I said to myself, is how war should be conducted by gentlemen.

The brave little tug pushed off from our side carrying 57 Commando all armed to the teeth, with Ian Gordon in the prow looking like a Viking and Tom at the helm, conspicuous in his yachting cap. The civilian crew were crouched down on the lee side, taking cover from the odd shots which by now were ranging across the boat from the other bank.

They were half-way across at 11.10 when I gave the order to open fire with the mortars, feeling mighty proud of myself and events in general. But my satisfaction was short-lived. Up went the first salvo with a mighty belch and all eyes followed the missiles, up, up, high into the air and then down, down, until wham!—they landed smack on the ferry we were going across to salvage.

Tom steered the tug in expertly with great skill—an error at this moment would have been costly—and the men stormed ashore. Two machine gun posts dug into the sand contained dead rebels killed by our air attack and the remainder had withdrawn to content themselves with some long distance sniping. The east bank was ours.

The Colonel congratulated us all and said he was sorry, but he had to get back to his office, where he was in danger of being overwhelmed, not by the enemy, but by the paper work. He had no typist, he said, and he was doing everything himself without the normal staff. He was S 1, S 2, S 3 and S 4 all rolled into one and to make matters worse, he had just received a top priority order to send a locomotive to Kongolo at once and he could not find a driver anywhere. He supposed he would have to drive the damn thing himself, he laughed. A few days later Alastair mentioned to him that he had seen the engine leave for Kongolo, but the Colonel was not driving.

"No," he said, "I was not. How could I? I was out chopping the wood."

Now that our blood had cooled and the enemy were contained on the other bank, Kindu felt safer and the war a little more distant, so that a posting across the river had a special significance—it was an invitation to the battle.

A few of my men who had seen what fighting was all about decided that it was not their cup of tea and began with one accord to make excuse. One such was wheeled up before me by the R.S.M., clutching a request for immediate repatriation on the grounds that his mother was going blind. I made sympathetic noises and asked for his supporting evidence. He produced a tatty letter which the R.S.M. read out—it said, "Well, son, I'm afraid I must end now as my poor old eyes are failing me!"

The Colonel visited me that evening. He was apologetic, but he had come to ask us to undertake a rescue operation at once. He knew that we were tired and needed sleep, but it was a matter of life and death. Forty-eight Belgian priests were being held captive at a place called Kalima and they were in grave danger of being chopped now that we had taken Kindu. A resident of Kalima had escaped and would give me all the information I needed.

I agreed at once and issued a warning order to the whole commando to cross the river that night. The general plan was to leave at dawn from the other side, dash the hundred odd kilometres to Kalima, hit the enemy with everything we had got, snatch the priests out of the mission and get back the same day. Ambitious, but feasible if all went well. Tom worked all night and by four in the morning had ferried our whole column across. By dawn we were ready to roll.

The dash to Kalima went off without incident other than having to abandon one truck with a burnt out clutch. The villagers coming out of their houses were amazed to see us flashing by and many gave the Lumumba salute in their astonishment, thinking we were Chinese or Russians. The enemy had just abandoned the Elila bridge, a sixty-yard iron span across a roaring torrent, so we left a section to safeguard it against our return. We arrived at the turn off for Kalima without seeing the enemy,

Kalima is a beautiful mining town built amongst wooded hills not unlike an Indian hill station. The enemy were preparing to decamp when we arrived and we hastened their departure, leaving a few of them spreadeagled on the roads. We went straight to the Mission, where we found the forty-eight Belgian priests imprisoned behind bolted doors guarded by a few Simbas. They were a tragic sight with their deathly white faces and grubby soutanes, crying out to us to come round the back and let them out. They gave us what I shall from now on refer to as a warm continental reception, much kissing and hugging and tears and emotion, so that no matter how phlegmatic one's approach, one was almost reduced to tears. But these were not all. The town was full of civilians, it appeared, all similarly imprisoned. We set off to release them realising it was now a race against time.

I chose a triangular plot of ground in the centre of the town by the Post Office as a clearing station and put Hider in charge, whilst the R.S.M. took details of a Belgian miner and his daughter, who were being held prisoner about ten kilometres away. With a flourish we mounted and tore off, only to find to my consternation that I was in the lead, Alastair was following and the commando was bringing up the rear! The road was too narrow to turn so the R.S.M. and I put a brave face on things and went like hell. We dashed up the hill to surround the house, hoping to catch the guards as they ran. There was a steep slope behind it covered with thick bush into which the rebels had run, when they had heard us coming. I decided to flush them out and ordered the men to fire bursts of automatic fire into the bush, calling on the rebels to surrender. Alastair, meanwhile, had released the miner who now prostrated himself at my feet and begged me to stop the firing.

"My daughter, my daughter," he wailed, tears streaming down his face, "she is in the bush!"

"My God," I thought, "I have killed the child."

She had run off to hide when she heard us coming. I ordered the men to fan out and search the bush, calling out her name—she was only four, and she would be so frightened she might lie still, pretending she was not there. After an agonising ten minutes, during which I prayed to God that she would be found unharmed, the R.S.M. came across her in some long grass, still clutching her rag doll, sobbing and trembling. The big man wrapped her in his arms and tears coursing down his face presented her to her stricken father with great relief.

"Would you like some beer, Major?" he asked as soon as he had recovered sufficiently, "I have two dozen bottles in my fridge and we might as well drink them before we go."

"Thank you, monsieur, but no," I answered, "you see we do not drink in the heat of the day," saying which I turned a defiant eye on my hard-bitten soldiery, some of whom would have drunk battery acid had there been nothing else to drink!

G

Back at the clearing station information was still pouring in about other civilians and patrols were going out to get them in. At two in the afternoon Hider informed me that there were ninety-four names on his roll, men, women and children. At one stage they were making such a noise that I was unable to make myself heard and fired a shot in the air to quieten them. This reduced them to a stunned silence, but not for long.

The R.S.M. mentioned to me that Volunteer X was missing and from his knowledge of the man, thought he might be up to no good. Jack and I went in search of the soldier in question. Seeing a jeep outside a house, we entered just in time to hear a hysterical mother promise Volunteer X anything he wanted, so grateful was she for her liberty. X had decided to take full advantage of her offer and had indicated that he would have the daughter, aged about fourteen, a full-bosomed girl, who now stood petrified in one corner of the drawing-room. Jack drew his pistol and put a shot through the ceiling in his anger.

"I don't think you will, you dirty bastard," he said, fetching him a clout across the back of the head with his enormous fist, felling him in one. "Shoot him, sir?" said Jack, hopefully, quivering with suppressed rage, and giving the prostrate figure a hearty kick in the guts.

In another house a minor tragedy was being acted out. Those that had got over their initial fright were now returning to salvage a few of their possessions and Volunteer Gary Cooper was assisting a Belgian to carry some of his stuff to the trucks. As they were leaving the house, a woman ran out from the kitchen, crying and screaming and begging her husband not to leave her behind. She was a Congolese. The husband treated her as though she was a piece of furniture he was obliged to abandon. She collapsed in a flood of tears, whilst Gary Cooper, a soft-hearted London Cockney, comforted her with, "There, there, ducks, don't take it so hard, love," not a word of which she could understand. His reaction was anger at the callous husband and reporting the matter to me, he said, "I've a good mind to bust that sod in the gob, wiv your permission, of course, sir."

All the civilians were delivered safe and sound into Kindu by midnight, complete with their hand luggage and Colonel Liegeois arranged for them to be flown out to Leo the next morning. The Colonel was overcome with gratitude and loud in our praise. We got to bed at two in the morning utterly exahusted, but with the warm feeling of having done something really worth while. There was another side to mercenary soldiering after all. We lingered some delicious moments over a final cup of tea. The R.S.M. was strangely pensive.

"What's up, Jack?" I asked.

"Nothing much, sir," he said, "I've just been thinking. I don't mind the fighting really. It's the bloody emotions that's going to kill me!"

The overall plan was now to build up our forces at Kindu for a final drive on Stanleyville and this would mean a halt of about ten days. In the meantime, it was vital that we should hold the bridge over the Elila, a main feature on our road to Stan.

The commandos took it in turn to defend the bridge and ran the gauntlet of the 20-kilometre drive every two days. The second time we bought it. Captain Calistrat ran into a well planned ambush in which the rebels fired from the grass verge, knowing it to be sheer suicide. The windscreens of the leading two trucks were shattered and Pat Kirton was blinded by flying glass and shrapnel and was evacuated later. I never saw him again. Volunteer Oosthuizen manned a machine gun on top of one of the trucks and fired on the enemy, covering his comrades who now made for the bush. Although he was hit almost immediately by a burst of machine gun fire, Oosthuizen stayed by his gun firing to the end until another burst killed him outright. He was the first 5 Commando man to be killed in the column and it was a sad 55 Commando that carried his body to Kindu for burial.

Wastage had set in already in the unit and I had signalled base urgently for reinforcements, notably for what was left of 51 Commando and for 2nd Lieutenant Wilson, their commander. On my return to H.Q. that evening two signals were handed to me, both distressing. The former read:

"Despatching 21 men ex 51 Commando yours to-morrow stop regret Wilson in pistol accident stop Dejager."

I was desperately short of officers and I needed Wilson badly. I heard later from his friend, Lieutenant Hogan, who was with him at the time, that he had been cleaning his pistol when it went off accidentally, removing his finger.

The second signal was more personal. It read:

"Feel I should advise you that there are certain difficulties your
wife's confinement mainly connected with breech presentation
stop as her general health is not good urgently suggest you arrive
here before twelfth November stop baby expected any day after that
stop regards Trott."

Ed Trott was the gynaecologist attending my wife with her first
baby. I had promised Phyllis I would be home for the birth of the
baby, come what may, and I intended to be there. It had been an
agonising decision leaving her in the first place and the last few
months had been hell for her.

I handed over to Alastair, cadged a lift to Leo in a T–28 and got
permission from Mobutu to visit my home in Durban for a few days.
He was sympathetic and did everything he could to help me. I
always found the General to be a man of great compassion, particularly where a man's wife or mother was concerned.

As the plane did not leave till the following morning, I went
round that evening to Mr. Tshombe's official residence at Kalina to
pay my respects. The residence was filled to capacity with important
looking people and champagne was flowing. It was Mr. Tshombe's
birthday and he looked happy and confident, circulating amongst
friends and members of the diplomatic corps. I stood behind a
curtain at the end of the room, hoping to catch his eye on his next
revolution. I had intended only that he should know I had passed
through Leo, but he would have none of it. With a loud hurrah he
welcomed me, filled my glass with champagne and escorted me into
one of the little curtained alcoves leading off the main reception hall.
He wanted to know all about Kindu, but more important still what
about Stanleyville?

"Take Stanleyville, Major," he announced, adding magnani-
mously, "and I will make you a Colonel and you will have a big
house with two sentries outside it!"

I laughed. It is just as well that I have a sense of humour. I have
been chasing that big house with the two sentries ever since!

The baby was born at ten o'clock on the fifteenth of November, a
beautiful boy, and his mother was well, thank God.

For some hours I moved in a different world. Everything was so
normal it was strange. Babies were born, people went about their

business and nobody feared death. Until a few hours ago, my world had been a vortex of emotions with death and violence in every spin of the wheel. In a few more hours I would be caught up in it again. I went the next morning to say good-bye to my wife. There have been fewer things in my life which I have found so hard to do. The sight of her beautiful face streaming with tears as I bent to kiss her good-bye, my new-born son nestling in the crook of her arm, haunted me for weeks to come.

My plane was due to leave Leopoldville for Kindu the next morning at dawn. I had the evening free and I spent it reminiscing with my old friend, John Bulloch of the London *Daily Telegraph*. It was a time for relaxation—wetting the baby's head he called it—and we had been making merry for some time in the Memling Bar. A lieutenant from 21 Squadron sought me out to announce that there was a young girl wishing to see me.

She was a nice looking lass of about eighteen with long blonde hair, well brushed to the shoulder. Bulloch and I scraped back our chairs and invited her to sit down, a little puzzled at the unexpected pleasure. She took her seat rather reluctantly, I thought, and said nothing. Bulloch shot me a glance of enquiry. We were in a happy and facetious mood and chaffed playfully with the girl who was really very pretty. She never smiled once or raised her eyes from the table. The conversation flagged. After a pause she asked, "You are Major Hoare?"

"Guilty," I replied.

"Were you at Kibombo on the fourth of November?"

"I was," I answered, falteringly, wondering what was to come next.

"Tell me how my father died," she said, without the smallest sign of emotion.

All the fun and happiness of the evening fled on the instant. My heart went out to the poor girl as the dreadful scene of Kibombo flashed through my mind. I smelt again the acrid smell of cordite and felt the starkness of that horrid little room.

I was nonplussed. I floundered. I lied. John Bulloch came to my rescue and comforted the girl, telling her the truth with great care, his melodious Welsh accent pouring a soothing balm on the awful wound.

After a while she rose, dry-eyed, and with great dignity bade us both good-night and apologised for disturbing us. She had to know, she said, and now that she knew, she was satisfied. She left, head held high.

The evening rang hollow after that and when Bulloch went I retired early to my bed. I was awakened a little later by one of my men, who brought me a signal marked "URGENT". It read:

"Regret advise you Jeremy Spencer killed fourteenth defending Elila Bridge displaying as always great courage stop Wicks."

I am not a soft man, but this went hard with me. The death of Jeremy, sensitive, courageous and lovable man that he was, struck at something deep down inside. I wept in the privacy of my room.

In the morning, before going out to catch the plane for Kindu, I sent a signal to my wife.

It read:

"Call the boy Jeremy."

# 7

## THE STANLEYVILLE COLUMN

Colonel Vanderwalle's plan for the capture of Stanleyville envisaged the use of four widely separated and hard-hitting columns, each led by a unit of 5 Commando, which would do the actual fighting.[1]

The main column, which was the most powerful, would attack along the axis Kindu-Punia-Wanie Rukulu. At the same time 54 Commando, who had already left Boende, would strike via Ikela and Opala. 52 Commando in the north would sweep down on Aketi and then take Paulis, whilst 53 Commando in the east would advance out of Beni to seize Mambasa. Air support had been built up in the last few days and our formidable little air force, based on Kindu, was well within range of all fronts.

The main column, known as the Stanleyville column, comprised over two hundred vehicles and now stood in Kindu, poised ready to strike. Lieut.-Colonel Liegeois was still in command and his general intention was to seize Punia, a town 240 kilometres north of us, and to make it a forward base. A second column to be called Lima Two would be flown in to Punia and then 5 Commando, the strike force, would clear the last main obstacle on the path to Stanleyville—the river crossing at Yumbi. After that there was nothing to stop us rushing down the new main road from Lubutu to Wanie Rukulu and hitting Stanleyville with the speed of a panzer division.

I arrived at the Elila Bridge on the evening of 18th November, féeling very much like a boy back at boarding-school. I was touched by the obvious pleasure with which my men greeted me; perhaps they thought I had gone for good. Excitement was in the air and all down the length of the column men were busy cleaning their weapons, filling machine-gun belts and checking their magazines.

[1] See Maps 1 and 3.

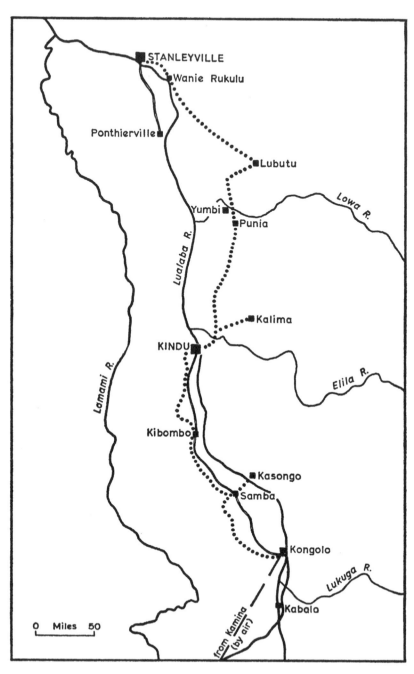

3. KINDU AND ORIENTALE: advance of the Stanleyville column

At the back of the column a Belgian priest, Father Demot, stood before a kneeling group of black and white Catholic soldiers, conducting a service.

My unit had taken on a character of its own and though there was intense rivalry between the Commandos, we closed our ranks when danger threatened to become one unit, 5 Commando, a band of brothers related by the blood of our fallen. By now every man was known for what he was, false reputations had been unmasked, and the hard core of the unit stood out proud and fearless. It was an honour to command them.

I was invited to dinner by Ian and astonished at the menu, which included fresh fish and roast meat, washed down with some uncertain red wine. 57 believed in living well. Any fool can be uncomfortable, they said, but it takes a soldier to make the best of his circumstances.

Over some after-dinner sherry Alastair brought me up to date with events. The day I had left Kindu the enemy had massed for an attack on the Elila Bridge. 57 were holding it at the time, when about two hundred rebels, in several groups, put in a concerted attack with tremendous fire power. Their leader was a sinister figure dressed in a black burnous. A black hood covered his face and this gave rise to some speculation as to whether he might be a white man, perhaps even a yellow man. John Peters had cautioned his men to hold their fire to the very last moment and as the rebels rushed the bridge he let them have it, machine guns, cannons and mortars, in a withering fire. The enemy retreated, leaving forty-five dead on the bridge, but try as they might Peters' men were unable to hit the gentleman in black. With disdain he turned on his heel and walked slowly back along the track, bullets whistling all round him.

A few days later they came again in larger numbers, led once more by the hooded one. This time Jeremy Spencer was commanding 56 and his men were dug-in and well prepared to receive them. When warned of the impending attack, Jeremy alerted his men to their stand-to positions and began to direct the battle from his deck-chair, waving his swagger stick in his usual manner, a means by which he imparted confidence to his men. A lone sniper, much in advance of their main party, took a long shot at Jeremy. The bullet hit him in the temple, killing him instantly.

A funeral High Mass was said for Jeremy in the Kindu Cathedral. The church was packed by all ranks, Belgian, Congolese, 5

Commando and hundreds of civilians, many of whom he had so lately helped to save. There was a special place for men of his own unit who were grieving his death bitterly. A choir of small Congolese boys, dressed in red cassocks and white surplices, sang hymns during the service which was conducted by the Bishop of Kindu. When the Mass ended, the coffin was carried down the long aisle by pallbearers from 56 Commando and all heads turned to follow it on its last sad journey. The little choirboys began to sing a haunting refrain with a sweetness and melancholy known only to the African. The words were in French, but the tune, which hung quivering in the air caught by the dusty sunbeams, was unmistakably "Auld Lang Syne". Recognising it brought many a tear and a lump in the throat to the men of 5 Commando.

Apart from that tragic episode there was nothing untoward, said Alastair, just a few minor happenings. Some of our deserters had sought refuge in the British Embassy in Leopoldville, where rumour had it they were received with the same awe as though they had been escapees from Devil's Island. John Peters was in bed with malaria. Lieutenant Hogan had arrived with 51 Commando from Kamina. Captain Mueller had taken over at Base.

I examined the column at first light. Substantially it was the same as the one which had left Kongolo, but Liegeois now had his own staff and presumably had put away his typewriter and his chopper. I went to the front of the column to have a word with Ian, as his unit was leading. It was a misty morning, but I noticed a forlorn figure, heavily swathed in blankets, shivering behind a machine gun on top of the leading truck. "Who's that?" I asked Ian. "John Peters," he replied. Malaria or not, there was just no keeping him down!

As the column seemed to be in good shape and everybody was rearing to go, I then gave the order in my best Stanley Holloway voice—"Let battle commence!"

The road to Punia was good by Congo standards and led through thick equatorial forest, still dripping from the early morning dew. The dense bush made its way right down to the edge of the track and given a year with no traffic it would swallow up the road without a trace. Already long green shoots reached out on to the middle of the metalled road and a profusion of smilax and buffalo bean made the verge impenetrable.

From a tactical point of view there was a possibility of ambush in every mile of the way and our nerves were keyed up as we approached each likely feature. We halted frequently to change the order of march to make it fairer on the leaders, but in fact it is not always they who get ambushed; more often the armour is allowed through and the soft skinned vehicles further down the line collect it. Every time we saw pineapple husks lying in the road, we knew an ambush would not be very far ahead—pineapples were the enemy's main source of food whilst they were on the run.

Thirty kilometres from Punia, Liegeois called a halt for the night. Ten kilometres back we had cleared a large ambush and I expected the survivors would give us trouble during the night. The rearguard of the column was commanded by Lieutenant Hogan, who took out a fighting patrol after dark to try and capture an enemy truck. He chose a sharp corner for his ambush position and had not long to wait. A large Mercedes Benz truck lumbered towards his position at midnight. As it rounded the bend Hogan stepped into the middle of the road and put up his hand. The truck slithered to a stop, the driver jumped out and was promptly shot dead. Those in the back were dealt with by the ambush party and Hogan drove the truck back to our lines in great style.

The new truck arrived at the right moment to replace one which had unfortunately been destroyed by an A.N.C. driver, who had been trying to make a cooking fire with an excess of zeal and petrol. It was an ammunition truck and was blazing merrily when a Belgian officer leapt on board, at great risk to himself, and started to throw off cases of ammunition. I ordered him off. A moment later the whole thing exploded with an impressive bang and a sparkling display of fireworks. I felt certain that anybody within thirty kilometres of us would know we had arrived.

I studied the map in the cold light of dawn, a hot cup of coffee in one hand. I doubted if the enemy would hold Punia, which appeared to have little tactical significance, but I was certain that they would defend the Lowa River at Yumbi with all the forces at their disposal. Once we were over that they could not stop us. I expected, therefore, a last ditch stand on the Lowa.

We dashed into Punia, which is a long, rambling mining town, all suffering from an overdose of nerves, and began what soldiers refer to euphemistically as "reconnaissance by fire"—in other words, firing without control at nothing to see who's not hiding where. I was annoyed at the fantastic wastage of ammunition and felt my men were behaving like a bunch of raw recruits in their first action, not at all like 5 Commando.

What upset me most was that Tom Harrison was as guilty as any of them. He had acquired an affinity for the Energa grenade, amounting almost to the pathological, and there was always one of these deadly contraptions to be seen on the end of his F.N. rifle. His men said he slept with one under his pillow. Coming round a sharp corner, I saw Tom blast off his block buster with commendable precision at a prison wall, blowing it to smithereens. A bank I might have understood, but a prison was beyond me.

The airfield was a long way out of Punia on the Yumbi road and was undefended. This was to have been 57 Commando's main task and I left a very disconsolate Ian to remove hundreds of saplings, which had been stuck into the ground as an obstruction to aircraft. The rest of the strike force hurried on for the Lowa river, forty kilometres away. Here at least, I thought, we must see some action. I was not wrong.

The Lowa River runs fast and deep and about one hundred yards wide between two very high banks at Yumbi. The village is a small collection of huts on the south bank. The moment the head of our column appeared on the crest of the hill overlooking the river, the enemy opened up with everything they had got. Heavy machine gun bullets whistled through the trees and mortar bombs began to fall in the middle of the river.

5 Commando halted at once and deployed into the bush on either side of the road to take cover, but unbelievably the remainder of the ponderous column closed up, bumper to bumper, until there was a solid mass of vehicles over three hundred yards long, all within range of the enemy. Hundreds of A.N.C. troops now disgorged on to the side of the road, oblivious of the danger.

55 Commando were sent through the bush on a left hook to engage the enemy on the opposite bank and 56, now commanded by Lieutenant Stevens, given the task of clearing the bush on the right and seizing the pontoon and landing stage. Meanwhile, the R.S.M. was screaming at the Congolese troops to disperse.

Mortar bombs began to fall close by with a fearful crump.

"Any minute now, Jack", I said to the R.S.M., "they'll have our range and God help us!"

The thing I feared most then happened. A mortar bomb fell in the middle of a group of A.N.C., killing one outright and wounding three others. Mass hysteria took hold of the soldiers, who flung themselves under their trucks, on top of each other, into the bush, anywhere they could find the smallest piece of cover. Seconds later they began to fire. Some had their eyes tight shut and their rifles pointing up in the air, others fired into the trucks before them, into the bush, anywhere so long as they could fire. It was a terrifying sight and when I realised that they were firing straight at my men, I yelled out, "Cease fire!"

*Arrêtez le feu! Cessez le feu!* I shouted out at the top of my voice, running up and down the panic-stricken column. When that had no effect I jumped on their hands and kicked the rifles out of their grasps. The R.S.M. and Sergeant Hider joined in the game and finally we got them under control. By the grace of God none of my men had been hit.

By this time Alan Stevens had got his men down to the landing stage and cleared it of enemy. I focussed my glasses on the other bank and picked up what I thought must be the main centre of resistance—a blockhouse about two thousand yards away. I was pretty sure the enemy mortars were behind that. I called up our heavy stuff. In a few moments we had mounted our 4·2 inch mortars, manned by Congolese troops, and their third shot put an end to the nonsense. As usual, all organised resistance stopped the minute the rebels saw we meant business and they broke up into small bands to snipe at us from cover.

As Hider and I walked back to my command post I heard a plaintive voice calling out, "Major, save me, save me, I'm dying." Hider nipped into the back of a truck which was stacked full of ammunition and staggered out carrying an Italian volunteer who had taken cover there during the battle. He was drenched in blood. A chance bullet had ricocheted through the side of the truck and then through his thigh, severing the main artery. We patched him up, but he was in great pain.

"You see that, Major", said Ralph, "you can duck into them as well!"

I made a quick plan to seize the other bank which was vital to us. 55 Commando were to do the job and for the occasion I promoted Jack to full Lieutenant and gave him command. Captain Calistrat was appointed Intelligence Officer and John Peters made second Lieutenant. I was sorry to see Jack go from my H.Q., we had grown close in the last few months, but his role as R.S.M. had outlived its usefulness since we had left barracks.

The operation took two hours to mount and included a full support programme with air, mortars and heavy machine guns to protect the strike force as it crossed the river. They used assault boats, powered by outboard motors, driven by Congolese sappers. Their first objective was to seize the ferry which, as always, was on the other bank, and their second to take the blockhouse overlooking the river. We would soon have to transport three hundred vehicles across the river and, realising its importance to us, Liegeois attached a Greek Adjudant-Chef mechanic to accompany the first wave to bring back the ferry.

The plan went exceptionally well. The air rocketed and blasted the other bank, the mortars softened up the area of the blockhouse and the heavy machine guns kept up a deafening clatter to discourage snipers. Jack's men got across without loss, stormed up the slope to the blockhouse, winkled out the defenders who were still dazed from the bombardment, and reported with joy the capture of fifty thousand Belga cigarettes!

Meanwhile, the Greek Adjudant-Chef, who was of a very nervous disposition, in his frantic attempts to pull the ferry away from the other bank pushed off without first securing the ramp. As they reached deeper water the ramp splashed down to hang vertically from the pontoon and gave us endless trouble until we cut it adrift.

Later in the morning 57 Commando rejoined us and brought with them John Latz, who had flown in on a helicopter to Punia from Kindu. He gave us some earth-shaking news. Belgian paratroops had landed at Ascension Island and were being held in readiness to drop on Stanleyville! That put a different complexion on things. Nothing official was said to us and the Belgians knew little more than we did, but staff officers began to dash to and from Punia through the day. I assumed we would be told in due course.

From a quick calculation of the time taken for one crossing, I imagined it would take a further thirty-six hours to get the whole of our enormous column across. This was a sobering thought and it began to gnaw at my vitals. Delay of this sort is one of the most difficult things to live with in the midst of action, it breaks the continuity of things and allows the blood to settle and generally upsets the men. I determined we should get 5 Commando and the armour across that day.

Once more Tom was invaluable. It was not just a case of steering a ferry across a swift river. Here the current was both fast and treacherous with sand banks near each landing place. To add to the difficulties the ferry had only one ramp and had to be turned around in mid-stream.

During the afternoon I relieved Tom at the helm for a short spell. Unaccountably the engine seized half-way across, the current caught the ferry and whirled it away merrily downstream at four knots, cheered good-bye by my men on both banks, who were delighted at the diversion and happier still when they saw who was at the helm. A knot of journalists, noting the disaster, reported the matter to the second-in-command who was enjoying his afternoon tea. Unperturbed, Alastair insisted on finishing his smoke, Sir Francis Drake fashion, and waved the whole thing aside with "Don't worry, the C.O. likes a bit of boating." Tom came to the rescue as always. By midnight we were all across.

Less than three hundred kilometres to the north the sprawling city of Stanleyville spanned both banks of the mighty Congo River, its vast population uneasily aware that the net was closing in. The A.N.C. had reached Mambasa, Aketi had fallen, Ikela was occupied and the Stanleyville column had overcome the last major obstacle in its path to the city. The momentum of the advance was gathering way. The hour of atonement was at hand.

Whilst we lay waiting impatiently on the banks of the Lowa River, seventeen hundred white hostages were being held prisoner by the leaders of the Popular Republic, three hundred of them in the centre of Stanleyville. The lives of the prisoners, Belgians and Americans in particular, were balanced precariously on a knife's edge. Despite repeated requests and entreaties on the part of the International Red Cross, who pleaded with the rebel Government to release the whites, who clearly had no part in the rebellion, Christopher Gbenye refused to allow one person to leave the city. He had been quick to appreciate that of all the weapons in his arsenal, none could be as potent as this one. It was obvious that merely being in the city constituted a threat to the safety of a white person.

It was not a threat to be taken lightly. Daily in Stanleyville dozens of Congolese were done to death before the Lumumba monument, a paved grotto surrounding a framed life-size photograph of the "martyr". Hundreds had already been slaughtered there in the most revolting circumstances, until the blood of the killed lay thick on the marble tiles. The Mayor of Stanleyville, Sylvere Bondekwe, a greatly respected and powerful man, who had done marvels for his fellow citizens since Independence, was one who was forced to stand naked before a frenzied crowd of Simbas, whilst one of the most blood-thirsty cut out his liver. This was given to the mob to eat, still hot and throbbing, as the victim died in agony before their eyes. When the scenes of bloodshed grew too horrible for the local population, the place of execution was moved to the Tshopo Bridge, four miles away. Here the unfortunates were hurled over the parapet into the roaring torrent below, where they were either drowned or smashed to pieces on the rocks. More than a thousand Congolese are known to have met their death in this way, their crimes being only that they refused to recognise the rebel régime.

Gbenye had been at pains to explain to his followers the reason why the Simbas were retreating on every front. He blamed the reverses entirely on the Americans. Part of the Communist Chinese technique is to declare the universal enemy to be American, regard-less of their actual race. America, he said, had sent planes to bomb their innocent women and children, America had sent arms and ammunition to help the A.N.C., and American soldiers were even then in the field fighting against their Simbas. Everything could be blamed on "les Americains". They had caught an American pris-oner, he told the mob, who would be tried shortly for espionage and the people would see for themselves the extent of American inter-vention. The name of the American spy was "Major" Carlson.

Amongst the prisoners held captive in Stanleyville and now guarded by the Simbas was the entire staff of the American Con-sulate, headed by Michael Hoyt, all arrested in defiance of dip-lomatic convention, and held in gaol for no reason other than that Gbenye saw in their lives a means of preserving his own tottering régime. The full fury of the rebel government fell on the unfortunate Dr. Carlson, a man whose life had been devoted to the healing of sick Congolese in the remote north-western corner of the Congo. On two occasions he was sentenced to death, but execution had been stayed at the last moment, when the rebels realised that his life represented a further bargaining counter against the Leopoldville Government.

America and Belgium reacted violently to the inhuman treatment of their nationals and warned Gbenye and his Government of the illegality of the actions committed in their name and the inevitable consequences. In Nairobi, American Ambassador William Attwood was all set to meet Thomas Kanza at a meeting arranged by Jomo Kenyatta in an effort to compromise, but Kanza refused to discuss the safety of the hostages without a guarantee that the Popular Government would not be attacked. It was an impossible situation for Mr. Attwood, and his Government instructed him to end the negotiations. The alternative was already in hand—the landing of a Belgian Parachute battalion on Stanleyville.

The Popular Republic had offered combat to the A.N.C., but now that they were being beaten on all sides, they resorted to the foulest blackmail imaginable—holding to ransom the lives of innocent spectators.

The world spotlight now converged on the bloody stage of Stanleyville, the players a handful of black megalomaniacs, incredibly stupid in their insanely arrogant demands, destroying on the one hand thousands of their own people whilst holding in the other, in mortal peril of their lives, seventeen hundred innocent non-combatants, men, women and children who had no part in the struggle.

The whole world held its breath as America, Belgium and England consulted feverishly in the wings. The stage was set for tragedy.

It was the morning of 21st November and the start of the long wait. I concentrated 5 Commando and the armour at a bridge ten kilometres down the road and reported back to Liegeois for the latest news. He was apologetic. There was nothing he could tell me except that the Belgian paratroops had been moved to Kamina Base. He did not know if it was intended to use them. He also had some sad news. During the night the Greek Adjutant-Chef had fallen off the ferry and had been drowned in the swift current. Liegeois had taken an assault boat out himself at three in the morning to search for him, but there was no trace of his body. It was a bad start and it cast a gloom over the day.

Liegeois confirmed that it would take at least another twenty-four hours before the rest of Lima One and Lima Two were across. His orders were to halt the column on the other side, possibly for several days. I gasped. To halt at this moment when we were within striking distance of Stanleyville filled me with apprehension. He said he was

H

sorry, but he knew nothing more and agreed that it was a hard order to obey.

The day dragged by interminably. I was conscious the whole time of an unspoken feeling of urgency, an overwhelming impulse to get going and to reach Stanleyville. The men's nerves were beginning to fray and they kept asking for news. I shook my head. I knew as much as they did.

I reasoned things out with Alastair. Every success we had had so far had resulted from one thing only—surprise. If only they would let us go, we could hit Stanleyville like a ton of bricks; the rebels would run, I was absolutely convinced of it, and we could get the hostages out unharmed. Alastair agreed that we had the power to do it. We certainly had the spirit.

I decided to act. I sent for Captain Calistrat. Ferdy was a personal friend of Mr. Tshombe. I gave him orders to get to Leo as quickly as he could to beg the Prime Minister to give me an overriding order to strike Stanleyville at once. I realised that this was most unmilitary and ran counter to everything Vanderwalle was trying to do, as I thought, so slowly. I pointed out to Mr. Tshombe in a letter that the fact of bringing Belgian troops to Kamina would only increase the danger to the hostages, apart from being a most questionable move in the eyes of O.A.U. We, 5 Commando, could do it, I assured him. There was no need to complicate the matter. The enemy would not expect us. I could be there within ten hours of his order! There would be no need for an international incident.

I fired Ferdy with enthusiasm for his mission and shot him off in a jeep to Punia, confident that one of the Cubans would give him a ride to Leo in a T-28. Meanwhile we waited.

It began to rain. My column was formed up at the bridge, a massive iron affair covered with dried out palm leaves. According to the rebel witch-doctors anything covered by a palm leaf was safe from attack. On either side of the road was thick equatorial jungle and my men amused themselves for a while chasing chimpanzees, which were screaming madly and leaping from tree to tree.

Night fell and the rain continued unabated. A solid sheet of water dropped from the heavens to rise again off the soggy road in a steamy cloud three feet high. Alastair and I sat in the front of the tentacle, miserable as sin. We discussed Stanleyville. In the past Alastair had always been the one to put the brakes on any wild scheme I came up with. Normally he counselled caution. This evening he surprised me.

"Mike," he said, "what's stopping you? Why don't you give it a go. You've got the whole of your commando plus the armour and the engineers on this side of the river. If we leave right now, we could reach Stanleyville by dawn tomorrow. They'd never know what hit them. I'm damn sure they are all expecting days to pass before anything is decided about the paras. We can't miss."

"What about Liegeois?" I asked. "It will be the end of him."

"No it won't. You can cover him with a letter, stating your reasons for doing it. He won't like it, of course, but we've got to think big. If we don't get there damn quick, every one of those hostages will be chopped, I'm certain of it."

We discussed the technicalities. There was no reason why we could not do it. There was nothing to stop us. Least of all the enemy!

"My God, Alastair," I said, "you're right. We'll leave at dawn. Call an O group for 23.00."

Looking back on it now, I am astonished how small a thing it was that altered the whole course of that decision, a decision which had it been carried out might have prevented an international incident and saved hundreds of lives.

As I ran back to my jeep through the rain, Fin Mills, my radio operator, called out to me.

"Sir—B.B.C. if you want them."

Over the abominable crackle in the earphones a voice announced:

"In Stanleyville Mr. Christopher Gbenye has stated that the white hostages have been taken to a place ten miles from the city. He says they are surrounded with barrels of petrol and that at the first sign of attack by Congolese troops or mercenaries, they will be burnt to death."

I spent the next two hours debating the matter within myself. If we were successful in the sudden dash for Stanleyville, it would be a victory of the first magnitude. I was in no doubt about the glittering prize it offered. But suppose that barbarian Gbenye actually did set fire to the hostages when he heard we were in the city, what then? The mere idea was terrifying.

I decided to give it more thought and sent word to Alastair to postpone the O group until 04.00 the next morning. I was incapable of making the final decision. In the end, tired and exhausted, I fell asleep. In the nightmare which followed I saw the tortured faces of the dying hostages, flames leaping hundreds of feet around them, and one was saying, "He did it to win some cheap fame!"

I woke up and decided against it. God help me, it was the wrong decision.

Finally, at ten the next day, orders came to move to Lubutu, a town about one hundred kilometres away. We were not to wait for the whole of Lima Two to cross. Lubutu would be a forward base for the final push on Stanleyville, and they would catch us up there.

We travelled fast through thick forest and began the climb up to Lubutu, which we reached at four in the afternoon. Not a shot was fired as we entered the town. It was deserted.

Lubutu is one of the prettiest of Congolese towns, set out in the usual superb Belgian fashion. It is built on the crest of a hill and on all sides there is a commanding view of the countryside, which now begins to open out.

If we were going to have to wait, then Lubutu seemed a much better place to wait in than the banks of the Lowa. I established my H.Q. in a house overlooking the valley.

During the night a sentry woke me up. He spoke softly.

"Sir, 55 Commando reports enemy truck approaching."

"Stand to!" I said. The word ran through the lines. The unit was good at this sort of thing, and within five minutes, without a cough or a sneeze, every man in 5 Commando was standing to his post, armed, ready for action. I looked out across the valley and picked up the headlights of a truck coming fast in our direction.

Now it was toiling up the steep hill into the town. It was a pitch black night and the two shafts of its headlights stabbed the air. Surely it would stop now. I felt certain this was a raiding party.

I was wrong. The truck entered the town to the right of our position. Not a shot was fired. Perhaps it is one of ours, I thought. It came on right past the bottom of our garden and went straight up to the hospital, which was occupied by Graham Hogan's 51 Commando. The truck stopped and a rebel lieutenant got out.

Our sentry shot him dead.

More rebels in the back who had been sleeping now jumped over the side and three more were killed. The rest disappeared into the bush. A lieutenant from the armoured cars, a Belgian colonial, jumped into the back of the truck and found another rebel hiding in a corner of the truck. He dragged him out, threw him on the ground and shot him dead. He was a boy of eight.

I inspected the scene in the morning. When I saw the body of the child, I was furious and demanded an explanation. My anger knew no bounds when the brave murderer was paraded before me—it was the same bastard who had given me all that trouble on the beach at Moba! This time I fixed him for ever.

It was apparent that the enemy did not know that we were in Lubutu. The hospital was still functioning and the rebels sent their sick and wounded there. The rebel Lieutenant was carrying an "Ordre de Mission" authorising him to take his son, the boy of eight, to the hospital for treatment. He had a broken arm.

Liegeois thought we might be in Lubutu for some time, so I moved my H.Q. into the hospital. Just before lunch, a helicopter arrived bringing some journalists. One of them was George Clay. George was the Africa correspondent of C.B.S. in America and I had met him before. He was popular and fearless. He asked if he could travel as near the front as possible when we advanced on Stan. He had brought all his sound recording apparatus with him and his photographer, Claus Kruge. It was his last mission of this type, he said, and he wanted to make it good.

A number of world-famous journalists had joined the column and I took this opportunity to discuss with them the frightful dangers of their job. The best they could hope to get was a good story at the risk of their lives. It is one thing to be an armed soldier, getting paid as such, and another to be an unarmed recorder of events. Danger of this sort was nothing new to George Clay. He had covered the whole of the Congo troubles from 1961 to 1963 and he was well aware of the risks involved in column warfare. None of the journalists saw anything extraordinary in what they were doing and it was not the last time I had occasion to admire their courage. One of them, Robin Mannoch, A.P. correspondent in Leopoldville, now asked me if he could accompany a patrol I was about to send out. When pressed, he told me that he was anxious to see how he reacted to enemy fire—his next assignment was Vietnam and he wanted to know if he could take it!

The purpose of this patrol was to find the new main road which had been constructed recently. It was a wide tarred highway, by-passing Lubutu and going straight to Wanie Rukulu. Wanie Rukulu was sixty kilometres from Stan. The patrol reported that they had found it. It was a magnificent road and we would be the first to use it. At two in the afternoon things began to hum. Helicopters flew in and out and at three Colonel Vanderwalle arrived to hold an immediate O Group. His orders were startling. The Belgian paratroops were to drop on Stan at 06.00 the next day, weather permitting. We must attack Stan from the east at the same time. The column would move at 16.00—in less than one hour's time!

I dashed back to my headquarters and issued my orders to Commando leaders. The column began to form up as I detailed the tasks of each unit, stating exactly who was to seize the Otraco Beach, the Tshopo Bridge, the American Consulate and so on. The vehicles were thirty yards apart and the column stretched far down the road. I decide to motor down it for a last inspection. It began to rain. I stood up in the jeep as Hider drove me slowly down the long column. It was an impressive sight. The men were in tremendous spirits and as I went by they shouted out, "Good Luck, sir, see you in Stanleyville!"

I stopped to talk to a truck-load of Cubans who had just joined me. I called them 58 Commando and they were proud of the title. They were as tough a bunch of men as I have ever had the honour to command. Their leader was a remarkable man and the most dedicated soldier I have known. I wished them luck. They would need it; I had given them the job of finding Hoyt and his compatriots the following morning.

I blew my whistle and the column moved forward into the coming night.

# 8

## STANLEYVILLE

It was obvious to every man in 5 Commando that it was going to be a hell of a night. I had impressed upon all ranks a hundred times the stupidity of moving by night through enemy controlled territory, and here we were, about to do that very thing. In one stroke we were throwing away every advantage we possessed and were sitting ducks to an ambush party, which could see us coming a mile off.

Colonel Vanderwalle, who now led the column, was in no doubt about the risks entailed. He regretted it, but it was one of those occasions where the dangers had to be accepted. There was no alternative. Perhaps there would have been if we had not delayed so maddeningly on the way, but it was useless to recriminate.

Hider and I sat in two inches of water in an open jeep, Mills in the back manning the radio. We pushed on as hard as we could whilst daylight lasted and as night fell we came to the end of the new road. The villages began again.

Frenchy shot up a Volkswagen at the side of the road which burned fiercely, and half-way thrugh the village the enemy opened up with rifle fire on our right. We answered with machine guns all down the length of the column and miraculously nobody was hurt. The same thing happened again a few miles further on, but the third time we bought it. One of the Cubans had stopped a bullet in the stomach and was seriously wounded. Green, our medical orderly, settled him on a stretcher on the back of a truck and we moved on again, the Cuban delirious with pain screaming out his agony in Spanish.

At the next village the enemy were prepared for us in some strength. They let the armour go through and then raked the leading trucks with fire. 57 Commando dismounted at once and engaged the enemy, who were hiding in the grass verge, in hand to hand combat. A burst of fire hit Sergeant Freddy Basson in the head almost at once and he dropped to the ground, mortally wounded. The same burst got young Bruce Harper in the arm, shattering his wrist. The lion-hearted youngster caught hold of the rebel who had fired and flattened him on the track with one swipe of his good arm, at the same time yelling out to his twin brother who was behind him, "Kill him, Wally!" Wally put a burst through the rebel. In the next truck Hans von Lieres was wounded twice, once in the leg and once in the head behind the ear.

A nurse came up from the back of the column. She was the only medically qualified person there. I admired her courage, she must have had nerves of steel. She applied a tourniquet to Bruce's arm and did what she could for Hans, but gave him little hope. The bullet was lodged in his skull. Ian walked back through the glare of the headlamps. "Freddy's dead," he said.

It was sheer murder. I was beginning to revolt against the stupidity of the advance, and I knew there was Wanie Rukulu yet to come. Wanie Rukulu by night would be madness.

The column moved on. George Clay had set up his recording apparatus in the back of the tentacle and was now recording the traffic on our P.R.C. 10 net. Alastair and I had just exchanged some comment on the heavy cannon fire coming from 57, when we ran the gauntlet of enemy fire once again.

"Stop the column," yelled Alastair down the P.R.C. 10, "George has been hit!" A burst of machine gun fire had caught the tentacle, riddling it with bullets. Two shots had gone through the loud-speaker in the roof and a third straight through George's head. He never knew what hit him. When I reached him he was dead in a pool of his own blood. John Latz and Alastair were riding in the front of the tentacle, one yard from George, and escaped by a miracle. Poor brilliant George! He was at his post to the end. He had said it was going to be his last assignment in the Congo and it was.

His death decided me. I was not in command of the column, but para drop or no para drop, I was not going to allow any further movement by 5 Commando that night. I put it to Vanderwalle bluntly. He was shaken by our losses and had already, I suspected, decided to halt the column.

We burnt down the village where George was killed and slept in the rain. When dawn showed red behind us on the track, we resumed the march for Stanleyville. I salute every man who took part in that column that night. It was the most terrifying and harrowing experience of my life.

With the dawn our confidence returned. An hour later we entered Wanie Rukulu just as our air appeared overhead. It was 06.00 hours and we wondered if the paras had already dropped on Stan.

The River Maiko runs through Wanie Rukulu and there are two large iron bridges in the centre of the town which is overlooked by a ring of hills. It is a perfect setting for a determined defence and Liegeois had previously told me that the Force Publique used it as a tactical training ground for this reason. Unexpectedly the enemy did not make a stand there and contented themselves with a sporadic fire on the column as it flashed through, the iron girders of the two bridges ringing with ricochets as we rattled across.

We halted on the hill leading out of the town. Our two dead were transferred to a school bus, which we had captured on the way and was placed in the charge of our Military Police. The bus was to bring up the rear.

The road was excellent and there was nothing to stop us. The column accelerated and sped down the road to Stanleyville, every moment bringing us nearer to the reckoning. My stomach knotted in a ball of apprehension as we passed a sign which said, "Stanleyville —30 kilometres." Mills passed me a signal from Vanderwalle. It read: "Paras dropped on Stan 06.35.' I looked down the column and spying his Land Rover, raised my hand in the V sign.

It was exactly nine o'clock.

Meanwhile in Stanleyville the last grim act of the tragedy was now about to be staged. The white hostages had been moved to the centre of the city and over three hundred of them were held prisoner at the Hotel Victoria. They had all long since given up hope. Only the previous day *Le Martyr*, Gbenye's newspaper, had screamed defiance in a hysterical tirade:

"We shall cut out the hearts of the Americans and Belgians and we shall wear them as fetishes. We shall dress ourselves in the skins of the Americans and Belgians."

That morning Radio Stanleyville had blared forth without stop, "Ciyuga! Ciyuga! Kill, kill! Kill all the white people. Kill all the men, women and children. Kill them all. Have no scruples. Use your knives and your pangas!"

For the hostages the end was near, it was just a matter of hours. At seven o'clock the Simbas came.

Two miles away a battalion of Belgian paratroops, the élite of the Belgian Army, led by the redoubtable Colonel Laurent, had seized the aerodrome and that very moment were forcing their way into the middle of the town, step by step, street by street. It was a race against time.

Now the Simbas were hammering on the doors, forcing the hostages into the street below. They formed them up into three ranks and made them sit down. In the distance the sound of firing grew louder with every minute, as the Simbas nervously fingered their rifles and spears itching for the order to kill. The leaders of the revolt had already fled the city and Colonel Opepe was now in command. The mild little man, who had so often befriended the whites, was torn with indecision. He was expected to kill them, but faced with the enormity of the crime, he could not bring himself to to do it.

But no-one looked at Opepe whilst Bubu was there. "Major" Bubu was Soumiallot's fetish, a gross monster of a man, a deaf and dumb mongoloid, who stood gesticulating in front of the prisoners, dressed in a monkey skin robe. "Kill, kill!" he grunted in pantomime acting out his orders in an inarticulate frenzy—until someone fired a shot. It was the signal for the massacre to begin. Machine guns blazed out at point blank range, the Simbas carefully selecting women and children for their first targets. Maddened by their blood lust, the Simbas sprayed the crowd with automatic fire. A little Belgian girl of six was cut in half by a hail of bullets. A Belgian priest had his leg severed above the ankle and bled to death. Phyllis Rine, a young American, was mortally wounded. She also bled to death. Many just toppled over and lay where they fell.

After the initial shock the prisoners broke and ran in every direction. A young Belgian woman, carrying her small baby, was forced back into the street by a Simba brandishing a spear. The terror-stricken mother dropped to the ground, bent double to protect her child. Another Simba held a rifle to her head and fired repeatedly until she was dead. The baby lived. A whole Belgian family was wiped out in a similar manner, each trying to protect the other.

At the other end of the column Michael Hoyt and Dr. Paul

Carlson made a dash for cover. Hoyt jumped over a low wall and escaped, but Carlson was gunned down by a burst at the very last moment. A bullet had struck his temple.

It was all over in four minutes.

Then the paras came. The leading scouts, rushing from cover to cover, cleared the Avenue Kitele finding over eighty people dead and wounded on the ground. Twenty-two lay in pools of blood and would never move again. Over forty were seriously wounded and of these, five died later.

It was an act of unparalleled savagery. Stanleyville bore witness on 24th November 1964, to one of the most hideous and barbaric crimes of the century, a premeditated act of murder, for which the leaders of the rebel régime must one day be held accountable.

Keyed up to a pitch of intense exceitement, the column moved fast towards Stanleyville. We expected to fight for Camp Kitele, which was on the road into the city from the east and was known to be Olenga's headquarters. We approached cautiously, only to find a Belgian paratrooper lying in the grass outside the main gate. We cheered at the sight of him. "Vive les paras!" we shouted, relief and anticlimax overwhelming us all. I was happy that we would not have to fight for Stan, but perversely I would have liked a showdown with the rebels, once and for all.

The column rolled on another four kilometres into the heart of the city and halted in Lumumba Square. Colonel Vanderwalle arrived. It was a moment of triumph for him. It was his plan, he organised it from the start and his mind guided the whole thing to a successful conclusion. Even in the last agonising approach, he had personally led the column. I felt proud of the little man and, as he walked past me looking old, tired, but unbeaten, the men gave him a cheer. The Colonel had earned our undying respect. In his turn, he had changed his mind about us, and subsequently I heard him defend us against extravagant accusations of bad behaviour. "They are not angels," he said, "but, by God, they can fight!"

I paraded the men formally and thanked them for their wonderful efforts and told them I was proud of them. We awaited orders from the Colonel, and I put the men on standby. In the meanwhile, I sent Tom down to the Otraco Beach to see if any of the tugs were working.

He was back within the hour having found the eighty-ton tug

*Geri* in perfect working order, complete with crew. The idea of striking the Rive Gauche at once leapt to my mind and I made urgent representations to Headquarters, but to no avail. We were too thin on the ground already, they said, to hold both banks on Day One. I realised that by that decision every single white person on the left bank was doomed to death.

Jack Carton-Barber stormed up from the back of the column, hopping mad. Thrusting a Greek volunteer in front of me, he explained that this was the military policeman who had been detailed off to guard the bodies of Freddy Basson and George Clay. Almost speechless with rage, Jack blurted out the story. The bodies were not here, they were still in Wanie Rukulu! I could hardly believe it possible, but when I heard the explanation, I was forced to accept it.

The Greek was to bring up the rear of the column as we left Wanie Rukulu, but try as he might he could not start the engine of the school bus. He stood in the middle of the road, waving down each lorry as it went by, but none would stop for him. As the last truck came rumbling up, he was forced to abandon his bus and leap on the tail-board as it passed him. He had no choice, he said, he was terrified of being left there alone.

It was impossible to go back straight away, but I promised Jack we would send for the bodies, as soon as it was humanly possible. Probably tomorrow.

"Tomorrow!" gasped Jack, "Christ, Major, you know what bastards these people are, you know what they are liable to do in the meantime."

I nodded.

John Latz and Robin Mannoch were typing their stories on portable typewriters, balanced on the hood of the tentacle. When they finished I took them round to Avenue Sergent Kitele.

The scene was too awful to look upon. I have never in my life seen such wanton butchery. I told Mills to take some photographs which we would show the world. People must see what can happen when savages lose control.

Jack and I walked round the corner to where the paras had set up a small H.Q. On the way we came across a tall young civilian, carrying in his arms a limp child of three. The Belgian was dazed. His clothes were torn and blood-stained. He had one shoe on, its lace undone. He was wandering about lost. I thought his mind might be unhinged.

Jack spoke to him in Afrikaans.

"Can we help you, meneer?" he asked.

"My boy, my boy," he cried, anguish torturing his face. He was beyond tears. His son was lost. The family had been together during the massacre, sitting there—he pointed out the place   "Then after the firing, we ran . . . and now he's gone. He's only five . . . fair hair . . . so high . . . "

"And your wife?"

His face fell as though he had suddenly remembered her. Dead.

God, I thought, how bloody tragic. I put my arm around his shoulder and let him cry. Jack took the little girl. I could not look at Jack, I knew he would be holding back his tears with difficulty.

Action was the answer.

"Jack. Two jeeps quick. Eight men. Go with this chap and scout the ruddy town until you've found the child."

The Belgian was past everything. He went with Jack, showing no emotion. His spirit had cracked.

We did not find the boy.

Orders now arrived for us to hold various parts of the city. The Colonel intended to occupy a very tight perimeter. Camp Kitele had been taken over by Lieut. Colonel Lamouline who was commanding Lima Two. 57 Commando took over the mission at the river's edge and set up heavy machine guns and 75-mm. cannons to engage the enemy on the opposite bank, 800 yards away. They began to raise a deafening din. 51 Commando rushed off to seize the Tshopo Bridge, whilst Alastair established my Headquarters in a small block of flats, known as "Pourquoi Pas," overlooking the river.

He showed me to my room. Very comfortable, I thought, double bed, own bathroom, nice view of the rebels, all mod. con. I flung myself on the bed, my arm hanging over the side. My hand rested on a dead body. I shot up like a flare.

"Alastair!" I yelled, "be kind enough to remove this corpse from my room, will you?"

A great guffaw of laughter came from the "servants quarters" as Sergeant Hider and his men were busy finding the bottom of a bottle of Cinzano. "C.O.'s getting fussy," said Mills, as two of them hurried up to my room. But the laugh was on them. As they picked the body up it came to life, literally! He was not dead, only shamming! We were all so shaken and our nerves so ragged that we took it in turns to give the "corpse" a good kick in the arse to relieve the tension before handing him over to the military police.

It was three in the afternoon and I was just about to doze off for five minutes shut-eye, when a runner arrived.

"Colonel Raudstein from the U.S. Embassy and the American Consul, Mr. Clingerman, to see you, sir."

I might have guessed that Knut Raudstein would have been in to Stan on the first C-130 available. He was dedicated to his job as Military Attaché. There was nothing diffident or withdrawn about Raudstein, and he wasted no time in getting to the point.

"Mike," he said, "you've got to do something for me. There are two American families in the middle of rebel-held Stan about eight kilometres from here. I want them out. Clingerman will show us the way." Mr. Clingerman was a slight man with a studious, happy face. He was bubbling over with enthusiasm.

To know Raudstein is to obey Raudstein.

"O.K., Colonel," I said, "but you better stay here. In your position as Mil . . ." He stopped me short.

"Not bloody likely," he said, "where you go I'm going. These are Americans, lad, Americans. Don't worry about me, I'm just going along for the ride. I'm under your orders, I'll do anything you say."

The opportunity of having a full colonel, American Army, under command was not one to be resisted. I raised a patrol in twenty minutes and accompanied by Clingerman we set off.

I put the Colonel in an armoured car and took the Consul with me in the tentacle. He kept up a steady chatter the whole way, oblivious of the gunfire, as though we were out for a Sunday afternoon drive. We arrived at the two houses in a residential area.

Clingerman dashed in while I set the field. John Peters sealed off one end of the avenue and engaged the enemy, whilst the other end was held by a group led by the Colonel. I just had time to see him kneeling behind an armoured car, blazing away with his M 14 before we got the two families out. A man, some women, and two children. I think he was a Professor at the University. I seated them in the back of the tentacle. One of the ladies was distraught.

"What about Aunt Millie's present?" she cried. "I've left it in the kitchen." The man said something crisp about Aunt Millie. The rest of the family shouted her down with protest. This was no time to be thinking about silly things like presents, they all said, let's get going for heaven's sake, they chorused.

In an effort to calm their nerves and show them there was nothing to worry about, I told the good lady to go back and get Aunt Millie's present and anything else she wanted. She would never see that house again. She wanted to go desperately, but she gave way to the others.

I blew my whistle and we were off. The sea of rebels which we had parted for a few brief moments closed in again, engulfing the house.

Half-way back we stopped to engage some snipers and the Colonel opened fire on the A.N.C. by mistake.

"Hold it Colonel," I screamed, "that's our side! That's the A.N.C.—furthermore, dammit, you're doing what I've always wanted to do!"

Clingerman delivered the party to the aerodrome and four hours later they were in Leopoldville.

At the Hotel des Chutes the A.N.C. were having a field day. Every minor clerk who had served the rebels was pushed down the stairs and shot out of hand. Nobody escaped. They were dragged from under beds and inside cupboards, some even shot whilst hiding behind bathroom doors. The city rang with the sound of fire. Snipers from the roof tops made things uncomfortable and men ran from house to house avoiding the open wherever they could.

A white soldier (not my unit) tried the handle of an upstairs bedroom. It was locked. He shot out the lock and bashed in the door with his boot. Inside he found a young Congolese girl, hiding in the shower cubicle. He stripped off her clothes till she was naked. He liked what he saw. "Shower," he ordered her, "then lie on that bed." Without a word she obeyed. He raped her.

Then he ordered her downstairs with the other prisoners and marched her to the river's edge some sixty yards away. A small pier ran out ten yards into the fast flowing water.

"Walk down that," he commanded.

She knew she was going to die. With the impulse of revenge, tinged with a spark of genius, she turned and screamed at the sadist, words which would last him the rest of his life . . . "You don't know how to make love . . . you're too small!"

With a derisory laugh she faced her death. It came a second later. Two shots rang out and with a pitiful "Oh!" in sad contrast to her brave speech, her body disappeared into the Congo for ever.

The road to the aerodrome was littered with the bodies of rebels. A few were killed when the paras came in, but small actions had been taking place since. The scene at the airfield was nothing short of heroic.

C-130 aircraft were landing and taking off whilst paratroops ringed the perimeter of the airfield. A chatter of a machine gun from time to time warned that the rebels were still holding on. In the huge hangar the wounded were lying in rows on stretchers and doors. Medical orderlies bustled around, carrying blood-soaked bandages. I heard an English accent and was introduced to an English army doctor. I could hardly believe my eyes. He was there with a section of the R.A.M.C. What I would not have given for them in my unit.

Civilians were piling up in knots of ten and twenty and Red Cross officials buzzed around, taking names and comforting the stricken. Consular officials arrived with every plane and tore into the task of finding their nationals. There was a low murmur of excitement pervading it all.

I went in search of my wounded. Hans was unconscious and a deadly white from loss of blood. They had decided not to operate, it was too risky. I wondered if he would make it; the young German was made of iron. It would not be for lack of spirit, of that I was sure; he had the guts of ten men. I waited for Bruce to come out of the operating room.

"My God, no!" I shouted, "you haven't!" I could not believe it. The doctor, a young Belgian attached to U.N.O., nodded to me as he took off his gloves and his mask.

"Sorry, Major," he said, "we had to do it. Gangrene had already set in." He had taken Bruce's arm off at the elbow.

I screwed down every emotion in me as I saw the two of them carried on to a C-130 for Leo.

At 3 Group Headquarters behind the Avenue Kitele, Lieut-. Colonel Liegeois set up his office. Lieut.-Colonel Grailly, an old

Congo hand and former member of the Force Publique, took over a bureau marked "S 4." A large blackboard ran the whole length of one wall. Grailly stared at it dumbfounded. On it was written in his own handwriting the Order of Battle of 3 Group—but dated 1960! Every unit was named in detail, but in four and a half years it had not been touched.

In the main street Sergeant Ross-Smith comforted an elderly Belgian. He was the owner of a Stanleyville Hotel. "Take what you want," he said, giving the Sergeant the keys. "Drink everything, use the place, I'm going home to Belgium and I shall never come back to this God-forsaken place." His wife had been killed that morning. His life was over.

The shops were full. Business must have continued until a few hours ago. Shelves were stacked with merchandise; jewellers' shops displayed trays of jewellery, wireless shops had radios and tape recorders, everything had been functioning normally.

Now the sack of Stanleyville began. I had warned my men that looting would be punishable by death. It was an absurd edict. Within minutes of our arrival in Stan the Congolese troops of the A.N.C. were bashing in the plate glass windows of the shops and selecting whatever they fancied. The case was put to me—we shall be blamed whether we loot or not. It was obviously so. My final word was—the order stands. "If any of you get caught looting, don't look to me for mercy. Looting is nothing but theft, and you will be treated as a criminal."

I know my men looted, but with the atrocities occurring all round me, I put it in its right perspective. I made no excuse for them, but I did not regard it as a shooting matter. Not after what I had seen.

I was introduced to Colonel Laurent, the Belgian commander of the paratroops. He was a quiet, efficient man and a brilliant commander. He was busy withdrawing his men from the town. "That was Operation Dragon Rouge," he said. "Now we must prepare for Dragon Noir." This was to be a drop on Paulis, a big town four hundred kilometres to the north-east of Stan, where a large number of hostages were being held. It was scheduled for the day after tomorrow.

The decision to use the paras was finally taken at ten o'clock the previous night. They were at Kamina in our old barracks when the

I

word came. Five C-130s were to be used for the actual drop. The drop would be made in two circuits, thirty-two from each plane each time.

They first saw Stan in the pale light of a grey dawn, low cloud obscuring the main features of the town. At seven hundred feet the jumpmaster despatched his men. Solid bundles tumbled from the doors, checked and blew into billowing puffs of silk. They hit the ground less than half a minute later. The Simbas opened up with ·50 Brownings, holing the aircraft as they banked steeply for a second run in. Down came the paras again, and in less than two minutes from the moment they had first appeared Colonel Laurent had his entire unit of three hundred and twenty men on the ground, one party engaging the enemy in the tower, another silencing the machine guns on the perimeter and the rest clearing the runway of obstructions. The C-130s circled round dropping bundles of heavy equipment and within a few minutes two armoured jeeps—Minerva Land-Rovers with three medium machine guns in each—rolled down the ramps of the first C-130 to land.

Now the dash for Stan began. Without waiting for more jeeps, the paras ran behind the two which were already out, brushing resistance aside and braving enemy fire aimed at them from houses on the way.

The leading elements broke into Avenue Kitele at 7.20. But for them every man, woman and child in Stanleyville that day would most certainly have met their death.

I congratulated the Colonel on his wonderful feat. He waved the compliment aside modestly. "We could never have done it without Colonel Isaacson," he said. Colonel Isaacson of the U.S. Air Force had been in command of the fourteen C-130s used for the operation. It was his drive and great organising ability which had ensured success. He received the American Order of Merit for his gallant work that day and Colonel Laurent was later decorated by a grateful Belgian Government.

I finally turned in to the sound of gunfire from the other bank and our own cannon on the esplanade below. Every time we fired the windows shook fit to break. I looked in at Alastair. He was sleeping like a baby, fully dressed.

I lay on my bed for a moment, wondering why it had all been necessary. Why had three of the great nations of the world allowed themselves to be messed around by a handful of semi-literate savages? This was something I would never be able to understand. My solution to the hostage problem would have been the landing of an airborne battalion damn quick, regardless of diplomatic niceties. Suit your tactics to your enemy. Queensbury rules when you are fighting gentlemen; no holds barred when you are up against savages. They do not think any the more of you if you use kid gloves and soft talk. Less, as a matter of fact; these are the traditional signs of weakness in Africa.

I fell asleep, sorting out the problems of the world.

Ian Gordon and ten men boarded a helicopter to rescue the bodies of George Clay and Freddy Basson. They were escorted by three T-28s. They landed on the road in front of the bus, throwing out a screen to hold off the enemy, whilst they got the bodies out. They had not been touched. In less than five minutes they were off again.

We buried them with full military honours in Stanleyville cemetery. It rained hard and the smell of the fresh brown earth rose up to mingle with our sorrow. The graves had been dug hastily and were too small for the bodies, which were on stretchers. Sergeant Parkinson gave crisp orders to the grave-diggers in Swahili and they set about enlarging the graves.

A close friend of George Clay, a well-known photographer, Ernie Christie, was overcome with grief at the loss of his great friend and in the depths of his sorrow jumped into the grave and widened it with his bare hands. It was a touching demonstration of the love one man can bear another and our hearts went out to him. I gave orders for wooden crosses to be erected at once, showing them both as members of 5 Commando. I looked at Ernie Christie for approval.

"I think George would have liked that," he said quietly.

On my return to "Pourquoi Pas" two shocks were waiting for me. The enemy had got our range from the other bank and had dropped a mortar bomb on the roof of my headquarters but fortunately there was little damage. Sufficient, however, to make me want to move. Graham Hogan escorted me to his jeep where a silent figure lay under a blanket. I pulled it back. It was our popular armourer, Van der Westhuizen.

Hogan had been holding the south bank of the Tshopo Bridge, the scene of the murder of over one thousand Congolese in the last hundred days, but the rebels still controlled the north bank and were sniping through the day. His position was almost untenable. In an effort to improve it, he attacked the enemy and Volunteer Van der Westhuizen was killed in the advance. Two other volunteers were badly wounded and these were evacuated to Leo at once.

The U.S. Consul asked me to take over the American Consulate. "It has just been used by Soumiallot", he said, "so you are in good company." He marched in fearlessly, whilst I cautioned him against this sort of bravado. A full day later we rid the adjoining house of a nest of rebels, any of whom could have taken a pot shot at the Consul.

The Consulate was in good condition and showed every sign of hasty evacuation. Copies of *Le Martyr* lay on a table and much Public Relations Equipment filled the rooms. In the official part of the Consulate we found the cipher room completely destroyed and saw a hole in the roof of the vault, where we understood Hoyt had made his escape on one occasion.

The residential part was sheer luxury and I settled in and prepared to enjoy it. As the Rive Gauche overlooked the lawn and there was still considerable fire coming from the other side, I gallantly put Alastair in the front bedroom, reserving the back one for myself. A locked door yielded to an axe and in it we found sixteen pieces of luggage belonging to the Consular staff. I had great pleasure in forwarding these "untouched by hand" to Colonel Raudstein and I hope they found their true owners in due course.

That night the heavens opened and a tropical storm struck Stanleyville. At midnight I heard a hammering on the kitchen door. The lights had failed and I groped my way through the lounge. Standing in the rain were three of my officers. Without a smile they came in. (For the purposes of this story, I will call them Captain, John and Jack, but these are not their right names.)

The Captain said, "Sorry to disturb you, sir, but it's rather important. Can you try a man for murder tonight," he paused, "now ?"

I am not at my best in the middle of the night, particularly when woken from a deep sleep.

"No," I said, "tomorrow."

That it was only the timing that upset me and not the subject matter gives some indication of how far my mind had acclimatised itself to this sort of life.

"It's got to be tonight or not at all," said John. "The bastard will get away during the night. He knows we are after him."

A trial for murder and the accused still at large—it quickened my interest. Jack poured out three large drinks—John did not drink—and we sat around the dining-room table.

"Go on then, tell me," I said with more than a touch of asperity.

Jack told the story of the man who had raped the girl and murdered her down by the river near the Hotel des Chutes. Of the three he was the most agitated.

"Why wish it on me, Jack? He's not a member of 5 Commando, you know that. Let his own C.O. try him."

"There's only one man in command here, sir, and that's you. You know it too, don't you? Don't let him get away with it, sir, please."

"You've tried him already, Jack?" He looked into his glass.

"If you let him get away with this, sir, it'll set a standard of behaviour in Stan which will sicken you. Every man will think he's got a licence to kill and rape."

"Not my men, Jack."

"How well do you think you know your men?" asked John.

The thing was getting away from the root cause of their visit. They were determined to find the man and have him tried that night and, if found guilty, executed, and all ranks should be told about it. That was the gist of it.

"Get him," I said, finally. "We'll try him next door. Will you need an interpreter?" Apparently not, his English was good enough.

An hour went by. I dressed and set up some candles in the front office, where there was a reception desk that looked oddly like a witness box. The Captain returned, followed by the accused—a man of about thirty, dark haired, heavy jowled, unshaven, and with a small forehead. He wore a jump jacket open at the front. His hair line came close to his eyebrows which were bushy. He was a bouncy type, fit and strong.

We sat down. I took his name and asked him how he pleaded to the charge of murdering the Congolese girl. Not guilty. I explained the seriousness of the charge and that if we should find him guilty, we would execute him that night. He sweated with terror. The lightning flashed and a gust of wind almost extinguished the four candles on the desk between us. They cast long shadows on the wall and ceilings. We lowered our voices unconsciously.

"Give your evidence, Captain."

He had been a police officer in Rhodesia and rattled it off expertly.

"Is that all?"

John had none and Jack had none, only what they had been told. It was all hearsay.

"It won't do, Captain," I said. "I must have someone who actually saw it with his own eyes and is prepared to say so."

In half an hour they returned with three Congolese, who had been eyewitnesses to the incident. They were wearing white bands round their heads, a sign that they were not rebels, officially, and must not be shot at. An interpreter came with them. Their evidence was irrefutable.

"What have you got to say?" I asked the accused after the witnesses had gone.

He did not deny what he had done. Spoils of war. She was a rebel. He did what he was entitled to do. It was a poor case. He saw it was going badly with me and he began to cry.

Jack was softening towards him. The Captain and John remained detached. He began to tell us about his home in Europe and his wife and kids and that he was a professional footballer in a minor league, and intimate details of his home life. He sensed that Jack would speak for him. He rambled on, addressing Jack pleadingly.

I stopped the irrelevant flow.

"The court will now consider the case," I said. "Take the accused outside." Jack delivered him to a sentry. We discussed the verdict. There was no possible argument. He was guilty.

Extenuating circumstances, any mercy to be shown?

None.

Sentence?

We thought deeply.

"We shall now each write down on a piece of paper the sentence we wish to pass on this man. If the sentence you give is confirmed, you will also be the executioner." We agreed that would be fair. After ten minutes during which not a word was exchanged, the slips of paper were handed to me. I opened them as a fresh peal of thunder rolled overhead.

I read them out.

"Jack; thirty-five strokes with a cat of nine tails and discharged the service."

"John; to be shot in the same circumstances as he shot the girl; at the river's edge with no mercy."

"Captain; he must be given a pistol with one bullet and told to commit suicide."

They looked at me. I summed up as best I could. The crime warranted death, of that there could be no possible shadow of doubt. But we were not a properly constituted court for this purpose and the taking of a man's life, even in these circumstances, was something from which I shrank. Therefore, we would visit on him a punishment that would be worse than death. I opened my piece of paper.

It read: "The big toe of each foot will be removed."

We all agreed, Jack with relief, the others reluctantly. As it was my sentence I must also be the executioner.

The four of us took him down to the water's edge to the spot where he had murdered the girl. It was the place of execution. A flash of lightning lit up the small pier and the black water rushing by.

The other three held the man, screaming and struggling in their grip. John quietened him with the butt of his pistol.

"Lucky bastard!" he said, with a grim sense of humour, "lucky to be getting away with it. If it was up to me . . . "

I took out my Colt 45 and with two quick shots blew the big toe off each foot.

He bled profusely. We took him to the hospital behind the airport and flung him off the jeep, in agony.

Five days later he was killed in a plane crash. Fate had confirmed the sentence.

# 9

## THE INNER STATION

Stanleyville is the most Congolese of all Congo cities. It is the "Inner Station" of Conrad's *Heart of Darkness*. It is the terminus for river traffic from Leopoldville, which cannot go further upstream because of the Stanley Falls. It is economically important as the clearing station for the produce of the eastern Congo, which finds a market in Leopoldville and the west, and it is the hub of the most densely populated province in the Congo, the Province of Orientale.

The European part of the city is as beautiful as Leopoldville with large modern buildings set out in gracious surroundings, paved streets and a planned spaciousness. The blocks of ultra-modern flats which overlook Lumumba Square are built to the very latest design with split level floors and every modern contrivance from lifts to air conditioning. Luxurious riverside villas, well-kept lawns and long, palm-shaded avenues are a living testimonial to their Belgian architects.

Two days after our arrival the city was a tragic sight. Nothing moved on its deserted streets, save army jeeps hurrying to and fro. Starving cats prowled through looted shops, worrying overturned trash cans. Empty boxes littered the sidewalks and broken glass lay in slabs on every street. Stanleyville had been saved and raped simultaneously.

The Congolese population of Stanleyville lives in three enormous *cités*, the largest of these called Mangobo. The rebels had taken refuge in these communes as soon as we arrived, and before Stanleyville could be considered safe, these rabbit warrens would have to be systematically cleared. At the moment our occupation of the city could only be described as tenuous. The small perimeter we held was constantly threatened and reinforcements were rushed into the city by air.

Belatedly the order finally came to undertake the most pressing operation of all—a raid on the Rive Gauche to rescue the twenty-eight Belgian priests and others who were known to be held captive near the cathedral. I had been horrified at the delay in mounting the operation, but gladly detailed off 56 Commando to cross the river at the head of an A.N.C. strike force to search out the hostages. Tom Harrison, who was now permanently employed on the river and had his own Congolese crew to help him, was at the helm of *Geri* and put the party ashore with little opposition. The raiding party arrived too late—two days too late. Every one of the Belgian priests had been massacred and the only survivors were a British woman missionary and her two children, who had hidden under the stairs of the vicarage, whilst the murder was being committed.

Tom ferried the bodies back to our side and they were all buried in a mass grave in Stanleyville cemetery. The rebels closed in again on the Rive Gauche.

There were a number of miners in my unit who held blasting certificates, issued by the Chamber of Mines in Johannesburg. I now gave them a task worthy of their combined talents—to blow up the Lumumba monument. The life-size photograph of Lumumba, framed behind heavy plate glass in a cabinet not unlike a telephone booth, flew into the air in a million pieces, destroying the blood-caked marble tiles which surrounded it. It was the most popular blast of the week.

Through the night I frequently heard lesser bangs of a similar nature, but I was forced to assume that my men were blowing up safes to see if any rebels were hiding inside them.

The same day I had a visit from Mr. Clare-White of the British Embassy in Leopoldville. He was a down-to-earth, energetic type and was greatly concerned about the safety of nine British missionaries at a place called Yakusu, nine or ten miles down the river. He begged me to lose no time in mounting a patrol to rescue them, as they were thought to be in great danger. I was happy to do it. The fact that the British Embassy considered us to be "scum" did not enter into it.

There were some difficulties involved in the operation, the main one being that we would have to cross the Lindi river and we had at

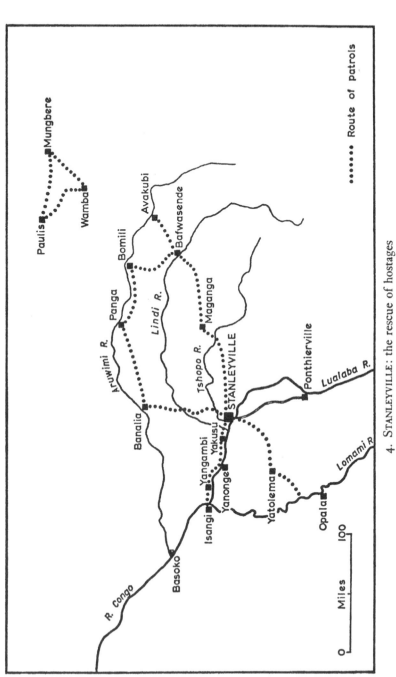

4. STANLEYVILLE: the rescue of hostages

this time no assault boats or river crossing equipment. I decided we would use canoes and march from the other bank. I alerted the patrol, who were to be on the start line at the aerodrome at 14.00 hours. Alastair nipped into the control tower and checked with the Cubans that they could hold an umbrella over us for the rest of the day and support us across the river, and then back again along the jungle track. It is always the return journey along the same route that is so dangerous.

I checked the column and dealt severely with one of my gentlemen who had the temerity to be drinking beer from a bottle at that unseasonable hour. Just as we were about to set off a jeep tore up and decanted an untidy figure on the road. He saluted, German style, clicked his heels, bowed from the waist and announced that he was my doctor.

"Doctor Germani, *à vos ordres,*" he announced. "Put me at the head of the column, if you please. Do not worry about Geneva convention, I intend to come as a soldier," he patted his F.N. For one glorious moment I thought he had come to take over command.

"Join Lieutenant Peters," I said. John had a built-in hatred of all foreigners—unless you were Yorkshire you were a lesser breed and not to be reckoned with—and I thought it was time he was educated. Here and there, I told him, you will find a good one, and this chap looked good to me. Oozing with character, I thought. Bulging might have been a more accurate description.

We approached the river bank cautiously and flushed out a few defenders and captured a canoe. The dug-out canoes of the Congo are magnificent pieces of craftsmanship, some as long as sixty feet and capable of carrying fifty men. Three, lashed together, will float a three-ton truck quite easily. I was contemplating the capture of the other bank, when Tom announced that he had got the ferry going, but its asthmatic Ford V8 engine needed constant attention. Now that we had the ferry we could use our transport on the other side and the whole thing would be completed in a matter of hours. We called up the air, who gave a scintillating display of aerobatics, firing on the other bank a bare fifty yards ahead of us, empty cartridge cases raining down in the water to one side. When half the column was over on the other bank, I realised we could not wait for the balance if we were to complete the mission in one day and I told Alastair on the radio he was now in command of the crossing and to expect us back about six that evening. He never forgave me.

We had no difficulty finding Yakusu, as it lay on the river bank, but to find the Protestant Mission posed a problem. After an initial resistance the Simba guards vanished into the bush and my men dispersed in groups, calling out the names of the hostages. Most of them were looking for the usual imposing residence which house Catholic Missions in the Congo, but I might have given them some guidance on that point.

I walked down the riverside path and noticed an unpretentious dwelling that could have been the Protestant Mission. I strolled down the path as Eriksen, my runner, called out their names. I banged on the door and saw some startled faces the other side of the glass panes. The door was unbolted and a woman said, "Major Hoare, how nice of you to come. We were expecting you!"

I was flabbergasted at her composure. I almost imagined she would ask me in, apologise for the state of the room and invite me to have a cup of tea. They were British all right. No tears, no laughter, no suffocating emotion, no warm continental welcome, just great relief that we had come. I called the roll and they were all there.

In one corner a matriarchal figure stood wonderfully erect, horribly bruised and beaten, with two black eyes, her broken arm in a sling. The brave Simbas were no respecters of age and the mighty warriors had thrashed the old lady within an inch of her life only the previous day. They had all been threatened with death and suffered unimaginable indignities. They were convinced that their time had come and began to say their final prayers.

There was no time to lose if we were to get back to Stanleyville before dark and we bundled them on to a truck. The air kept a close watch on the road as we sped for the river, firing ahead of us to keep down any possibility of ambush. Four miles from the river a T-28 peeled off from its circuit and dived down on us, as though to loose off one of its rockets. I watched dumbfounded as it came nearer and nearer, and finally, to my horror I saw the tell-tale puffs of smoke as the rockets were discharged—straight at us! There was no time to duck or take cover—the rocket exploded with a shattering bang under the leading jeep, shrapnel flying everywhere.

When the smoke cleared we found the jeep totally destroyed and young Volunteer Menzies seriously wounded in the thigh and all others in it peppered with shrapnel—including Robin Mannoch, who had come along for the ride. We screamed in anger at the plane which circled and swooped again. Terrified that it was going to loose off another salvo, we dived for cover, cursing and swearing. As the good missionary doctor, a Scotsman, said to the Press later, "You should have heard the language!"

The plane headed for home seeing the damage he had caused and in twenty minutes a helicopter dropped on the track to evacuate the wounded. I thought this would be a good time to despatch the British and put them aboard, too.

From there to the Lindi was only a matter of minutes. The enemy were still hiding in the deep bush on either side and from time to time took a shot at us. Tom was bringing the ferry back from the other bank when he noticed a sudden movement in the heavy foliage, fifty yards upstream. He fired off a burst with his F.N. just in case. A short sharp scream and a small canoe slid out from under the overhanging trees and floated downstream, nobody paddling. It circled slowly, caught by the current, until it was quite close to us. Now we could see into it. An elderly man lay motionless, his back against a bundle of white clothing, a handkerchief over his face. It was blotched with blood. A woman lay dead in the bottom. The canoe circled closer in deadly silence as the blood-stain spread over the man's shirt.

"Bloody murderer!" one of the men said.

Nobody would talk to Tom for the rest of the day.

Four hundred kilometres north-east of Stanleyville the railhead town of Paulis lay deep in a pall of red dust. The events of Stanleyville had placed the lives of every European in the gravest jeopardy.

"Dragon Noir" began that day, and shortly after dawn the Belgian paras dropped again, seized the airfield, and set about evacuating the white hostages in the town. Once more Colonel Laurent and his men added lustre to their shining record and saved two hundred and fifty people from certain death. Even a few hours' delay would have proved disastrous.

For twenty priests in the Dominican Mission, however, it was already too late. In a typical frenzy of rage and hate, after the news of the fall of Stanleyville, the twenty had been lined up and killed with spears and pangas. Many were tortured before death and their bodies left to rot on the Mission steps. An American priest, Joseph Tucker, was killed first. He was tied to a chair and the Simbas gouged out his eyes with a broken bottle. Then they trussed him up like a chicken and beat him mercilessly along his spinal column with rifle butts and clubs until he died. It took them forty-five minutes to kill him. With his last breath he called on God to forgive them.

In Paulis itself the rebel régime had followed slavishly the Communist pattern of horror in its efforts to break down law and order. Over four thousand of the Congolese population—almost an eighth of the total inhabitants of Paulis—were murdered by the Simbas in the last one hundred days. For the majority of the killed, it was enough that they were "intellectuals"—people who were able to read and write, and held clerical posts. To be well-dressed was to court almost certain death, and those who did not agree whole-heartedly with the concepts of the new régime were instantly put to death.

The Provincial President, a man known to be loyal to Mr. Tshombe's Government, was executed in front of hundreds of jeering rebels with ritual bestiality, as a warning to all others. The ritual followed the age-old custom. First his tongue was cut out. Then his ears, his hands and his feet were hacked off with razor-sharp pangas. Finally, a bamboo stake was driven into his rectum. He lasted fifteen minutes, watched by the insane mob of hooligans.

The savages had not moved one inch towards civilisation in the last eighty years, despite the noble self-sacrifice of hundreds of missionaries.

America and Belgium now bore the full brunt of their humani-tarian action and brought down on their heads the displeasure of the Communist bloc and the bulk of the Afro-Asian peoples. The land-ing of Belgian paratroops had, as its sole purpose, the rescue of innocent white and black hostages and was thoroughly understood by the people for what it was. Furthermore, the plan had been endorsed by N.A.T.O. before execution, and then only after Mr. Tshombe had appealed to all African countries for assistance, either by actively supporting his attempts to stop the rebellion or passively, by refusing to aid them. The fact that Ghana, Algeria and Burundi were stoking the fires of rebellion with arms and ammunition from Russia and China was left conveniently unmentioned.

If the joint action had a fault, in my opinion, it was that America and Belgium had been too slow about it, too voluble before the event, and too meek after it. And while they were about it they should have taken every white hostage out of Orientale Province, simultaneously. The pause between "Dragon Rouge" and "Dragon Noir" was militarily unsound.

Reaction to the slaughter of innocent people at Stanleyville and the rescue operation sparked off comment at a tangent to the truth. The opportunity for anti-American, anti-colonialist propaganda was too good to be missed by the Communists. A Communist-inspired outcry now rang around the world that made the Belgians and the Americans responsible for the Stanleyville atrocities and not the Simbas! Fantastic as it sounds, the story was blown up to represent the rebirth of Belgium's colonial administration and shown as a flagrant piece of imperialism on the part of the United States.

African countries went berserk. Algeria screamed she would send arms and ammunition to help the rebel cause. In Cairo a mob of Egyptian students burnt down the John F. Kennedy memorial library. In Moscow, Sofia, and Prague, African students rioted at the U.S. embassies in reaction to this absurd perversion of the truth.

In Peking, Mao Tse-Tung made one of his rare appearances at a rally of over 700,000 Chinese, protesting at U.S. action in the Congo, the crowd carrying huge cartoons, showing the Congolese people heroically repelling the enemy. Others showed "U.S. imperialists" massacring Congolese, while wearing a cloak inscribed "humanitarianism." In Accra, President Nkrumah declared the action to be a "flagrant act of aggression against Africa and a warning that colonialism is not dead." Finally, in Tanzania, in a moment of mental aberration, Julius Nyerere, hitherto regarded as a moderate, deplored the combined U.S.-Belgian para drop as "reminiscent of Pearl Harbour".

In the face of this hysteria, America and Belgium remained stoically unrepentant but, to my mind, regrettably silent. Propaganda is a two-handled sword and in the Congo we looked in vain for some word from the great powers to defend their humanitarian action. Finally, to the everlasting credit of the United States, that great statesman, Adlai Stevenson, gave the lie to the monstrous and ill-considered accusations of a number of African countries by declaring in the United Nations:

"Never before have I heard such irrational, irresponsible, insulting and repugnant language in these chambers—and language used, if you please, contemptuously to impugn and slander a gallant and successful effort to save human lives of many nationalities and colours."

The Belgian paras came, delivered and departed. We were now left to get on with it.

The time had come for a determined effort to rid Stanleyville of the rebels. Colonel Vanderwalle divided the City up into so many areas and began a giant push to sweep the enemy out of the three enormous *cités*. Lieut.-Colonel Lamouline, a Belgian regular officer, was in control of the A.N.C., together with a number of Belgian mercenaries who now formed a new unit called 6 Commando. Their main purpose was to provide stiffening to the A.N.C.

The sweep was a great success. Captain Gordon was in command of our sector and announced that evening that Mangobo was clear, but better still, that we had captured the butcher of Stanleyville, the infamous Khingisa.

"Bring him to me, Ian," I said. I had plans for Khingisa, alive.

"Too late, sir. The A.N.C. got at him before I could do anything about it." He tugged at his moustache. "Not to worry, I had his body dragged round the city for all to see. The mob cheered when they saw it. I've dumped what remains on the Lumumba Monument."

I went up to have a look for myself the next day. The body was swollen to twice its normal size and covered with flies. The stench of putrefaction was so overpowering that I could get no nearer than ten yards. Parts of the body were missing. They had been chopped off during the night.

Before ringing down the curtain on the horrors of Stanleyville, I must record one last abomination. Late one evening Jack Carton-Barber asked for a truck-load of rice to feed the starving thousands of Congolese prisoners, penned up in the stadium. It was a humanitarian act on his part and not part of his duties. I went with him. The stadium was jammed tight with over twenty thousand citizens of Stanleyville, packed shoulder to shoulder, a seething mass of black humanity illuminated by a chain of arc lamps. A pelting rain made the scene even more miserable.

On a flood-lit platform a tribunal was in session. It was a "trial by acclamation." As I watched it, I realised the clock had been put back two thousand years. A rebel was paraded on the dais and his name announced over the public address system. If he was cheered, he was released. If he was hissed, he was taken out and shot.

This was the "Inner Station" all right.

The following day I flew to Leopoldville to visit Mr. Tshombe and to see my sick and wounded. The Prime Minister was at Binza and saw me at once. If I had expected to find him jubilant over the events of Stanleyville and the apparent collapse of the rebel régime, I was to be disappointed. The Prime Minister was tired, overworked and dejected.

We discussed the next phase of the campaign and the coming meeting of the United Nations, which he had decided not to attend. His eyes were sadder than ever.

"Some people think that this is the end of our troubles in the Congo. It is not the end. It is the beginning. Our task in Orientale is a challenge to every man of peace, and until we have sealed off the country from outside intervention, we can never call the Congo our own. Major, do you think we shall ever see a happy, united and peaceful Congo?" I was glad he did not press me for an answer.

If the Prime Minister was less than jubilant it was understandable. His action to hire mercenary troops to help put down the rebellion, his agreement to the joint American-Belgian action to rescue the hostages, and his firm government domestically, successful though they were, had brought him nothing but hostile criticism and savage abuse. In the face of it all, this remarkable man saw his destiny clearly—to lead the Congolese people along the path to peace and self-dependence.

I visited the General. His attitude to me was as ever formal, correct and distant. He agreed readily to my proposal to recruit another one hundred and fifty men to replace wastage in the unit.

I visited the Louvanium Hospital with Ian. Hans had already been flown to Johannesburg, where the bullet had been removed from his head and he stood every chance of a quick recovery. The colder climate of South Africa would assist him, whereas here on the equator, the slightest wound or scratch produced complications. Gangrene and tetanus threatened every casualty.

Bruce Harper was in a private ward. The corridors were full of the Stanleyville wounded and the reek of anaesthetics filled the air. I sat next to his bed. His voice was barely audible. I put my ear next to his mouth.

"Sorry, I can't . . . offer you . . . a drink, sir," he said with effort. I looked at Ian, my eyes filling with tears. A flutter of panic shot through my chest. I rushed into the corridor and stopped a doctor.

"What are you doing for young Harper?" I demanded. "Can't we

K

do anything more? He's dying, I tell you, and all from bloody gangrene."

I was distraught. I wanted to blame it on somebody, unreasonably. Ian calmed me down.

"We are doing all we can, Major," said the doctor. "He stands a fifty-fifty chance."

We visited my other men. They were all doing well and were being well cared for.

During the night Bruce died.

I hurried back to Stanleyville and sent Alastair off to Salisbury to get the new men.

Nothing had moved in my absence. There seemed to be no plan for the exploitation of the successful capture of the city. It was as though the Belgian staff had planned as far as this and had no ideas for the next phase. It was apparently the end for them, but, as Mr. Tshombe had said, it was far from the end, it was in fact the beginning.

I asked about the bigger plan for the outstanding operations. What was the intention with regard to the hundreds of white hostages dotted around the city and in the Province? Did they intend clearing the "Old Elephant Camp"—a known rebel stronghold, only seventeen kilometres from the centre of the city? What were they going to do about the left bank of the river, still held by the enemy?

Nobody could tell me. Worse still, nobody seemed to care. The only thing which was certain was that the original 5 Brigade staff, members of the Belgian Technical Assistance, had been engaged only for a period of three months, and this had now expired. "Home for Christmas" was their watchword and with one accord they began to pack their bags and leave. I was sorry to see them go, they had done a good job, and I hoped we would see Colonel Vanderwalle again before the whole thing was over. It was a forlorn hope.

Our old friend, Liegeois, was unlucky. A B.I.A.S. Skymaster, which had been on charter to the Congo Government, was due to return to Brussels on completion of its contract. It was its last trip. As it took off that morning, bound for Leo and Brussels, the tail-plane hit a pile of drums stacked on the side of the runway. The aircraft turned over, killing all the crew and two passengers. Liegeois was dug out of the wreckage with a broken back, a cigarette still dangling from his lip. It was a sad end to his wonderful fight in the Congo.[1]

With a battalion of A.N.C. under command I now undertook the capture of the Rive Gauche. By this time we had the drill for river crossing off pat and after the air had softened up the other bank and our 4·2 inch mortars prepared the way, we met little in the way of solid resistance to our actual landing. The river had risen five feet overnight and Tom put us down, to our chagrin, in six feet of water.

I held a small perimeter to begin with around the area of the docks and enlarged it to include the cathedral, when all opposition had been quelled. One of my men was shot in the shoulder and another suffered a spear wound in the face, before we got the situation under control. Before nightfall, we had overcome an enemy heavy machine gun post and an 81 mm. mortar emplacement and could truthfully say we were in command of the left bank.

The next day I decided to attack the large army camp, known as Camp Leopold. I saw this as an entirely routine infantry operation. By noon it was all over and Jack, who had been in charge of the centre sector, announced with pride the capture of one hundred prisoners, ex-A.N.C., who had surrendered to him complete with uniforms and weapons. I waited for Jack on the corner of a football field. Down the road he came, as proud as Punch, standing in his jeep at the head of the prisoners, who were marching in perfect formation, flanked by our guards. A huge white flag preceded them.

As they approached my corner, which was to be a saluting base, Jack murmured to his driver, Proetti, out of the corner of his mouth, "Turn left." Alfredo thought he said, "Turn right," and proceeded to decant a much crestfallen Jack on the track, amidst hoots of laughter. Jack clipped the Italian on the ear, saying, "Bloody fool— I've a good mind to charge you with loss of dignity!"

That afternoon we captured the "Poudriere." The enormous ammunition dump, consisting of over three hundred separate small buildings, covered an area of several hundred acres and contained enough ammunition to supply the rebels for years to come. In two of the houses we found vast quantities of ammunition which had originated in China and had apparently come via Algeria.

[1] When I last heard from Lieut.-Colonel Liegeois he had spent over six months in hospital and had practically recovered.

Now that the left bank was securely in our hands, all that remained was to garrison it with a unit from the A.N.C. and one of my
Commandos, and then to patrol extensively along the two main
roads leading out of it.

I hurried back to my Headquarters on the right bank, anxious to
come to grips with the bigger problem, the one nobody seemed to
care about—the rescue of the remaining hostages.

# 10

## A NUN'S KISS

The beautiful town of Isangi stands at the confluence of the Lomami and the Congo rivers and is about one hundred and fifty kilometres downstream from Stanleyville. For several weeks no word had been received of the fifty Belgian priests and nuns and the large number of Congolese nuns, who ran the Catholic Mission, and we were now asked to undertake their rescue.

It was a task to try our mettle. The river crossings in themselves would be a major problem, as we would have to cross the Congo to reach Isangi and the river ran over a mile wide at that point. I prepared a strong force from 5 Commando to travel as light as possible with maximum speed. We took with us a unit of Congolese sappers, but left our armour behind for greater mobility.

We swept into Yangambi to overcome a light resistance, brought in the tug, *Geri*, anchored it against the picturesque jetty, and left a holding force to form a base from which we could operate and get assistance in case of trouble. The main column pushed on for the village Yakusa. Air had already told me that the village was empty and there was no sign of life in the neighbourhood. Judge of our surprise, as they used to say, when we burst into the village to find over three thousand villagers dashing for their canoes in a mad state of panic. It would have been sheer murder to have opened up on them and I am glad to say not a shot was fired. The unit had learned its fire control.

Yakusa was the most miserable spot in the Congo that night. The mud was a foot thick and every vehicle sunk in up to its axle. Mosquitoes came down in droves and nothing kept them off but the smoke of our fires. The final discomfort was a plague of red ants, no respecters of rank, and the cause of many an impromptu cabaret. Heavy soaking rain put the finishing touches to a night of unparalleled misery and we longed for the dawn, which was slow in coming.

At first light 57 Commando under Ian Gordon chugged away for the opposite bank in four assault boats, Tom navigating through the rocks, and battling to beat the current midstream. In another hour we were all across safely and formed a beach-head seven kilometres west of the town. We began the march into Isangi, scouts well forward. The Simba guards vanished from the Mission at the first sight of us and we found all the Congolese nuns hiding in the outhouses, petrified with fear. Many of them wept copiously and had to be coaxed out of hiding. Jack comforted them as best he could and somebody took his photograph as he pulled one of the nuns up from the ground, where she was lying. (This picture was subsequently published in a French magazine with a caption stating that he had just knocked her down!)

In another building we released a Belgian priest, quite overcome with emotion. He was a mechanic, he told us, and had been spared by the rebels in order to keep the ferry running across the river. He did not know where the white priests and nuns had gone to, but knew they had been removed about ten days ago. He thought Yangambi was the most likely place, but the villagers were sure to know. As for the civilians of Isangi, he feared for their lives.

We marched into the town which was deserted and despite a thorough search, we failed to find the seven civilians. In one place by the river's edge there was an overpowering stench of putrefaction, with somebody's pet dog whining over it, which led me to believe the worst had happened, but we had not the time nor, to be truthful, the inclination to dig.

By ten I called off the search and withdrew to our beach-head, stopping on the way to blow up the Lumumba monument and set fire to it with palm oil. I noticed that all the Lumumba monuments in this area were erected on the same pattern. A few natives hung around our boats in a surly fashion, unhelpful and unco-operative. One was the village headman, who was immediately recognised by the priest we had just liberated. It was obvious that he must know something about the civilians of Isangi and where the priests and nuns had been taken. I sent for him.

"Kneel down," I said. He knelt in the mud at my feet. Volunteer Schoeman examined his head and his stomach for the Mulele marks, which all rebels are presumed to carry—a small cross knicked into the flesh by a sharp knife.

"He's a rebel all right," he announced triumphantly, "look!" An infinitesmal cross showed white on his forehead. Schoeman pulled out his 9 mm. Browning and cocked it.

"Shoot him, sir?"

I gave Schoeman a look which said, "Lay off." I admired his enthusiasm, but could not share his conviction.

"Not yet, Boet. Later perhaps."

Schoeman had been a hunter in Kenya and spoke fluent Swahili.

"Ask him where the white people have been taken."

No reply.

"Ask him if he has seen any white fathers cross over the river recently."

No reply. Just a helpless mumbling. He knew nothing.

A man kicked him in the small of the back and flattened him in the mud. A large boot trod on his neck to help him remember. His memory returned. Yes, he had seen about fifty people cross the river some days ago, but he did not know where they had gone.

"And the civilians?" He did not know. The mumbling act again.

The man was being incredibly stupid. The headman of every African village knows exactly what is going on for a radius of many miles around, as well as the intimate secrets of his own village. I was determined to have no more of it.

"I will give you fifteen minutes to tell me exactly where the white fathers have been taken and what has happened to the civilians of Isangi. If you fail, I shall burn down your village and kill every man, woman and child here."

If he was in any doubt that I meant what I said, he had only to look at Boet for instant confirmation.

He ran to the village talking drum—a section of hollow tree trunk three feet thick with a slit in the top—and began to beat out a message with two rubber-ended mallets.

Miraculously people appeared from nowhere. In less than ten minutes five thousand villagers materialised out of the bush, running out of their huts and stumbling out of the fields. The Chief drummed on. In the distance we could hear an answering drum. He was assembling the village. He addressed the crowd, told them what I had threatened to do and asked their advice. Should he tell us the truth? A low hubbub answered him.

"The priests are in Yangambi Mission," he said.

"And the civilians?"

"They are dead. They were drowned in the river ten days ago." Later I heard that the civilians had been murdered by the rebels and eaten, but I was never able to substantiate it.

We withdrew to the other bank, after ferrying the Congolese nuns, chattering like magpies, across to the south bank. We took the Chief's son with us as insurance.

The road to Yangambi was ambushed, but we swept through without stopping to do battle, intent on reaching the Mission, which lay at the back of the town off the main road, without further delay. The Belgian priest rode with me in the tentacle to show us the way. He had regained his composure, but was nervous of the outcome of our action. A mile from the Mission we stopped so that I could give out my orders for the attack.

"Any questions?" I asked, the usual termination to an O group. The bearded father raised his hand timidly.

"Major, may I ask you one thing in the Name of the Lord?"

"Please do."

"Major, I beg of you, have mercy on the Simbas."

Sergeant Wepener spat on the ground with an elaborate show of disgust.

"Mercy," he said, "I'll show them mercy. Quick bullet is all the mercy they'll get from me." It was the general mood of my men.

We screamed into the Mission. The hostages were all in one building. My men surrounded it hardly before I had time to walk down the corridor and kick in the door.

What I saw tore out my heart. The room was full of nuns and priests, so badly bruised and beaten that some were difficult to recognise as normal human beings. They looked like grotesque caricatures. Nuns lay stripped of their clothing, their bodies black and blue with bruises and red with marks of the lash, teeth broken and lips swollen. Priests lay naked and ashamed, their bodies tortured beyond human endurance.

A young nun in strips of clothing stumbled to the door, and with tears in her eyes, flung her arms round my neck and kissed me on the cheek. She may have been beautiful once.

"God has answered our prayers, God has answered our prayers," she cried out, over and over again. The poor girl was in a state of advanced hysteria and on the point of collapse. I took her arms from my neck and handed her to Germani. I was choking with suppressed emotion. Ian took over from me.

Hans busied himself with those who were too far gone to walk and his medical orderlies improvised stretchers to get them out into the trucks. Once the captives were in the warm sunshine and knew themselves to be safe again, they revived like Karroo flowers after the rain. They began to smile, even to laugh, as my gentle ruffians escorted them to their houses, where they screamed with childlike delight at finding some of their precious belongings untouched by the rebels. One nun, who was the treasurer of their group, mystified us all by demanding a spade to dig in the garden outside her bungalow. Up came a flower-pot stuffed with 5,000 Belgian francs!

The Italians in my unit were busy collecting the vestments from the church—they had taken this upon themselves as a sacred duty; loot anything else, if you must, they said, but these things are God's—when they came upon the tabernacle, still holding the consecrated hosts. Five of them knelt before the altar and, in the presence of a priest, took Holy Communion.

Stories of the dreadful sufferings the priests and nuns had suffered percolated through to me. A Bishop had been forced to eat his own excreta, nuns had been made to drink urine, whilst many had died under the inhuman and calculated savagery of the Simbas. Rapings in public, whippings, slow torture and other bestialities had been performed for the amusement of the rebel guards, some of them too frightful and shameful to record.

I was anxious to get away quickly. I feared a sudden counter-attack when the priests and nuns would be an encumbrance to us in the fight. I took a quick look at the Mission, as we formed up the column. It was the most beautiful mission in the Congo, without exception, and the town of Yangambi a fitting counterpart. Every house was slate roofed and built to the latest architectural design. Nothing had been spared that money could buy. The huge school and its lovely playgrounds slid away from us, as we gathered speed for the escape from nightmare back to reality.

Some of the Congolese nuns were put on the *Geri*, which I had anchored at Yangambi, and despatched up the river to Stan, whilst the remainder rode with us in the trucks, now grossly overloaded. We reached Stan late that night and I handed over the fifty or more nuns and priests to Colonel Vanderwalle outside the Hotel des Chutes. He looked into the back of the trucks. Infinite pity saddened his face. It was the only time I ever saw him overcome with grief. "They are Belgians, and you have saved them," he said, "they are my countrymen. Thank you, Major, thank you. Thank all your men, thank all your men."

He turned to hide his emotion.

The British Military Attaché, Lieut.-Colonel Kirk, had been greatly concerned about the safety of a number of British nationals still locked up in various parts of Orientale. He had prepared a list of names, showing where they might be. One group of eleven were thought to be at Banalia, a place one hundred kilometres due north of Stanleyville on the banks of the Aruwimi River. Another group were at Bafwasende, two hundred and fifty kilometres east of Stanleyville in the heart of rebel-held territory. He asked me to do everything I could to get these people out without delay. Speed was obviously of the essence and every day was vital.

I put the matter to the Chief-of-Staff. He was the same awkward cuss that we had been cursed with at Kamina in our training days. The months between had done nothing to mellow his charm. He looked at the wall map in the Ops. Room.

"You are no doubt aware, Major, that you have a unit of brave soldiers lying idle on the south bank of the Lomami River, here, near Opala. Despite our repeated orders, they refuse to move. They have just announced that the only order they will obey is one from you." He paused. "In that case, I suggest you had better go and give it to them. As soon as you return, we can talk about Banalia and Bafwasende."

I protested that the delay would be fatal and that we must see the two operations in their right perspective, the one could wait, the other could not. But all to no avail.

54 Commando had apparently shown little enterprise once they had reached Opala. The initial plan for the attack on Stanleyville had envisaged their advance simultaneously with the Stanleyville column, but nothing had been heard of them for over fourteen days. There was nothing for it, but to take a strong fighting patrol down to the north bank of the Lomami and find out why they had not moved. The resulting delay in the Banalia operation worried me, but I determined we should leave the following morning.

That night I entertained Mr. Nendaka to dinner. Graham Hogan had gathered a crowd of over twenty-five thousand people into the Cathedral square on the left bank that morning to hear what Mr. Nendaka had to say. The Minister was late getting across the river and the vast crowd had grown a little restless. Hogan had led them in community singing, much to their joy, until Nendaka arrived to harangue them. I congratulated Mr. Nendaka on his obvious success, but he was far from pleased with the results himself.

"Perhaps you did not notice," he said, "the crowd contained no young men, only old men and women. The young men are still in the bush, waiting. We still have a long way to go."

We left the Rive Gauche at dawn the next morning, travelling as light and as fast as we could, and without armour. I had been warned that the rebels in this area were fanatical and I felt in my water that we were going to have a rough passage. We did not have long to wait before this was confirmed. At the entrance to one village the enemy fired from the grass verge into the middle of the column. The lorry behind me was sprayed with automatic fire and two men were wounded, one of them the cheerful Sergeant Gary Cooper. In the same action, a bullet smashed through the cab of the tentacle, nicking a piece out of my eyebrow. It left a disappointingly small scar, but I made the most of it with large pieces of plaster.

I don't know which I feared most, the wound or the doctor. Hans Germani was rusty, he confessed, had not practised for years, but stitching a wound, poof, nothing to it—and the patient jumped a foot in the air.

At Yatolema we ran the gauntlet of enemy fire again, with small loss, and finally rested for the night on the north bank of the Lobaye, which we took after a small skirmish. The men had just finished filling their dixies for tea when a dead body, bloated and foul, floated past on the surface of the water. I took an extra tea-spoonful of sugar with my cup, just in case!

We found the ferry hidden in the bank, some way downstream, camouflaged with palm fronds. Tom worked on it through the night with success. Most of the ferries in the Congo had engines which were just about to give up the ghost and only the regular skippers knew their idiosyncrasies. Tom never failed and coaxed life out of them when all hope had fled. We were across the next morning in under three hours and left a small party to guard the crossing against our return.

On the final stretch we heard the drums. I had never really appreciated the efficiency of the jungle drums and had always been rather sceptical about their reputed performance. Now I heard for myself their urgent warning, reverberating through the thick Congo jungle. A moment later the rhythm was taken up by another drum further down and the message passed on. Little wonder news travels through the Congo with the speed of the telegraph.

Every village we passed through had its drum, which was always given pride of place beneath a neatly thatched roof. The drums themselves were impervious to damage and many were hundreds of years old. A bullet hole made no difference to their tone and the only way to destroy them would be by fire.

We halted a few miles from the Lomami. Now the drums were both loud and near. Hans Germani asked an A.N.C. Lieutenant if he knew what they were saying. The officer consulted a *fundi* in his ranks.

"The White Giants are coming," he said.

The phrase delighted Hans, but the throbbing of the drums filled many of us with foreboding. The "white giants" were distinctly on edge. We had lost one truck that morning through enemy action and had to fight for the river crossing behind us. Every man was thinking about the journey back, when we could most certainly expect trouble.

The Lomami River was almost a mile wide and 54 Commando were waiting patiently on the southern bank. I was displeased with their commander's lack of initiative in failing to float his transport across on home-made rafts, which could have been built from canoes, and later removed him from his command.

The men were in good shape, however, and glad to be united with us once again. They had come a long way since I last saw them in Bikili and had taken Boende and Ikela in good style. I congratulated them, overlooking a slight rash of fancy dress which had mush-roomed in my absence. The A.N.C. sappers quickly assembled a floating pontoon and ferried the light vehicles across without delay.

Two of my men stood by the village drum. One hammered out a message in faultless rhythm. In the far distance we heard a muted reply. Our man hammered out another message. We strained our ears. Again the same reply.

"What's he saying?" asked his mate.

"Wrong number!" said the drummer.

The return to Stanleyville was, as anticipated, sheer agony. It was a running fight most of the way and the enemy were now using "stand cannons." The stand cannon is a home-made weapon consisting of a section of iron tube four or five inches wide—a truck propeller shaft sawn in two is ideal—and stuffed with gunpowder and pieces of scrap iron. A length of fuse is pressed into the bottom of the contraption. The instructions for use are simple—point cannon at enemy, light fuse and retire pronto.

On the return journey a stand cannon exploded four feet from Ian, who was travelling in the leading jeep, but it missed him. On another occasion a stand cannon went off whilst we were halted to clear a road-block. We investigated at once. The rebel gunner had not read his instructions; he had lit the fuse, but failed to retire soon enough. We could have put what was left of him in a large size suitcase.

We regained the sanctuary of our lines on the Rive Gauche with relief. Within an hour I issued a warning order to move on Banalia the next day. Every Briton in the unit was detailed off for the patrol.

My general plan was to do a circular tour, taking in Banalia and Bafwasende. A Hollander, working for the United Nations, gave me all the information I needed about the roads. He confirmed that we could get from Banalia to Bomili via Panga along a little-used track, and then could descend on Bafwasende from the rear. I liked the sound of that. There were two things to consider, he warned me. The first was that the track would be plagued with broken bridges and the second that the tribes in the Bafwasende area were the fiercest in the Congo. This was the home of the infamous "leopard men" that I had heard so much about. A witch-doctor would dress up in a leopard skin, kill his victim for *muti* (medicine), and then leave his body covered with the marks of leopard claws. The ritual was well known.

Once more I decided to put my trust in speed and decided against taking armour, which would slow us down. We loaded the column with bridging equipment, planks and P.S.P. The patrol would take us in a circle 850 kilometres behind the enemy lines. It was a thrilling challenge and the men responded to it eagerly. Just before we set off, a Seychellois begged me to take him with us, so that we could rescue his entire family who were marooned at a place called Mangaga, one hundred kilometres from Bafwasende.

We crossed the Tshopo into enemy territory and hurried north. The further we got from Stan, the safer I felt. It would be quite impossible for the enemy to know we were coming and there was safety in speed. From time to time, we would surprise a group of rebels on the road and the leading jeep would open fire. One of our difficulties was in recognising our enemy and my general rule was that a man with a weapon was a rebel, all others were to be regarded as civilians and left alone.

This order proved difficult to obey, particularly when nerves were strung up and the enemy were seen indistinctly in the distance, so that I was forced to halt the column and choke off the leaders for failing to comply. After that every rebel killed had a weapon in his hand. At the next halt to clear a road-block, I noticed John Peters' jeep was stacked full of spears. One was issued to each dead rebel, posthumously, just in case!

We burst in on Banalia just before dusk, catching a small number of rebels before they melted into the bush. The wide river ran around two sides of the town, which was set out under shady trees and wide avenues. We made straight for the hospital which was supposed to hold the hostages. It was deserted. The operating table had been used in the last few hours and blood-soaked cotton-wool lay in a basket.

We searched the town twice, from top to bottom. There was an air of death about the place and I was filled with a presentiment of disaster. Just before dark I sent Hider and Cramer down to the landing stage to search the long grass on either side of it. They came running back.

"It's them, sir," said Ralph, bitterly.

We examined the wooden planking. It was clotted with blood. In the grass were separate heaps of clothing. The hostages had been forced to strip and were then murdered and their bodies flung into the river. The men brought out the clothing, piece by piece, as they found them. A little girl's dress. A small boy's shirt, labelled "St. Michael's."

"Marks and Spencers," said John Peters. He picked up a slipper, "Hush Puppies," he said. He knew all the British trade names. There was no doubt about it now, these were the clothes of the British. We gathered up the rest of the clothing, which included the complete habit of a nun, her ring and her prayer book, and left the horrid scene. Hider brought me the passports of the children. They were aged five and seven.

In the morning we examined the blood again to try and estimate how old it was. The general opinion was that it could not have been shed more than four days ago. Too bloody late again. My blood began to boil at the thought of our senseless delay in reaching Banalia. If the Chief of Staff had been there at that moment, I would gladly have flung him in the river myself.

The men were greatly affected by the scene of the murder and the death of the little children, in particular, went hard with them. Jack would not be consoled. Almost half the men in the patrol were British and they were muttering darkly amongst themselves, when someone picked up a dress out of the bush which might have belonged to a seventeen-year-old girl. I had been instructed to look for a seventeen-year-old girl, who had come out from England to spend her school holidays with her Missionary parents. This looked as though it was the end of her. Months later, I heard the true story. The poor kid had been forced to submit to some swine of a Simba Captain, who had taken a fancy to her. When the group of British were killed, she was offered her life in exchange for her body. She preferred death and met it at the side of her parents.

Carter, my wireless operator, brought me a signal pad. I sat by the landing stage and composed a signal. It read:

"British Embassy Leopoldville stop for Colonel Kirk stop deeply regret must conclude all eleven British at Banalia cruelly done to death last three or four days stop kindly tender abject apologies Ambassador our failure arrive in time stop we weep we mourn our British dead stop Hoare."

Every man in the column felt a rising resentment against the Simbas and a renewed sense of urgency to reach Bafwesande before it was too late there as well. Every man with small children saw his own kids cruelly done to death. It was a poignant moment.

The column was all set to roll. I took a last look at the ferry as though it might release some final secret. There was a thick morning mist clinging to the surface of the river and it lifted for a moment to reveal a startled native in a canoe, fifty yards from the bank. He paddled fast to get away, but one shot from Wepener persuaded him otherwise. He pulled in to the side. He was armed with a spear.

"Kneel down," I said. This was routine for the interrogation of prisoners. Stupidly he played dumb. Wepener cracked him on the back of the head with the butt of his F.N. rifle and three boots thudded into his guts.

"Speak, you swine," said Jack.

"Where are the white people?" I asked. He did not know. He showed me his M.N.C. card. He was from another village. He knew nothing. He was visiting the hospital to see a friend.

I could find no fault in him.

The mood of the men was such that they had already decided he was one of the murderers and should be convicted out of hand. It was quite obvious to them, there could be no argument about it.

"Kill the bastard," they yelled from the trucks, "and let's get going."

"Let him go," I told Ian.

"Let him go!" they echoed. My officers looked at me as though I had gone mad.

"That's what I said. Let him go, he had nothing to do with it."

Thunderstruck they released him. He disappeared downstream in a hurry.

I walked over to my jeep amidst low mutterings, conscious that resentment was building up against me.

"Bloody Major's going soft," said one of the men in a private soldier's whisper.

The track ran through thickly populated villages, full of startled people who did not know whether to sit still or run. The jungle grew darker and more lush as we closed with the river. Enormous trees shut out the sunlight even at midday and exotic blooms flourished in the hot-house humidity beneath them. Vines and lianas as thick as a man's arm wound their way around the giants of the forest, threatening to choke their very existence. Orchids blossomed in the shade of the giant trees near unhealthy-looking toadstools. The track was perpetually wet for want of sun and the wooden plank bridges were rotted through and incapable of taking our weight. The routine of bridge building under cover of forward patrols grew tedious and tiresome.

We made a dash for the Mission at Panga, but it was deserted and already ransacked. Volunteer Fabri collected the church ornaments, all of which were in good condition, except for a large gilt cross which had lost its semi-precious stones. Some vandal had prised them out with a knife.

That night we stopped fifteen kilometres short of Bomili. I was not tired and spent much of the night talking to my men around a camp fire. I never ceased to wonder at the extraordinary types which went to make up my unit, but they all had one thing in common— they were real men and were unafraid. Whatever their failings may have been, they were real men, fearless and big, the last of a vanishing breed. I never found anything small or petty in any of them. To have command of men such as these, men whom you trusted and respected, and whom you felt with pride respected you, was something which was not given to everyone. The joy and the responsibility of command was, to me, a happiness in itself.

We advanced on foot in the morning, my usual tactics after a halt, and cleared a big road-block which was unmanned. We pressed hard for Bomili. One kilometre out of the town an enemy Volkswagen came head-on to our leading jeep. Tom Harrison and Joe Wepener gave them a belt of automatic fire, killing the occupants. By the time I arrived on the scene, the car had already been searched for papers and the bodies were lying in the road. The driver was carrying a letter, addressed to the Commandant at Bafwasende, ordering him to kill all the whites in his hands at once! That meant they were still alive. We rushed for our vehicles to continue the march. We destroyed the barrier guard at Bomili and turned south for Bafwasende.

The track left the jungle behind as we began to climb the side of a mountain. Mist swirled around us and the vehicles slithered along the muddy track. We shivered deliciously for a change. 57 Commando were leading and Ian reported over the radio:

"We have stopped in a big village. We are surrounded by about five hundred pygmies, all armed with bows and poisoned arrows. They are threatening us. Some are giving us the Lumumba salute. Perhaps they think we are Russians. Shall I open fire?"

"Hold it as long as you can, Ian," I said, adding, "Try laughing at them."

When I arrived Ian had saved what could have been an ugly situation by the skin of his teeth. The huge crowd of little men, naked except for a string around their loins, were laughing and yelling with glee. Now they were convinced that we were on their side and the Lumumba salutes were thick on all sides. Ian's men had fun throwing them cigarettes and candy.

We left them hooting with laughter at nothing. Thank God, Ian

L

had held his fire. It would have been murder. The wretched pygmies had been forced to help the rebels against their will and were no more rebel minded than we were.

We reached the outskirts of Bafwasende at 13.00 hours. To hit the enemy from the rear, after an outflanking patrol of six hundred kilometres, gave us a feeling of overwhelming superiority. Total surprise was ours. We rushed the town and clobbered the enemy on the bridge leading out of the town, all looking the wrong way. After the action, we searched for the hostages.

Sergeant Ross-Smith found them in the Mission house. They were all women. There were fourteen altogether, four being Sisters of the Precious Blood, seven Sisters of the Order "Pa madri della negrezia," and three British missionaries. Their welcome was truly continental. One of the nuns was a beautiful young novice of about eighteen, who won everybody's heart, and the men fell in love with her straight away. They fought like adolescents to be her bodyguard!

The Italians in my unit jabbered away for life with the Italian nuns and I had difficulty in trying to interrogate them. Where were the priests? There should be over forty of them in Bafwasende. They did not know. All they could say was that one morning all the priests had been herded together in the main street and shortly after that they had heard firing. They were sure they were all dead.

They told us how they had fared. All the nuns and missionaries had been paraded at the bridge and stripped naked and forced to parade around the town, jeered at by the Simbas. They wept for shame at the retelling. Some had been beaten and outraged. Some had been killed and their bodies thrown into the Lindi. They were happy to be alive.

A rebel captain was brought in by my men. He had been taken prisoner in the bush behind the mission.

The nuns were terrified that we were going to kill him out of hand and cried out, "No, don't! Not him. He saved our lives. He has been so good to us. Please, Major, promise you will be kind to him." Some of them were actually crying and one caught me round the ankles, pleading for his life.

"Tie him to a tree," said Ian, "we will deal with him later."

The rebel looked a crafty swine to me. I got the impression that he befriended the nuns only when he saw which way things would go for him. He now volunteered some information. He knew where all the priests had been taken. There were forty-two of them at the mission at Avakubi. The number tallied with my estimate. Avakubi was only sixty kilometres away and the road was excellent. Go at once, he urged, and you will save them. Tomorrow may be too late. I had already alerted a helicopter from Stan in order to despatch the hostages. I decided to attack Avakubi the following day. I signalled the British Embassy at Leo:

"For Colonel Kirk stop have rescued three British missionaries ex Bafwasende ex Boyulu stop Miss McCarten Miss Rimmer Mrs. Chester Burke stop despatched by helicopter to Stan 16.00 hours 19 Dec. stop every hope rescuing further British hostages operation Avakubi 20 Dec."

I held an O group to consult with my officers. I had already decided to attack Avakubi the next day with a strong force to leave at dawn, but a suggestion was now put to me that a hand-picked patrol leaving at once could get there before dark and stop any possibility of a massacre during the night. It had its points. Furthermore, it was feasible. Whilst I like to listen to suggestions, I invariably make the plan myself. I am not a believer in leadership by soviet, or by vote of a committee, and I was to regret the departure on this occasion. I reversed my original decision and decided to go hard for Avakubi at once.

The defence of Bafwasende was given over to Lieutenant Florence, an Australian, who would hold the fort until we returned early the next day. We took eleven of my best officers and men, all hand-picked, in two armoured jeeps and the tentacle. We reached Avakubi half an hour before dusk. The moment we left the main road to branch off down the narrow tree-lined avenue leading to the Mission, I realised we were being led into a trap.

The Mission stood at the end of the drive, its back up against the river. It was a cul-de-sac and the Mission was deserted. It was too late to go back now that dusk had fallen. During the night the rebels attacked. Tom Harrison leapt across the balcony we were sleeping on and engaged the enemy with his machine gun, kneeling on my neck as he did so. A burst of automatic fire splattered the plaster of the wall all around Wepener, but he escaped unscathed. The enemy had crept up to within twenty yards of our position but retreated when we opened up in retaliation. In the morning, we found that they had jumped out of their boots, literally, and abandoned piles of ammunition.

The long avenue was road-blocked four times, but the rebels had not the guts to man them. By a show of force out of all proportion to our size, we blasted our way back on to the main road and tore off for Bafwasende.

An armed rebel, pushing a bicycle, ran when he saw us. He scrambled up the bank on the side of the road. John Peters gave him a burst as he tried to escape. Later, I asked John why he had fired. "He ran," he said. It was sufficient.

Ten kilometres from Bafwasende a rebel truck, going hell for leather, came straight towards us. It was still a quarter of a mile away.

"Bazooka, sir?" said Ian, stroking his moustache. The rocket hit the truck as it came over the rise of the hill. Ian was a master with the weapon. The truck had two drums of petrol on the back and was still blazing when we reached Bafwasende. Nobody escaped.

We were lucky to have got out of Avakubi alive.

"Send me the Simba Captain," I said.

We returned to Stan the next day, stopping only to raid the larder of the Mission at Boyulu, which had a three-year supply of tinned food. Every man now had a can of Bartlett pears. At Mangaga we rescued the Seychellois family and reunited them with the father. It was a touching scene and the look of gratitude on their faces made the long patrol seem well worth while, every kilometre of it.

We entered Stan from the east, cheered by the A.N.C. garrison at Camp Kitele, who thought we were fresh reinforcements. Alastair had returned from his recruiting mission and announced that the new men had arrived at Kamina. We sat down to an evening of good music, good food and relaxation, the knowledge of a successful trip behind us.

After dinner John Peters announced the arrival of some gentlemen whom he called "newsagents", much to our glee and their annoyance. They were some internationally renowned journalists. Inevitably we were asked to describe our worst horror of the campaign. We took it in turn to impress our receptive audience. It was Alastair's turn.

"Without question," he began, "the dreadful occurrence in the Indian Embassy next door takes the cake. I can hardly bring myself to tell it." The "newsagents" leaned forward, notebooks mentally at the ready. "To think that a swine could do a thing like that, one of our own men too, passes all comprehension." He continued, pausing to sip at his five-star Napoleon. "If I had not seen it with my own eyes, I would never have believed it possible, but I can vouch for the hideousness of the act as I am sitting here." He led them on.

"Grow to the point, man," muttered Bulloch.

"The man should be hanged for it," Alastair went on, unabashed. "The wretch actually cut a piece of cloth out of the middle of a full-sized billiard table to make himself a pair of green epaulettes!"

# 11

## THE FACE OF SADNESS

There could be only one answer. If the hostages from Bafwasende were still alive, then they must be at Wamba. Wamba was another hundred kilometres north of Avakubi. I put my plan to the Belgian staff—two helicopters could drop a small raiding party on the road ten kilometres from Wamba and get the hostages out. It was turned down flat.

A new Belgian staff had now arrived to take over 3 Group Headquarters and they were headed by a Congolese full Colonel—Leonard Mulamba. Mulamba was a short thickset man of about thirty-six, who had received a thorough training in the Force Publique. He was quiet, modest and efficient. He had already made a name for himself in the Congo by his defence of Bukavu in August and he had proved himself to be a fearless leader. He did things according to the book, which he knew by heart and he was that rare thing in the A.N.C.—a stickler for discipline. He attracted loyalty and we all took to him at once.

The new draft, which Alastair had recruited, had now arrived in Stanleyville and they were billeted with my other men at the Stanley Hotel. I interviewed each man separately and was astonished to find an old friend in the ranks. Brian Glyn had been hunting in Kenya for some years and lately had been running safaris in Bechuanaland, my old stamping ground, and I was delighted to see him. I earmarked him for command of one of the units and gave him a few days in which to settle down as a volunteer to learn the ropes. The new draft was of a fair standard and included two men who took my eye. One was an ex-Scots Guardsman, named Sam Cassidy, whom I promoted to Sergeant on the spot and the other a Swedish ex-U.N.O. Forces officer, named Roy Larsen, who began as a Lieutenant. Larsen was small, tough and capable and spoke with an attractive brogue, which he had picked up from his Irish wife.

John Peters took the new draft under his wing for training and on 23rd December conducted an exercise-cum-fighting patrol along the road to the Old Elephant Camp, which was still held by the enemy. On the way back they ran into severe ambush and several men were wounded. I was sitting in my Headquarters, when the telephone rang from the hospital. I knew exactly what it was going to say. Brian Glyn had been seriously wounded and was asking for me. Could I come straight away? They were sorry, but there was little hope. I dashed up the airport road at breakneck speed and bumped into John Peters, as I entered the hospital. "Glyn's dead," he said. Brian had been in the Congo exactly seven days. It was a sad and tragic end to his exciting career.

It was a miserable evening in my Headquarters and we retired early to our beds. At eleven that night, Alastair and I were summoned urgently to 3 Group Headquarters. Colonel Mulamba was not there, but the new Belgian Staff had been busy hatching a plot by means of which the Wamba hostages could be rescued. They had also been drinking. After an hour in the Ops Room, Alastair and I agreed we had never attended an O group in such fantastic circumstances. Everybody was jabbering, people were coming and going, and there was an atmosphere of cordiality, bred of much whisky and beer. In due course we gained the impression that 5 Commando were to undertake a raid on Wamba the next morning at dawn! I presented my compliments to the Chief of Staff—not the previous holder of this post who had now been replaced—and told him politely, but firmly, what he could do with his half-baked plan and went back to bed. We heard no more about it. The "second eleven" were evidently rank amateurs.

52 Commando now returned to the fold from Paulis. They had been under the command of Major Jennis, a Belgian regular Army Officer, and had gained for themselves an enviable record for hard fighting. They had liberated over eight hundred whites, mostly Belgians, from the Paulis area, and had burst their way through the country from Aketi, Buta and Poko to do it. At Poko, they had entered the town from the back and taken the enemy completely by surprise. The Simbas rushed out to meet them with open arms, thinking they were Russians reinforcements! Ben Louw and his boys disillusioned them. Not one escaped. They repeated their success at

Paulis, where they came in from the north, having travelled via Niangara, and overtook a huge pantechnicon filled with Simbas. They engaged the truck from the rear, killing over forty. Tragedy, however, finally struck the column and in one battle Major Jennis, a great and much loved soldier, was killed in action. 3 Group then decided to halt the column at Paulis, where 52 Commando became garrison troops for the time being. As soon as Christmas was over, 54 and 57 Commandos under Captain Peters, would be sent to replace them.

The Stanley Hotel had a reputation in "peace-time" of having the finest wine cellar in Africa. 5 Commando had lately been in a position to verify this statement. Nothing amused me more than to hear two of my hairy-backed volunteers discussing their choice of wine for dinner—the Nuit, St. George, or the Mouton Rothschild? They invariably ended up with both. The bar was run on a non-payment basis for a few days—a fairyland existence—until we could bring back the owner from Leopoldville to take over his hotel again.

Christmas dinner was to be a full-blown affair in the Stanley Hotel and I asked the Spanish Chargé d'Affaires to join us. He had arrived to take part in the long planned raid on Wamba, which would now start from Paulis and be spearheaded by 54 Commando. His particular interest in Wamba was the contingent of thirty Spanish nuns, who had been held hostage there since August.

Signor Valera was a born diplomat with all the charm and grace of his countrymen—the last race of noblemen on earth. He looked at the sign over the bar, which said, "One more looting day to Christmas!", and smiled. If he was concerned about the swash-buckling appearance of some of my men, who had just returned from a patrol, he did not betray it by so much as a twinkling of his eye. During the course of the dinner, however, a shot rang out in the dining-hall. He could contain his curiosity no longer. "It is perhaps a normal occurrence?" he said, without raising his voice a semi-tone.

Alastair investigated. It was nothing, he said, just a little good-natured buffoonery. One man had shot another by mistake. The wounded volunteer was removed and the happy meal went on.

On Boxing Day I began to hand over to Ian Gordon, who was to be the new commander of 5 Commando. Jack Maiden was brought in from Bunia and was to be Ian's second-in-command. I was pleased to see Jack after his long spell in action in the east of the country and he rapidly brought me up to date with events in 53 Commando. When the Stanleyville column left Kongolo on 1st November, 53 Commando were stationed in Butembo, which they had just captured. As part of the Vanderwalle plan for the advance on Stanleyville, they then moved forward to seize Beni, an important town sixty kilometres to the north. The capture of Beni on 2nd November sparked off immediate repercussions in Stanleyville, where it was seen as the beginning of the A.N.C. advance. At the same time, to make excuses for the loss of the town, Olenga fulminated against the Americans whom, he said, had dropped an atomic bomb on his Simbas!

53 Commando consolidated their position in Beni and awaited orders to advance on Mambasa, which they captured five days after the main column entered Stanleyville. Two days later they stormed into Bunia, a large town 250 kilometres to the east, and took the Simbas completely by surprise, catching a large number of them drilling on a lawn in the centre of the town. Jack Maiden's men then released several hundred Congolese nuns, who had been trapped in the mission under rebel guards, and rescued a further seventy Belgian priests and nuns in other parts of the town. The hostages had undergone the most hellish experiences during their captivity. Only eight days before Stanleyville fell, the Simbas had staged a drug-crazed orgy, in which they forced the white nuns to strip in public. Many of them were raped, but Sister Marie Therese was one who resisted. She was shot through both kneecaps and left to die a slow death on the main street of Bunia.

The scene at the Mission when Maiden's men came to rescue the Congolese nuns was heroic. Hundreds of them were brought out into the bright sunlight, weeping and moaning, to be transported in five-ton lorries to the airport. The tail boards hung down to provide a step into the back of the trucks, but these were too high off the ground for the Congolese nuns. Without any fuss or bother, the South African mercenaries of 53 Commando knelt in the mud to let the black nuns step on their backs and into the trucks to safety!

Joe Wepener attacked Wamba with 54 Commando on New Year's Eve with tremendous verve and dash and made short work of the Simba guards. About one hundred white hostages were rescued and hurried back to Paulis, where they were immediately evacuated in a

C-130, crammed to capacity. The priests from Avakubi were not amongst the people liberated at Wamba and must now be reckoned as killed.

A slight fault in the aircraft forced the C-130 to make an unscheduled stop at Stan on its way to Leo and, after some persuasion, Alastair and I were allowed to board the plane. I looked around for familiar faces and barely recognised the brave Signor Valera, who was bubbling with joy at the rescue of all the Spanish nuns. His normally immaculate clothing was torn and dirty and he was covered with the red dust of Paulis, but he was grateful his people were all alive and well.

The hostages looked beaten and spent. Reaction to their escape was setting in and many sat silent with their thoughts in the overpowering hum of the powerful engines. I spoke to a bright-eyed little party, who looked as though she was already fit for another tour of Congo duty. She was Doctor Helen Roseveare. Her mind was sharp and her spirits bright and untarnished by her ghastly experiences. Her companions spoke of the little missionary doctor with unstinted admiration. When surgical instruments were unobtainable, she performed an urgent hernia operation with a razor blade! She had kept the whole group going, cheerful and brave, a shining example of how a strong mind, buoyed up with faith, can rise triumphant above the worst disasters. I felt honoured to talk to her.

Two small boys and a girl sat on their luggage close by. The boys were playing quite happily with their toys, but the little girl took no part in the games. She was about twelve, I would have guessed, and had long black hair, which hung down her back. She was quite beautiful. I played with the little boys for a moment and spoke to the girl. She did not answer. She continued to look straight into the middle distance, unsmiling and detached. Her parents touched me on the sleeve and shook their heads and began to cry. I looked again at the child. She had an expression of resignation, such as one only sees on the faces of people who have known some great sorrow. Her face, now that I came to look into it, was unnaturally lined and incredibly sad.

Her story shocked me to the core of my being. For the last three months she had been kept locked in a dark room and raped night after night by the Simba soldiers. Her mind was unhinged. She wished that she was dead.

For me, it was the final horror. With difficulty I swallowed back my emotions and determined I wanted no more of this damnable country.

We arrived in Leopoldville in the early evening and escaped quickly from the flashlights and turbulence of sympathetic Red Cross officials, Consular Corps and newspapermen. It was New Year's Eve, after all, and Alastair, who loves a party and sensed my lowered spirits, dragged me with him on a round of enforced merry-making. It was useless. The child's face haunted me and would not be drowned in endless glasses of whisky. In the small hours of the morning I realised clearly that my time in the Congo was up. I was a spent force.

Alastair and I got to bed, as the first light of New Year's Day, 1965, made the night club cheap and tawdry.

I had lunch with the Prime Minister the next day. We discussed the political situation in the Congo and I was surprised to find it basically not greatly improved. Mr. Tshombe still had a long way to go with his Government of Reconciliation and it became obvious to me that, until there was complete victory in the field and the rebel movement was finally put down once and for all, the politicians could not really get the country going again. Elections were impossible whilst the whole of Orientale was in rebel hands and now a new and more dangerous threat to the Congo was fast becoming apparent. A red cloud, no bigger than a man's hand, appeared on the eastern horizon.

"You are leaving with your work half done, Major," said Mr. Tshombe. "Can you not see what is happening on our Sudan and Uganda borders? Every day the rebels are being aided by Algeria, Ghana, Uganda and Burundi. Communist arms and advisers are flooding into Orientale Province. We have absolute proof of these things. Think carefully, Major, before you decide to go. We still need you."

I promised to see the Commander-in-Chief before making a final decision. General Mobutu, who was well aware that there was a number of things irking me, took a new line. He promised me a new deal. I was weary of remote control by a Belgian Staff, in whom, now that the efficient Vanderwalle had gone, I had absolutely no faith. I was angry and aggrieved that no indemnities had been paid out to the dependents of my men killed in action—seven thousand pounds for death—and there were a number of administrative problems, apparently insoluble at my level, which were making me old.

The General handed me a sheet of paper. "Put down on that," he said with a smile, "everything that bothers you." I thought I would need a ream of paper and was surprised at the shortness of the list. He had me cornered. He looked at the list. "But, my dear Major, there is nothing here which we cannot put right at once. Your own Pay Section, two doctors, your own hospital, etc., these are simple matters to solve. Furthermore, I promise you your own command with the whole of 5 Commando concentrated under your hand. How's that? Go home for fourteen days, give orders to recruit a new 5 Commando, now that the old one has finished its contract, and return here ready to tackle a big job in Orientale."

Some Generals can inspire you with enthusiasm, some cannot. General Mobutu was one who could, and did. I borrowed two hundred dollars off the first of my men I met in the street and caught a Pan-Am. flight for Johannesburg.

The fourteen days passed all too quickly, the first three being spent in bed, throwing off a malignant malaria, which I had brought home from the Congo with me. With much sleep and rest, my nervous system recovered slowly, and the horrors of the last few months slid into the limbo of half forgotten things. I spent two glorious days at the helm of my cutter, *Colin Archer*, and the fresh breeze off the coast of Natal blew away what remained of my Congo misery.

The Press had been kind to me and a light shower of notoriety had fallen on my shoulders. This led to an amusing incident one day, when I took my wife to lunch at The Edward, my favourite hotel, on Durban's magnificent beachfront.

A glamorous female swept across the floor of the Causerie and introduced herself in a charming foreign accent.

"Major Hoare, I have been dying to meet you," she said. My naïve and unsophisticated soul was thrilled, flattered and delighted.

"Do join us for a drink," I said, pulling out a chair and conscious of small darts entering the side of my head.

"Is it true what they say about you in the local papers?" she went on, looking me straight in the face with puppy-dog eyes.

"Oh!" said my hero, "you mustn't believe everything you read in the Press. Most of it is pure fiction."

"But I love reading fiction!" gushed she.

A well aimed shoe connected with my shin-bone and brought me back to the Edward pronto. Collapse of flattered party, as they say!

I stopped off in Johannesburg to raise a Liaison Office, which would keep in touch with relatives of men in my unit, instituted a system with the efficient International Red Cross to notify the next of kin of our killed and seriously wounded, and placed Darby de Jaeger, now a Captain, in charge of the office and our affairs in South Africa. We recruited two doctors, one to be the unit Medical Officer and the other to run our own hospital, which we were to set up at Bunia. Finally, we set up our own Pay Section under a painstaking German, named Von Blottnitz. I felt for the first time that we were getting on top of some of the administrative matters which were clogging the fighting machine.

Back in Leopoldville, I sensed that our mercenary image had improved but slightly. Although we had now been in existence for six months, we were still regarded in certain official quarters as not quite respectable, if effective, types. I had been to great pains to erase the memory of *les Affreux* and I was distressed that we should be looked upon by some as a gang of ruffians, unkempt and ill-disciplined. Frequently, however, my own men were their worst enemies in this respect. They basked in a reputation for toughness, which followed in their wake, and the speed with which they donned "fancy dress"—camouflage smocks, etc., which formed no part of our uniform—when out of my sight, did not help any either. Many talked big in the bars and nightclubs of Leo, leading a few undiscerning journalists to build freely on their imaginative stories of action and bloodshed. The stories were usually in indirect proportion to their prowess as soldiers. Good soldiers, of course, do not talk. I imagine they do not write books either! However, it is human nature to play it big once in a while and many of my men did just that.

We were pleasantly surprised, therefore, on our return to Leo when Alastair and I were invited to a cocktail party at the British Embassy. We had arrived! But our new found aura of respectability lasted a bare four hours before we were put back in our place again.

"Frightful error, old chap," said the Embassy spokesman with the five pound voice, explaining it all to John Bulloch, who had passed on the invitation to us, "sorry and all that, but we can't really have these er, um, er, mercenary types at the Embassy, don't you know?"

The social slight went hard with Alastair, a blue-blooded Englishman if ever there was one, but for my part, I was only a little saddened at the sorry spectacle of one of the world's great powers bending over backwards to placate newly arrived African States in even such a small matter as this. I supposed that I had been born too late and would have been more at home in Victorian times, when old-fashioned ideas of leadership and industry were qualities which shone in the British race and made its name a byword of integrity and ability—rather than the pitiable, self-effacing diplomatic grovelling, which I had witnessed up and down the new Africa of the last five years. It made me sick.

If there was any vigour and virility in Britain's African policies during 1964 and 1965, these were certainly not manifest in Leopoldville. By contrast, my visits to the energetic Americans convinced me, as an objective observer of the African scene, that the mantle of world leadership, with all it implies in the spending of blood and treasure, had fallen squarely in the right place—on the shoulders of the American people.

If I was *persona non grata* at the British Embassy, this was certainly not the case at Q.G.-A.N.C. General Mobutu's attitude towards me had undergone a complete change and, whereas in the past he had been cold and distant, now he was warm and friendly whenever I visited him.

He wrote out an order promoting me to the rank of Lieut.-Colonel and Alastair to Major and escorted us to his door.

"Good-bye, Mike," he said in English (he always pronounced it "Mark"), "and good luck."

The General's recognition cheered me as nothing else could. I had wanted nothing so much as to have 5 Commando known as an integral part of the A.N.C.—after all, were we not fighting for the very existence of the Congo?—and in the fullness of time it had come.

I went happily on my way with a lightness of heart and a premonition of the great success in the field, which was to be ours in good measure, pressed down, and running over. I flew on to Kamina, prepared to build a new and better 5 Commando, a 5 Commando destined to strike a blow to rid the Congo of the greatest cancer the world has ever known—the creeping, insidious disease of Communism.

# 12

## BUNIA

The Commander-in-Chief took a cane, walked over to the large wall-map and described an arc around the north-east corner of the Congo. The top of the arc was the Sudan border, the bottom was Uganda. Heavy Russian transport planes had been landing in southern Sudan, he said, and an immense quantity of arms and ammunition was being trucked over the Congo border into Aba via Juba and Yei. The flow into the Congo of Communist aid was not less than thirty tons per day. His latest information was that Algerian and Egyptian "technical advisers" were presently in Aba. It was possible also that troops might be sent from Algeria. Gbenye had boasted that a unit of six hundred men were already on their way down the Nile.

On the Uganda border Aru was the focal point of Communist aid arriving from Entebbe and Dar es Salaam. The rebels were paying for it in gold from the rich Watsa gold mine and ivory, of which there were vast stocks in the provinces.

The situation inside Orientale Province was deteriorating rapidly said the General. River traffic from Leo to Stan was blocked at Elizabetha by the enemy and Stanleyville itself was merely an island in rebel-held territory. The rebels were still active within seven miles of the centre of the city! Their lines of communication to Sudan and Uganda were unmolested. Communist infiltration into Orientale Province under the guise of aid to the rebels might turn the theatre into another Vietnam.

To counter the threat, he intended to raise a new operational area to be called "Operations North-east." This would be commanded by Lieut.-Colonel Hoare, who would have a two-battalion group under command and be given the role of sealing off the frontiers with Uganda and Sudan. He would rely on 3 Group at Stan, whose

Chief of Staff would now be Lieut.-Colonel Jacques Noel. 5 Commando would be based at Bunia in the new area and all available air would be given to Ops. North-east.

The General ended by saying that until Orientale Province was restored to the Congo, there could be no political settlement in the Congo, and that the parliamentary elections, which had been set down for March, would have to be postponed. He wished me luck, advised me to keep a tight grip on my men—he made a hand movement as though turning off a tap—emphasised once again the importance of my task and the far-reaching effects it would have on the future of the Congo, and withdrew. I could not help admiring the General's empirical approach to the problem and his clear-cut directive for its solution. For a young man he had a sense of perspective and history more in keeping with an elder statesman.

Jacques Noel was a Belgian regular army officer and since his arrival in Stanleyville had transformed 3 Group Headquarters into a smooth running machine. He was a large, handsome man with a calm, dignified manner, knowledgeable and shrewd. His presence cast an optimistic glow over the impending operations and resulted in the happiest collaboration between the staff of 3 Group and 5 Commando.

The old 5 Commando were stationed in Paulis. They were in the phasing out stage of their contracts and many of them indicated they would sign on again for another term. In the event, less than ten came back after their leave, but I did not blame them. Six months in the Congo at this sort of thing is a lifetime.

Major Ian Gordon gave me the details of the abortive raid on Niangara which had cost the lives of two men, Volunteer Roberts and Volunteer Coetzee, and fourteen wounded. The enemy had caught them in a skilfully prepared ambush and trapped the patrol in a murderous cross fire. The leading Ferret scout car had fallen into a monstrous elephant trap, and Joe Wepener had been badly concussed. The pit was apparently the work of an expert who had constructed it with the aid of architectural drawings. The top had been camouflaged, even to a tyre mark across the surface, made, Ian thought, by rolling a spare wheel over the soft earth.

The men were stationed in the famous Makasi Brewery and their most compelling task had been to get it working again, but their product was generally voted barely drinkable. Somebody had "flogged" one of the vital ingredients!

M

Ian reported that there had been an ugly incident the day before. One of his men had gone berserk and held up a number of others with his F.N. rifle, firing at their feet and threatening them with death if they moved. Fortunately, Lieutenant Roy Larsen had come upon the scene unexpectedly, sized it up in a second and put a couple of quick shots into the madman. He was now recovering in hospital.

The new 5 Commando was in training at Kamina. It was still the same hateful place, said Alastair, but at least there was one great improvement—we now had electricity. Our new pay section was working well. The Q.M. stores were full. Gino was at it again. The men's Mess was first-class. That brought me up to date, he said, and, oh yes, he had almost forgotten, the two doctors had arrived. So had the doctor's secretary, he added, deadpan. I realised in a flash that he had been saving up that little tidbit of information for days to relish its presentation in this casual manner. He burnished the shining moment with a broad grin.

"I assumed the secretary had your approval, so I took her on the strength. You must see her. She is a terrific blonde, German, twenty-three and answers to 36-24-36. I know, of course, because I was obliged to fit her uniform myself."

My reaction made his day! Kind hands led me away, frothing at the mouth.

I sent for her and explained that, desirable though her presence might be, and it certainly was, I regretted that the thing was not really practical. She left on the next plane, waved good-bye by three hundred disappointed men.

I concluded from this episode that our new German doctor, Brenhardt, whose secretary she was, was a man with an over-active sense of humour. He was a robust forty-five, with thick, greying hair and a jovial air. Nothing worried him. His very presence was enough to cheer one up; he seemed to carry around with him the recipe for instant fun. He was popular with the men.

The other doctor, John Flemming was the unit medical officer. He was everything I had hoped for. Young, tough, adventurous and efficient, with just the right touch with malingerers. "What are you going to give me for it, Doc?" one asked. "Twenty-four hours to get better," replied "Doctor Kildare." At times I felt he was wasted as a doctor, he would have made a magnificent infantry officer. He had tremendous dash and courage. His ambulance is the only one I have ever seen leading a column into battle!

His orderly was a gentle chap, named Petersen, who was the outright favourite of all ranks in 5 Commando. This arose largely from what I called "Petersen's Elixir," the genuine sympathy which he ladled out in great dollops to the sick and wounded. During this campaign I was amazed at the healing power of straightforward, honest-to-goodness sympathy, as dispensed by Petersen. Great pity it could not be bottled and sold over the counter, I thought, but there again everything depended on the way it was administered.

I was glad we were leaving Kamina. The place was full of ghosts. The bleak corridors rang with the memory of the first 5 Commando and the laughter of the men we had lost, killed and wounded in action. Walking back to my quarters one evening, I heard the men singing "Alouetta" in the canteen. It had been the marching song of 57 Commando. It took me straight back to the frightful night before Stanleyville, the night Freddy Basson had been killed. Freddy, happy soul that he was, always led the verse, the men belting out the chorus behind him. I could hear again the tramp of marching feet, the crunch of boots on gravel, and Freddy singing . . . "Week-end pass . . . week-end pass . . . big fat blonde . . . big fat blonde . . . hotel room . . . hotel room . . . knock on door . . . knock on door . . . ooooooooh . . . Alouetta, chantez Alouetta . . ."

I was glad we were leaving Kamina.

Bunia is 4,000 feet above sea level and the nearest thing to an English climate in the Congo. It is cool and bracing and blankets are needed at night. It is the vegetable garden for the entire province. Forty miles east is Lake Albert where fish are plentiful. After Stanleyville's humid heat and Kamina's misery, it was an absolute paradise. Green fields, rolling downs, high hills, good roads, everything combined to make it an ideal station, so different from the sweltering jungle of the Congo basin.

I studied the tactical position. Two hundred kilometres north of us lay Uganda, with the border towns of Mahagi and Port Mahagi at the northern end of Lake Albert in rebel hands. Our most forward position, half-way to Mahagi, was at Nioka which was held by units of the A.N.C. Jack Maiden knew the area pretty well as far as Nioka, where 53 Commando had done battle with the rebels last December and lost Volunteer Linton, a Salisbury solicitor, in some fierce fighting. On another occasion 53 Commando had dashed to Mahagi to rescue a Cuban airman who had just been shot down. His T-28 crashed near the Lake, but Jack's men got there too late. All they found was his mutilated body with the hands cut off.

Ngote was a small village, twenty kilometres the other side of Nioka, and these two villages controlled the roads leading north-west towards Aru. It seemed to me that if I concentrated my two-battalion group in the Nioka-Ngote area, after capturing Mahagi and Port Mahagi to secure my flank, I would then be in a position to launch the campaign. The strength and calibre of the enemy were still an unknown quantity and vigorous patrolling would be neces-sary once we were in position. With this general plan before me, I got down to the training of the new unit.

The ability to manoeuvre once more in open country gave me a feeling of strength and superiority. The whole area was honey-combed with roads and sustained a vast population. It rapidly dawned on me that a steady advance on foot, covered by strong air support, would provide the surest and safest form of attack. But everything would depend on the attitude of the local population. If they were with the rebels I could foresee a winkling out operation, comparable with Malaya and the necessity for thousands of troops. If not, we should be able to go through them like a knife through butter and wrap the whole operation up in a matter of three months.

My first task once again was the raising of new officers and new N.C.O.s. In this I was very fortunate in having Peter Johnstone. Peter had recently been a major in the British Army and joined me taking a chance on whatever rank was given to him. He began as a captain, but did not have to wait very long before his proper rank was restored to him. He was a thorough professional, mature and efficient, and took over at once the training of an N.C.O.s' cadre. After fourteen days' intensive course he produced eighteen sergeants he thought would make the grade. They were a keen bunch and very soon the new unit came into line, organised into eight rifle com-mandos, an armoured troop and a mortar platoon. Commando leaders were selected, who took their men under their wing straight away to foster the commando spirit, for in this campaign we would need several self-reliant bodies, our sector stretching over a distance of over three hundred miles.

To boost morale, I had recruited an old soldier, Pipe-Major

Sandy King, as regimental piper. Although he was nearly sixty years old, he was as fit as the next man and strong as an ox. His whole life had been spent soldiering, with a chest full of medals to prove it. He was a walking training manual, for ever spouting bits of knowledge. "DRINK," he would shout at a recruit, "what does that stand for? Designation, Range, Indication, Number of rounds, Kind of fire!" he would rattle off parrot fashion.

With his bagpipes under his arm and his kilt swaying on the march, he was an impressive sight. He was officially Q.M. storeman, but he was also piper, bugler, adviser to young recruits and C.O.'s confidant, as became his years as an old soldier.

Sandy and the chimpanzee were the great attractions in our camp. The chimp was an unmitigated nuisance and frightened the life out of me late one evening when I was driving a Land-Rover. I did not know he was lying there quietly in the back until he put a hairy arm round my neck in the dark. He met his end prematurely one sad day, when he broke into Dr. Flemming's surgery and ate too many pills.

Things went well, but the new unit was not to be born without travail. In the middle of one night I was called. Some men had run amok, fighting had broken out in the camp and shots were fired. The inexperienced Orderly Officer had ordered all men on parade at eleven at night, with a view to taking their arms from them. This had sparked off further trouble, but the root cause appeared to be our old friend, Pay, or the lack of it. It invariably took six weeks for a man's pay to come through to his home, owing to the roundabout fashion in which we were paid. Many men appreciated this, whilst a number made it an excuse for causing trouble. A further element, knowing that we were due for battle fairly shortly, latched on to it as a means of getting out without too great a loss of face. The upshot was mutiny.

I mounted the back of a Ferret armoured car and divided those who had no complaints from those who wanted trouble. I subdivided those again into groups according to their special groans. A very small party of malcontents now stood out rather shamefacedly. It all ended surprisingly with a call for "three cheers" and "let's get on with it." I sent home twenty of the hard core bad eggs that day, fifteen of whom pleaded to come back as soon as they reached Leopoldville.

The labour pains continued. Sam Cassidy, who was my new

Regimental Sergeant-Major, a severe disciplinarian and a hard man to boot, knocked me up again a few nights later.

"Verra serious, sir," he said in his Glasgow accent. "Ye'll never believe it! I've got twelve men locked up in the cooler on a charge of treason!" He rolled the "R" in treason, making it sound like a cross between rape and stealing the crown jewels.

"Treason!" I jumped out of bed. "What in the name of thunder can you find treasonable in Bunia?"

Incredible as it sounded two or three hotheads had persuaded two or three softheads to overpower the guard, steal arms, ammunition, and rations, and desert to the enemy in some of our transport. They claimed they did it to make their fortunes. The rebels would pay them a fantastic sum to fight for them.

I reflected that they were taking their mercenary calling a little too seriously. There was some logic in selling their arms to the highest bidder, which was only in the best tradition of mercenary troops, but it was a transaction I did not intend to countenance. I awarded them a sentence which would give them ample time to consider the mercenary market in all its phases and expelled them with ignominy from our proud unit. Once more the dross had been burned off and we were able to get on with the soldiering, fewer in number, but of a higher calibre. Daily we marched round Bunia showing the flag, led by Sandy King and his pipes, mystifying the wide-eyed Congolese who had never seen this instrument of torture before. The villagers talked and the enemy would know what was coming to them. I felt sorry for the rebels when I looked at my men, bronzed, tough, and ready for anything.

Once more I was faced with the apparently insoluble problem of transport. I had gathered every available vehicle from far and wide and lined them up on the barrack square. They were a sorry sight and many looked ready for the breaker's yard. Service in the A.N.C. had taught me how sweet were the uses of adversity. I decided to take a startling decision. I marked the vehicles with the numbers of the Commandos in chalk, so many old wrecks to each. I then paraded the men.

"Gentlemen," I said, "there lies your transport for the campaign. Today is 10th March. By first parade on 12th March, you will have those vehicles ready to fight and travel a distance of one thousand kilometres. I don't care how you do it, but do it. Beg, borrow or steal, but get them on the road. The alternative is marching, carrying everything on your backs!"

I blew my whistle and the men ran to their prizes like a pack of harriers. Groans of dismay filled the air, but they set to work. In two days the vehicles underwent an astonishing change. New engines appeared, tyres, starter motors, distributers, even bodies, were interchanged and on the morning of the twelfth the column actually rolled out of the barracks on time—a little shakily here and there, but the intention to roll was manifest.

Then the fun began. Complaints came in from the town by the score. My innocent looking men were actually accused of removing engines from parked vehicles at night. A garage complained that its entire stock of spare parts had vanished mysteriously in twenty-four hours. And so it went on. Finally the telephone rang in my office. It was the local Commandant de Place.

"Monsieur le Colonel?"

"Oui!"

"Colonel, I regret to advise you of a matter of very grave importance. The townspeople . . ."

"Hold on a moment," I said, "you've got the wrong chap . . . Alastair, it's for you."

We left Bunia on the morning of 15th March and by nightfall the whole of 5 Commando, less those taking part in Operation Kingfisher, were concentrated at Nioka. Lieutenant Roy Larsen with 58 and 59 Commandos had embarked at the southern end of Lake Albert in several large fishing boats to strike Port Mahagi at the top of the Lake at the same time as a strong column led by Major Wicks would seize Mahagi.

Alastair got off early the next day. It was one of those occasions when a sun spot or something blacks out all radio communication and soon I had lost touch with his column. "Kingfisher" had got off to a bad start when a large wave submerged their T.R.T. set and put it out of action. Apart from local contact with my patrols to test the strength of the enemy, I had contact only with Peter Johnstone at base, and this only through the brilliance of my Belgian wireless operator, Adjudant Bouve.

Bouve had asked specially to join 5 Commando, which had flattered me, but I had previously admired his courage on the Stanleyville column before Lubutu. He had been wounded by an enemy bullet in the shoulder and refused evacuation. For two days he lay in agony in the back of the truck, until he was well enough to man his set again. He was a member of the famous Belgian Parachute Regiment and the finest example of the Belgian fighting man that I met in the Congo. Later in the campaign he was to prove himself invaluable in a number of ways, his natural ability as a civil administrator being one of them.

The lack of radio contact worried me and I was concerned about the patrols I had sent out from Nioka. It was to be our first brush with the enemy and we were still unblooded. At four that afternoon the P.R.C. 10 crackled into life. It was Sergeant von Brandis 56 Commando. "Helicopter needed . . . Sergeant's been hit . . . badly wounded . . . bringing him in now . . . ambush."

We carried the Sergeant into a bare bedroom at my H.Q. while von Brandis gave a quick report. They had bumped the enemy in some strength. During the action the Sergeant had trodden on a small mine. He had lost a lot of blood.

Sandy worked on the Sergeant, helped by a medical orderly from 56 Commando. His shin-bone was broken and there were pieces of shrapnel under his chin. The Sergeant, a highly strung chap, was convinced he was dying. He was badly wounded, but he had every chance if he would fight. I spoke firmly to the Sergeant in an effort to rally him.

"Get a grip on yourself, son. You're not dying. Do you hear me, you're not dying. You've got a broken leg and you've lost a bit of blood, but you're going to be O.K.; isn't he, Sandy?" Sandy reassured him, wiping cold sweat from the Sergeant's brow. He was a ghastly grey colour. His pulse was barely perceptible and his breathing was laboured. No matter how convinced we were that he had a chance to live, there was no question about it, he was dying in front of our eyes. He was sinking fast.

"You're not dying, Sergeant," I said, over and over again, trying to make myself believe it was true, but it was no good. He was not fighting. He had given up hope and I think he knew he was going. He groaned and tried to speak. I put my ear to his mouth.

"Say . . . prayer," he whispered. I looked at Sandy.

"Can't we save him, Sandy, he's not that badly wounded?"

Sandy shook his head and put his hands together in prayer. After a pause we began.

"Our Father . . . Our Father," he whispered. "Which art in

heaven . . . Which art . . ." The dying Sergeant tried to repeat the words as Sandy took his hand to ease him on his way. We got as far as "Thy kingdom come . . ." when he died.

Sandy looked at me with compassion in his eyes. "He should never have died you know, sir," he said, "I wish I'd been there when it first happened, I could have saved him. Very highly strung he was. Shock must have done it, I think."

His mates laid him gently in the back of a truck to take him to Bunia. They rigged up a screen to shield his eyes from the sun. They had seen so little of death they did not know he was already dead.

With nightfall wireless reception improved. I still could not get Alastair, but 54 Commando who were near Ngote were loud and clear. At seven o'clock they reported their patrol had returned after bumping a large party of rebels. Volunteer Killen had been seriously wounded and Volunteer de Beer grazed by a bullet through his hair. Fifteen minutes later they announced that Killen had died and they were bringing his body to my headquarters that night.

It was a grim start to the campaign. Two dead, one wounded, and all units out of radio contact. Everything could be going wrong in Mahagi and Port Mahagi and the enemy were reported strong on all sides. I was feeling pretty low when Adjudant Bouve joined me for supper. He had something on his mind.

"I have just heard some very bad news on the air," he said, "but it is not official, just signallers' chat. Would you rather wait until you get an official report or shall I tell you now?" I nodded to him to tell me. The news shattered what remained of my peace of mind. At a training session at our camp in Bunia a Bazooka rocket had exploded inside the men's mess hall, killing three men and wounding fourteen!

At 23.00 hours I received the official report from Peter Johnstone. He was O.C. Base and it had been a day of agony for him. He had done everything he could for the wounded, but some of them were in a bad way. Fortunately a C-130 had landed at Bunia with an American doctor on board and he had done marvels for our men. I was indeed grateful to him.

It was the worst day of my life, but it ended on a better note. "By the way," added Peter, "John Peters came in on tonight's plane from Stan. Do you want him sent up to you?"

"At once," I replied, "give him the rank of Captain."

The 17th March dawned grey and wet. Bouve had worked deep into the night to make contact with Major Wicks' column, but still there was nothing. Nothing with Kingfisher either. At ten Bouve got through. Alastair was barely readable, but I could understand him, I knew his phraseology so well I could guess the gaps in the transmission. He had taken Mahagi the previous day and had motored down the escarpment to help "Kingfisher" who had landed safely and captured the port. The enemy were giving trouble at Port Mahagi and dodging into Uganda whenever we went for them. He wanted me to protest strongly against the Uganda border posts, who had fired on his column. It provoked an international incident and he hoped I would report it for what it was, a flagrant breach, etc. I did, of course, but the incident was smoothed over. He was leaving holding forces in both places and would be back in Ngote by the following evening. I was delighted with his success. That news raised my spirits considerably and I signalled Jacques Noel at once.

Nioka stood at the top of some high ground and to the west, the country rolled away into large pine forests and open green fields. The mission church, red-bricked and square-towered, stood on the highest ground in the vicinity, watching over the sprawling village like a medieval castle. In the late afternoon we buried Volunteer Killen in the long shadow of the Mission wall.

Sandy King was in charge of the last rites and conducted the burial party with dignity. It was a simple, but moving affair. We marched down to the graveside, attended by a large number of sympathetic A.N.C. soldiers. Sandy played a lament on the pipes, which curled away across the valley into the pine-clad hills.

I read the burial service from a Prayer Book, the majesty of the English language matching the solemnity of the occasion.

"Man that is born of a woman hath but a short time to live, and is full of trouble. He cometh up, and is cut down, like a flower; he fleeth as it were a shadow; and never continueth in one stay."

His friends threw some clods of earth into the grave and saluted. Sergeant Roberts handed me a Bible, open at the 23rd Psalm and asked me to read it.

We filed away to the drone of the pipes. It was the "Flowers of the Forest."

My second battalion came up the next day. They were nearly seven hundred strong and were mostly Katangese. They were commanded by Commandant Tavernier and had a number of European officers, mostly Belgian and German. Tavernier was a tall, thin Belgian with a keen sense of humour, always smiling. His habitual expression reminded me of a surprised ostrich looking over the top of long grass. He was capable, alive, and willing to tackle anything. His unit, he declared, were the best in the A.N.C. and "ever ready"—nothing was too difficult for them. He was to prove his words very shortly and to show us that 14 Commando were indeed matchless in the A.N.C.

I gave him Nioka to defend, whilst we moved forward to concentrate at Ngote. Phase one was over. Nioka–Ngote was my start line and I would begin the operation when I felt the time was right. I was shaken at the loss of my two men so soon, but the capture of Mahagi and Port Mahagi had put us in a strong position, tactically.

Alastair's force arrived the next evening and the village throbbed with the hum of three hundred men preparing for war. I walked round the camp fires that night to listen to the men. They were in great heart. If spirit counted for anything, I was in no doubt of the outcome of the campaign before us.

# 13

## OPERATION WHITE GIANT

A large crowd assembled on the hill at Ngote and waited patiently through the day for Colonel Mulamba to speak. By four in the afternoon over two thousand villagers had gathered in the biting cold. The Colonel spoke passionately for twenty minutes, appealing to the tribesmen to come forward now and help the A.N.C. rid the land of the hated Simbas. This was the moment, he declared, when they must all combine to restore peace to their beautiful land. It was exactly what the harassed villagers wanted themselves, and with one accord they rose to their feet, brandishing a forest of bows and arrows, and pledged loyalty to the little Colonel. They had suffered too long at the hands of the rebels, they cried, now they would act.

I was greatly relieved at the outcome of the Colonel's speech. Indifference on the part of the villagers was something I had feared, but now that we had the local population on our side, the battle was half won. All that remained was to mobilise their goodwill.

Sandy King stepped forward. The Congolese, like most Africans, love a show of strength and a strong man is universally admired. Sandy drew himself up to his full six feet six, his kilt stirring in the breeze and a murmur of approval ran through the crowd. They had never seen anything like this giant. Sandy took a rifle and demonstrated some drill, giving himself the words of command. Then he entertained them with conjuring tricks. He opened his right hand and showed them it was empty. Then he placed a walnut between thumb and forefinger. There, he said, now watch. A smack with the other hand and the walnut vanished into thin air. The crowd gasped. Sandy produced the walnut out of the Chief's nose and they were convinced he was a magician. The men nudged each other. Of course he was the white man's witch doctor, look at the strange way he was dressed. Conscious of his success, Sandy ran through the rest of his repertoire. The villagers were intrigued, mystified and delighted. They roared their approval, the children cried for more.

Sandy tucked his "secret weapon" under his arm and blew hard to inflate the skin bag. A few tortured notes escaped with a squeal and the mob backed away in dismay. A moment later their faces lit up with wonder at the strange music of the pipes. It was "Scotland the Brave," and the high notes pierced the thin air in all their glory, as Sandy paced to and fro.

The performance was part of our recruiting campaign and when the music died away we chose a hundred of the boldest spirits to be our scouts and guides. Hans Germani, who was now my staff officer and had laid aside his scalpel, was placed in command of the new unit. With a skirl of the pipes he and Sandy led the motley crew away down the hill, cheered by us all, bows and arrows at the trail, ancient shotguns and spears at the slope.

"Queen's Own Mobutu Highlanders!" said the R.S.M., his imagination boggling at the thought.

" 'A' Company, the Black Watch," suggested someone else, and so they came to be called. The gallant little band stayed with us all the way to Aba, rendering invaluable service, probing the land ahead and bringing back vital information. In so doing many of them including the Chief's son, laid down their lives for their country.

They were proud to serve with us. We were proud to serve with them. I salute the men of Ngote.

I called the operation to capture Aru, Aba and Faradje "Operation White Giant." It began cautiously. The area between our start-line and Golu, a village one-third of the way to Aru, was honeycombed with rebel positions and apparently strongly held. The first phase of the operation was the capture of Golu. Commandant Tavernier took the left flank from Nioka, the main column took the centre, and Force John-John the extreme right. I had created a special force of one hundred men for Captain Peters, which I now called Force John-John. There was an unknown magic in the name and the men of this force came to regard themselves, under John's inspiring leadership as the élite of 5 Commando. They certainly did their best to prove it.

Within an hour John-John struck the enemy. In a short sharp action they killed twelve rebels and captured two heavy machine guns, typical Chinese armament mounted on solid iron wheels. The rebels were heavily armed, some of them carrying two personal weapons, and most had the Russian 7·62 mm. Kalashnikov assault rifle, the "banana gun", so-called from the shape of its curved magazine.

By nightfall we had succeeded beyond our wildest hopes and were ten kilometres from Golu on all our axes. I sent John–John off on an outflanking movement up along the Uganda border, with a view to cutting off the rebels behind Golu, using a little-known track which Volunteer Grobler had told me about. Murray Grobler knew the countryside intimately and when he joined the unit in Bunia, I placed him in the Intelligence Section. He was a South African who had been born and bred in the Congo; in fact his farm was just this side of Golu. He had suffered at the hands of the rebels and had been lucky to escape with his life last October, when the Simbas descended on Ngote from the north. Since then, he had heard nothing of his wife and family or of his farm. He waited for the next day with some trepidation.

Early next morning we stood in the wreckage of what had been Grobler's homestead. The house had been systematically destroyed, door by door, window by window, until there was nothing left worth salvaging, not so much as a door knob. The ceilings had been pulled down, the floors ripped up and the fittings looted. It was a wanton act of vandalism. Grobler kicked the rubble with his foot and looked again at the scenes of his childhood, dazed and bewildered. He was a man of some character and accepted the blow stoically, but murmured softly that he was glad his father was not alive to see it. The old man had laboured fifty years to build this lovely farm. It had been his life's work. There was no trace of his family, and the cattle had gone. We moved on down the long driveway. Murray never looked back.

We took Golu easily after straddling it with mortar bombs but not without loss. The entrance to the village had been mined and Sergeant Lang, who was leading the assault, was blown up on a land mine and critically wounded. Doctor Flemming turned a dusty hut into an emergency operating theatre and worked on Lang's badly mutilated leg. The Sergeant fought for his life with a brave show of guts and determination and the will to live. He survived, but a year later was still in hospital.

The R.S.M. was an expert in the handling of high explosives and

5. ORIENTALE: Operation White Giant

went down on his knees to clear the minefield. He felt carefully in
the topsoil, sifting it gently with his hands until the outlines of a
box-like mine came to the surface. I found myself some urgent
employment at the back of the column at that moment! The R.S.M.
called me after an hour had passed to examine thirteen Chinese
land mines, each powerful enough to blow up a three-ton truck.

We that day captured an enemy courier and learnt from the letters
he was carrying that the rebels were demanding five thousand
*Jeunesse* from Army Headquarters at Aba, if they were to fight against
"*les Americains*", whom they declared had been "*bien reinforcés.*"
This information, coupled with the fact that in many instances the
Simbas had abandoned their well fortified positions without firing a

shot, convinced me that we could now accelerate the speed of our advance. I revised my plan.

Djalasiga and Kerekere were two hotbeds of rebel activity, halfway between Golu and Aru, where we could expect to find the local population whole-heartedly in support of the rebel régime. Generally it was a question of the local chief's allegiance which governed the villager's course of action, but I was fast forming the impression that the average Congolese was heartily sick of the rebellion and would welcome a strong hand to restore law and order and the peaceful life.

I decided to strike these two towns with the strongest force I could muster, whilst at the same time putting in a direct thrust for Aru across country. Alastair led the armoured column and part of his plan was to send Force John-John around the back of Kerekere on foot to cut off the enemy's retreat.

The cross-country force for Aru would start from Ambesi and comprise one hundred and twenty men, plus the "Black Watch" as guides and scouts. Its task would be to sever the main road into Aru at a point four kilometres from it, and then to march on northwards to attack the Mission at Essebi, which was known to be the rebel training centre. If this was successful it could swing round east and cut the road to Aba whilst the main column attacked Aru frontally. I would lead this column myself.

A thrill of excitement ran down the Aru column as we prepared for the long march. Unnecessary baggage was discarded as every man saw to his load. The heavy weapons were distributed amongst the Black Watch for the rough journey across the hills. A steady rain fell as we began the march in single file and well spaced out, covering a distance of over two miles. Piquets flanked the column North-west Frontier style and the men had to run to keep up with the main body. From time to time snipers took shots at us, when we went to ground, but after several delays we pushed on without stopping, accepting the small risk.

Dark fell and we were still two miles from the main road. I called a halt for a rest and we lay on the track, soaking wet and miserable. I went forward to speak to Lieutenant Griffin, whose Commando was in the lead. His men had all taken cover as a solitary figure approached in the dark, whistling softly to himself. Griffin stood up and called out to him in Swahili. He came on. When he was a yard away Lucky made a dive for him and pinned him to the ground in a rugby dive. It was a rebel officer, armed to the teeth with Chinese Grenades and a Russian Tokarev pistol! He began by saying he knew nothing, but a knife blade on his genitals under the guidance of the Black Watch soon made him sing. The barrier ahead was held by twelve men, the road to Essebi was clear, but Aru was well defended.

We dropped six mortar bombs on the barrier position and advanced through the pouring rain. The rebels had gone. We took shelter in some houses at the road junction, wet through, hungry and unhappy.

It was probable that the Simba lieutenant was telling the truth about the defence of Aru, so I decided to leave a holding force where we were and to continue with the plan to attack Essebi and outflank Aru.

Somebody took my wet trousers to dry them in front of a fire and lost them. I gave out my orders for the advance on Essebi at three in the morning, shivering in my shirt tails, but it had been such a grim night we were in no mood for laughter.

The rain stopped and we moved off at four, sections staggered on either side of the road in the approved manner, a watery moonlight glistening on the light frost. All was quiet, but for the sound of our boots ringing on the metalled road. With the first rays of dawn, firing broke out from the leading commando and the whole column took cover. The R.S.M. and I doubled forward to see what had happened. Lieutenant Maurice Lucien-Brun, who was commanding 53 Commando, lay wounded on the ground, a hideous gash from a bullet wound over his right eye. Another half inch and he would have been stone dead.

The explanation was almost unbelievable. During the night march a section of rebel soldiers had joined the column, under the impression that we were some of their own troops. For over an hour we had all marched along merrily together, but with the first rays of dawn they realised the error of their ways and started shooting!

John Flemming sewed up the wound and although Maurice had lost a lot of blood and was very badly shocked, he was able to march slowly at the back of the column. Lucien-Brun was a Frenchman who had contacted me during my January leave. He had just sailed in to Durban on his 38-foot ketch, *Sinbad*, from the Seychelles, having set out from Brittany. He was looking for adventure and I snapped him up when I heard that he had been an officer in the

N

French Army in Algeria. He was young and handsome and added tone to the unit. Furthermore, he spoke English like Charles Boyer. We marched all morning, but the final assault on Essebi was denied us. Alastair's column had overcome Djalasiga and pressed on to Kerekere to meet John-John, who had already taken the enemy by surprise. John-John had then mounted their vehicles and dashed down side roads for Essebi, arriving an hour before us, capturing a vast amount of equipment and killing about thirty rebels. They stole our thunder, but we were so worn out from the fifty-kilometre march that we were happy to concede them the honour. Captain Peters' column completed the outflanking of Aru, whilst the main column concentrated at my position four kilometres from Aru.

I gave 14 Commando the task of seizing Aru early the next morning. Commandant Tavernier appreciated the importance of his role and the effect success would have on his unit and the A.N.C. generally. He tackled it with his usual vigour and by noon Aru was his. I sent Hans Germani along with him for liaison purposes, with particular instructions to collect all Communist matter, Russian and Chinese, for immediate transmission to G 2 at Leo. He borrowed my camera to make a record of the more important papers.

Tavernier met me with some startling news. A Belgian priest whom he had liberated on entering the town had informed him that three lorry loads of Ugandese mercenary troops in bright green uniforms had crossed the border into the Congo only a few days ago!

It was obvious that we had achieved maximum surprise and I intended to exploit it fully. Leaving Alastair with 14 Commando to defend Aru, the main column prepared to pursue the enemy up the road to Aba before he had time to dig in anywhere and organise a defensive position. Meanwhile, the R.S.M. was to take a small party along the Uganda road to destroy a large iron bridge which would effectively seal the border with Uganda in this sector.

Just as the main column was about to move, Germani's familiar figure came waddling down the road at some speed. Under his arm he carried a bundle of captured documents. Some of them implicated Russia and China in the supply of arms to the rebels and others showed that the Uganda Army in Entebbe was sending small arms ammunition to Aru in exchange for gold and ivory. A letter from Gbenye to Soumiallot made a cryptic reference to his "young artillery" which we were unable to understand. I wondered if the

Simbas had got hold of some screw guns or field howitzers and consulted with the Chief of Staff immediately. If they had, this could alter the shape of things, especially if they were manned by Algerians with the necessary knowledge to use them.

Hans had gone through Gbenye's house with a fine-tooth comb and now produced a worn copy of a book in French, which he had found on Gbenye's bedside table. Given a hundred guesses I could never have told him it was Dale Carnegie's *How to Win Friends and Influence People*.

Amongst the papers he had found were some printed attestation forms to be used when Simbas were inducted into the army. We became quite excited when we read them at first, but their real meaning sank in later. One phrase in the form said the Simba would be recruited *"en qualité de Chinois."* If we were *"les Americains"* they were *"les Chinois."* It was all part of the Communist doctrine.

Hans was extremely well informed on African affairs and a brilliant conversationalist. I enjoyed his company and admired two things about him—his enthusiasm for life and his magnificent appetite. The Germans in my unit were all good trenchermen and this prompted Hans to remind me of the story current amongst the A.N.C. soldiers that they could always tell the nationality of *les mercenaires* from their habits. "The Germans," they said, "are always eating. The South Africans are always drinking, and the Belgians are always chasing our girls!"

The column was now formed up ready to leave Aru. Germani-was deep in conversation with the R.S.M. He looked agitated and passed his hands over his bulging pockets a few times, performing what the Americans call the "lost wallet routine." They exchanged a few words, which went like this:

Hans:  "R.S.M., I hate to admit it, but I've lost the C.O.'s camera. He'll flay me alive if I tell him. What do you think I should do?"
R.S.M.: "Desairt, sir!"

Although the Congolese are, to my mind, amongst the most intelligent people in Africa, I found that they did not adapt well to modern soldiering. The African, generally, has not the makings of a good soldier and lacks the necessary self-discipline and courage essential to the task. His lack of sophistication in the use of modern weapons and tactics are things which can undoubtedly be overcome with training and time, but in the long term I see no probability of vast African armies rampaging up and down the continent, if only for the basic reason that the average African at heart is not a soldier. Economically, one imagines, it will not be possible for many African countries to maintain large standing armies, but in any case the idea of taking arms to redress their wrongs is not one which is likely to prove attractive to many Africans.

Basically the African is a realist and does not readily assimilate any idealistic doctrine. Old Congo hands see in this the salvation of the Congo, declaring that the Congolese are incapable of the self-sacrifice and the effort required to embrace Communism. I am not so sure.

During my campaigning I came to meet a large number of Congolese officers and civilians with whom I was able to discuss intimate matters of this nature quite objectively. One of the favourite subjects for debate was the difference which exists between the European and African character. The Congolese conceded that they did not understand the meaning of chivalry, in fact there is no word for it in Swahili or Lingala, and the concept of sportsmanship, the son of chivalry, was completely unknown to them. These were distinctly European attributes for which they could see little use in the African context. Gratitude was another, but I agreed readily that their sense of loyalty and devotion to their family unit far surpassed anything of which we were capable.

The foregoing comment is not intended to be adverse criticism of a fine people so much as a bald statement of fact. Arising out of these discussions, my Congolese friends came to understand how shocked the European mind can be at cruelty, although this is something which is accepted as quite normal up and down the African Continent. I recall seeing a soldier of the A.N.C. pluck the feathers from a living dove and then throw the naked bird, still alive, on to a bed of red-hot coals to cook it. He was genuinely unable to understand my rancour.

On the other hand I was genuinely unable to understand their attitude to ritual torture, something which had been handed down to them through the centuries. A prisoner of war must be killed after ritual torture, it was always thus, and nobody expected anything different. This acceptance of torture as the normal thing may help one understand the scene which I now describe, even though it cannot excuse it. A platoon of A.N.C. troops had caught a rebel in Aru and decided to torture him before death. The majority voted that the best way to do it would be to boil him alive in a forty-five gallon drum of water. A fire was lit and the rebel roped up and dropped in. The soldiers stoked the fire, encouraged it with petrol and laughed at the agony of their prisoner. At this moment one of my men, a South African from Durban, chanced by and ordered the men to stop it at once. They refused to obey him until he pulled out a pistol. They doused the flames reluctantly and threw the rebel out with the water on to the ground. It was, however, too late.

The affair was reported to me and I was as disgusted with the episode as the next man, but savagery begets savagery and two months later I had occasion to revise my own standards of civilised behaviour. As I stood over the tortured remains of a small European boy of eight, done to death by the rebels in the most barbarous fashion, I thought back to the boiling alive episode in Aru and wondered why I had been so shocked. I felt then that it was far too good for them.

The column halted fifteen kilometres from Aru, waiting for the armour to come through from Essebi. Sergeant-Major Chaloner was in command. He was a small wiry little fire eater, and sported a bristly moustache, which adequately camouflaged his twenty-four years. Davy Chaloner was always where the fighting was thickest, and in a tight spot his pugnacious and aggressive character was worth forty men. In a careless moment he had bogged down a Ferret scout car and a heavy M 8 was trying to get him out. I decided to go on without him.

The advance was led by Lieutenant Hobbins and Lieutenant von Lieres. Hans von Lieres had recovered from his wounds before Stanleyville and had returned after a spell in our Johannesburg Liaison Office. I had been so impressed with his efficiency that I promoted him to Lieutenant in command of 52 Commando. Barry Hobbins was a Canadian, about 28, calm and efficient and an expert on all firearms. I had noticed his flair for leadership and had given him 55 Commando at Bunia. He was one of the very few who had been right through every action we had fought, beginning with Lisala. Both of these good men were now to be tried again by fire.

Lieutenant Hobbins led both Commandos to seize Wawa, a village twenty kilometres away. There was a prominent bend in the road before Wawa, which suggested it might be a likely spot for enemy ambush. And so it proved. The enemy were well concealed and opened fire on Barry's armoured jeep at thirty yards' range, shattering the bullet-proof windshield with five bullets. Volunteer White, his driver, raced for cover, but was killed by another burst of fire. In the next jeep Hans von Lieres had his forearm shattered and his driver, a Hungarian, was wounded in the stomach, another shot passing through his buttocks. The action was going badly for Hobbins, when Force John-John arrived in the nick of time. John Peters deployed his men in extended order and swept through the enemy killing fourteen. They were dressed in new bright green uniforms and I was pretty certain these were the "Ugandese mercenaries."

Captain Flemming and Petersen erected a roadside surgery and attended to Hans who was bleeding badly, his main artery severed. He was a ghastly colour. The Hungarian was put out of his pain with morphine. The doctor offered to take the wounded back to Aru himself and have them flown out by helicopter. The return journey entailed a considerable risk, as I could spare only a small escort, but the doctor was his own escort and feared nothing and went.

Poor, unlucky Hans, a man with an enormous heart and an unyielding spirit. As he drove off, white and shocked from loss of blood, he raised a feeble smile and said, "I'll be back, sir, you can't win without me."

After the battle was over, I examined a white Mercedes Benz car which was lying at the side of the road. General Olenga was known to be travelling in something similar and I wondered whether the car had been searched for secret papers. Our men had certainly gone through it, to judge by the litter lying around and I was assured that nothing of value had been found. I walked into the adjoining bush and turned a few loose papers over with my foot. One had been used for toilet purposes within the last hour and I screamed with rage when I saw what it was. Bold as brass, the heading announced that it was the Top Secret list of Code Names to be used at cabinet level between the Rebels, Uganda and Tanzania. I gave the task of smoothing it out to Hans Germani! It was not one he appreciated fully.

The column halted this side of Wawa. I was expecting the enemy to make a determined stand somewhere in this area and thought this might be it. We probed around vigorously on foot before night fell, but saw nobody. I closed the column of vehicles up head to tail and accepted the risk of enemy mortar fire during the night. This way the maximum number of men could sleep and we could keep going. We must not let up our pressure for one moment, I felt sure of it, and every advantage lay in getting to the enemy before he could recover from his shock. Morale was low with the death of White, a popular chap, and when the R.S.M. asked me to give a ruling on fires I decided fires would be lit, as many as we wanted, and the enemy advised that we were coming, and to hell with them. Let them all come—three hundred of us were a force to be reckoned with.

The aggressive spirit fired the column from top to bottom and every man waited impatiently for the dawn.

The column sped forward like an avenging flame, striking Wawa and all villages to the north in quick succession. At midday we entered Adi, one of the mission stations of the African Inland Mission, an American body, and found it in good condition. At four in that afternoon we crossed a long iron bridge and the road to Aba stood clear ahead. From now on the country was sparsely populated and bordered on the Sudan. Open green fields gave way to low savannah and rocky outcrops, a sure sign of the desert beyond.

From time to time I lost wireless contact with units in the column, but Bouve worked incessantly to keep me in touch with everybody. I was anxious to hear from our signaller with 14 Commando, whom I had ordered to join us. Finally we got him.

"State your position", said Bouve. There was a pause the other end. A new signaller was on the set. Haltingly, he ventured a reply. "We are on a rough track next to a kaffir hut, man."

"In Africa!" said Bouve, sardonically, looking to heaven for comfort in his affliction from 5 Commando signallers.

John-John were leading and reported an astounding capture. A brand new Willys jeep was standing abandoned in the middle of the road in perfect condition. All it needed was petrol. It was a welcome addition to our fleet and the first of over thirty vehicles we captured during this campaign to fit ourselves out with the best motor transport in the Congo. Whoever had left the jeep had done so in a hurry. It was another indication that we were breathing on the enemy's neck and we dashed back to our vehicles to continue the advance.

As the convoy bowled along a single shot rang out from behind a hill and Volunteer Brock slumped to the floor of his truck, mortally wounded in the head. Volunteer Petersen, the medical orderly's brother, who was standing behind Brock, got the same bullet through his wrist. Most of us thought that this was the work of the abandoned jeep driver, who had fired a shot in the general direction of the convoy. We searched the surrounding hills, but found nothing.

The tragedy delayed us by ninety minutes. I examined my map and came to the conclusion that if the enemy was to make a stand, then it must be on the line of the Nzoro River, which lay twenty kilometres ahead of us. After that there was only the town of Dramba between us and Aba. It had to be the Nzoro or nothing. I gave the order to dash for the Nzoro, accepting all risks. It was a race against time which we lost. Night dropped suddenly and I was obliged to call a halt.

I was convinced that the enemy would try to hold the line of the Nzoro, but if we could get to it that night, I was equally certain we would frustrate his plans. I sent for John Peters. I explained the tactical position as I saw it and affirmed that I would never give the order for our column to move at night, particularly after Stanleyville, but that if he could find sufficient volunteers to do the job, it would be a valuable night's work. Without so much as a second thought, he decided to take the whole of John-John at once. With a flourish they mounted and disappeared into the night.

Twenty minutes later the whole sky was lit up with a gigantic fireworks display. Force John-John had met the enemy column in the act of trundling on to the bridge! A lucky shot from Peters' jeep hit an ammunition truck and blew it sky high. The battle lasted ten minutes at the end of which Force John-John had annihilated the whole of the enemy column and captured eleven trucks, and mountains of arms and ammunition.

Once more John Peters had risen to the occasion and by his magnificent personal example and bravery had turned the day. If the enemy had dug in on the Nzoro we would certainly have been held up for days, during which time Aba and Faradje could have been reinforced and the whole course of the campaign altered. General Mobutu raised John to the rank of Commandant in the field for this particular action. There was no holding the men of Force John-John now. One almost needed permission to talk to them. The main column occupied a poor position ringed by rocky hills. Despite patrols sent out during dusk and the early part of the night I was worried. An aggressive enemy, using the cover of the nearby hills, could have inflicted fantastic damage on the column. I slept uneasily. During the night a single shot rang out. After dawn stand-to the R.S.M. took me to the last truck in the column, where ten feet away a rebel was lying dead with half his head blown off. Sergeant Smith, our sentry, had seen the rebel as he walked towards the column in the moonlight. The rebel was under the impression that the convoy was one of theirs. Sergeant Smith was lying in the shadow of a truck and challenged the rebel when he came within earshot. "Mulamba," he called out, the counterpart was "Mobutu." The rebel replied, "Lumumba." It was the last sound he ever uttered.

I was greatly impressed with Smith's nerve. It took some presence of mind to let the rebel come so close before challenging him. If he had scared him off at fifty yards, he might have opened up on us with his machine gun and done untold damage. The rebel was armed with a brand new Russian light machine gun, the 7·62 mm. Degtyarev, complete with fifty-round drum of ammunition.

Force John-John led the attack on Dramba. Davy Chaloner stormed up to the cross-roads at top speed, narrowly missed by two bazooka rockets which exploded in the hedge behind him. He opened his turret and loosed off his own rocket launcher. The rocket struck the enemy control post dead centre and parts of rebels flew into the air. The remaider of the garrison fled.

Dramba was chock-full of Russian hospital equipment, field dressings and drugs, all of which were wrapped with a slip of paper wishing their comrades well. We helped ourselves to these, for the time being we were all comrades. Another house contained rooms full of ammunition, lately the property of the Uganda National Army, Box 20, Entebbe, or so the printing read. We took photographs of these for the record. The whole place was a veritable arsenal and ought never to have been abandoned without a last ditch defence.

Aba was barely twenty-five kilometres away. We approached it carefully and on foot. It was the known Headquarters of the entire rebel movement in Orientale and the funnel through which aid was reaching them via Sudan. If we captured it, we would smash the core of their resistance.

Captain Peters led the advance and apart from a little skirmish at the entrance to the town, where we captured an enemy 76 mm. cannon, we found the town completely deserted. It was unbelievable. Patrols went out and brought in a 120 mm. mortar with Algerian markings. We tried it out on the retreating enemy. It made a comforting boom.

I sent a strong patrol at once to blow the bridge on the road from Aba to the Sudan, eighteen kilometres away. They returned to report total success. The Sudan border was now sealed to wheeled traffic.

Early the following morning Alastair left to attack Faradje, the key town sixty-five kilometres to the west of Aba. He took with him 54 Commando, the mortars, and the whole of 14 Commando, less the company at Dramba. It was a sizeable force. He gave me a look which said it was about time the understudy got the part and disappeared with glee in a cloud of dust. Fifteen minutes later he ran into a fierce ambush in which three Congolese soldiers were killed. 14 Commando spread out through the village, like a plague of ants, destroying everything in their path. The village was completely razed to the ground and the column rolled on for Faradje. War, as fought by the Congolese, is a harsh and revengeful business and, although he tried hard to restrain his men, Tavernier was unable to stop the slaughter.

Alastair's force brushed all resistance aside and entered Faradje a few minutes before sunset to capture the airfield, which he found in perfect condition. He signalled to tell me how well the A.N.C. had done and I passed on the message to Colonel Mulamba at once.

Meanwhile, in Aba, it was our sad duty to bury Volunteer Brock. Father Demot, the hardy Belgian priest who had accompanied us all the way from Kamina, conducted the ceremony with full military honours. The dying notes of the Last Post were still quivering in the air, when the enemy opened fire on us. We ran for cover. Quite by chance, at precisely this moment, two B 26 aircraft circled overhead, but mistaking us for the enemy, swooped down and blasted off their rockets. One of the mission houses was blown to pieces by a direct hit and two of my men were wounded. They received medical treatment, whilst I composed a blistering signal for Stan.

Back at my Headquarters, the Aba Country Club, Lieutenant

Griffin had lined up some enemy captured material. Seven 76 mm. cannons, mounted on two-wheel trailers, stood side by side in a formidable array of fire power. I saw at once what Gbenye meant when he referred to his "young artillery!"

I busied myself with the defence of Aba, realising that we were now as far from Stanleyville as it was possible to be. With that sobering thought in mind I set about making the place impregnable and addressed myself to the next phase in the campaign.

# 14

## WATSA

With the capture of Aba and Faradje the first phase of our mission was completed. My orders had been to take Aru, Aba and Faradje, and to close the borders with Uganda and the Sudan. This we had done. My command now stretched over a distance of three hundred miles.

Phase two of the overall plan for the recapture of Orientale envisaged the seizure of the remaining big towns in the Province. Chief of these was Watsa, whose gold-mine had financed the rebel movement and paid for their arms and equipment. It had been part of the plan that 6 Commando, a unit of Belgian and other mercenaries, would leave Paulis and strike Watsa at the same time as we struck Aba, but for a variety of reasons 6 Commando were unable to move.

I discussed phase two with Jacques Noel over my S.S.B. He agreed with me that it would be tragic if our advance lost its momentum at this critical stage, when we had the enemy on the run. I suggested to Jacques that, tired though we were, and thin on the ground as we would be, 5 Commando should now strike Watsa. He agreed readily.

I called an O group at the Country Club. Overnight my men had given themselves the impression that Aba was to be journey's end and had already found themselves cosy nooks as is the habit with good soldiers everywhere. I was sorry to disillusion them.

I gave out the plan. Move to Faradje today. Capture Watsa tomorrow. Lieutenant Griffin's 51 Commando and two hundred Katangese to hold Dramba and Aba. My officers whistled. "The men are bushed," they said. "With respect, sir," they added, "one can only push them so far. Furthermore, we are all out of petrol."

"Gentlemen," I said, "it is now ten o'clock. The column will move to Faradje at 13.00 hours. Every vehicle will have sufficient petrol to reach Watsa, a distance of 165 kilometres."

Excitement will beat fatigue at any time. The reckoning would come in due course, I realised that, but meanwhile we must seize this unrepeatable chance of taking Watsa by surprise. It was too good to lose. Petrol appeared miraculously from everywhere. The men responded, as always, with cheerful grumbling and "Who does he think we are, bloody supermen?" That is exactly what I did think. They would never know how impressed I had been with their behaviour on the long march from Golu to Aba. Each night they had slept rough, but their rifles were always cleaned and ready for action. Every man snatched sleep during the day when he could. No man wasted his energies unnecessarily. Sentries were keen, alert and responsible. Vehicles were clean and shipshape. They were a unit to be proud of and worked as a team. Above it all, the men were happy and confident. They had the bright gleam of victory in their eyes.

The column rolled out of Aba at exactly 13.00 hours and in high spirits. By this time the men had decorated their trucks with souvenirs, ranging from ivory tusks to parrots. The "Black Watch" were distributed evenly throughout the column and counted themselves part of 5 Commando. Firm friendships were struck up between the men of Ngote and the men of South Africa, with names like Viljoen and Pretorius. Fear, the great equaliser, had forged a new understanding in many of us, black and white.

"All right for you," my men shouted, as we left "Lucky" Griffin and his boys to hold the town. The column accelerated and was lost in the swirl of dust, which swallowed the last vehicle. Nine miles from Aba we patrolled the African Inland Mission. Its hilltop houses were deserted but undamaged and still watched over by a group of faithful servants. I thought of my American friend, Mrs. Kleinschmidt, whose mission station it had been, and her eagerness to return to Aba to continue her ministry, despite the rough treatment meted out to her so recently by the rebels. Her husband, the good doctor, had lived and died working in this remote corner of Africa for these same people. Of such are the Kingdom of Heaven.

I was not worried about the safety of Aba, thinly held though it was. I placed great confidence in Lieutenant Griffin and knew him to be quite capable of holding the town in our absence. "Lucky" Griffin was a quiet, self-effacing man with the slightly worried look of the really conscientious. He was gentle with his men, but commanded their natural respect. They never took advantage of him. His career in Kenya, where he had spent all his life, had come to a sudden end like so many of his compatriots, with the advent of the new régime, but he was by no means bitter. He spoke Swahili fluently.

Griffin's immediate task was to encourage the civilian population of Aba to return to take up their normal occupation once more. He sent out patrols with the "Black Watch" to spread the news that the soldiers were here to protect the people, not to harm them, and that they must come back out of the bush. He would feed them and help them.

In a few days thousands flocked back to Aba. The presence of the civilian population was our surest safeguard against the rebels and a buffer against sudden counter-attack. Rewards were promised to all who gave information about the rebels with special sums for those actually bringing them in with arms. The armoury bulged with weapons and the gaol swelled to bursting point!

"Lucky" Griffin set up a civil administration. Soon the post office was working again, then the clinic, then a garage workshop and now perhaps a school, if he could find some school-teachers. As a soldier, he was one of my best. As a civil administrator, he was invaluable. The Congolese loved him. He administered justice with a fair hand, a father figure, stern but kind, and his fame spread through the land, until finally it reached Mr. Tshombe and the General. Both asked me to ensure that he stayed on in the Congo at the end of his contract. These are the men we want, said Mobutu, men who understand us and are prepared to work with us. Griffin was certainly that man. That there were some others in my unit with similar talents was my very good fortune.

We arrived at Faradje without trouble. The place that had figured so often in my imagination was every bit as romantic as its reputation. Broad red gravel avenues radiated from the centre of the town and the abundance of palm and mango trees lining their sides spoke of the Arab civilisation which had created it. It was, of course, originally one of the old slave stations which stretched across the Congo. The Belgians had superimposed a Catholic presence on the town and the red brick church and mission school were a living tribute to their genius.

The main feature of the approach march to Watsa was the Kibali River, which was spanned by a long iron bridge. Our latest information was that Watsa, which was ten miles from the bridge, was held by a thousand rebels. I anticipated trouble at the bridge and ordered maximum air over the target at eleven o'clock the next morning.

Late that evening a truck coming from Watsa motored straight into our lines. All the occupants were killed, except for the driver, a mulatto who claimed to be the director of the Watsa Gold-mine. His party were on their way to draw wages for the garrison and were unaware that we had captured both Aba and Faradje. It was a fantastic stroke of luck. All we had to do was to make him talk and we would know the enemy strength and all his positions in detail. I handed him to my military police.

The mulatto had been shot below the right knee and it looked as though his shin-bone was broken from the angle his foot made with the rest of his leg. He was only concerned with the gold-mine, he said, he knew nothing about the defence of Watsa. He thought there might be about 1,200 soldiers there, but he could give no details of the barriers on the hundred-kilometre stretch from Faradje to Watsa.

It was nonsense, of course. The mulatto was being incredibly dumb if he thought we believed him. The lives of my men were at stake and I gave permission to use whatever force was needed to get the truth. Horrible screams came from the mulatto, as one of my military policemen twisted his wounded leg. There was a spine chilling crunch of jagged bones, but he spoke. It was enough. He knew everything and he told us all. In return, I promised him his life, subject to his information being correct.

Sergeant Carter drove the tentacle, the wounded mulatto sitting between us. Howard Carter was my chief signaller and an unspoken comradeship existed between us. It was born the day we both paddled for eighteen hours across Lake Tanganyika, right back in the beginning of 5 Commando. It seemed like an age ago. Carter was a Birmingham boy with a pleasant Midlands accent, to him a truck was a "lurry." He was stolid and unimaginative, which may have gone some way to account for his coolness in action. He had a detached look and seemed to live in another world most of the time, as though constantly deciphering the morse code. It was a solitary attitude which I often noticed amongst signallers. Perhaps the much wearing of earphones had something to do with it.

We ticked off the kilometres. Every defended barrier was now know to us, thanks to the Director of the Gold-mines and, so far, he had not lied. Force John-John was leading once more with Davy Chaloner forcing the pace in front, his machine gun swivelling round and round, ready to deal out instant death at the slightest provocation. Tavernier brought up the rear. Four T-28s appeared high above us with two B-26s. This was our first wave. Alastair signalled them to strike the Kibali Bridge and to ease up as soon as they saw us appear. I intended to rush it. If the enemy did not know we were coming, then the sooner we got there the better. The planes peeled off and splattered the bridge with machine gun bullets, the B-26s coughing out their rockets in a stream of smoke. I hated these smash and grab tactics, but the risk was reasonable.

Force John-John crossed the bridge just as the enemy defence opened up. Machine gun bullets ricocheted off the heavy iron girders and the air was filled with whistling bullets. John-John ran for cover as the rest of the column came on across. The firing was too fierce for safety and I stopped the column as soon as my tentacle was over and ordered everyone to take cover. 14 Commando fanned out on foot from the rear of the column and cleared the jungle on either side of the road. There was a lull in the firing and I could hear the sound of escaping air—it was the front wheel of the tentacle going down.

Sergeant Patterson was carrying a P.R.C. 10 on his back. The antenna had been shot off at its base four inches from his head. He ran up with a grin—"Permission to change my aerial and my pants, sir?" he said.

We were still laughing at this when the enemy started firing again. Captain Peters took a patrol into the bush on my left to seek out the rebels and returned in five minutes triumphantly pushing a new Austin Gypsy pick-up, which he had found hidden in the bush. Some of his men were firing from the hip and three rebels who had been lying in the long grass not twenty yards from us rolled over, dead. Four men dragged out another who was horribly wounded and threw him on the track in front of me. Most of his guts were missing and he left a trail of blood behind him.

"See what he knows, Hans," I ordered. Hans bent down close to the dying rebel. *Tu parle Francais?* he asked, in all earnestness. The absurdity of the question at that moment and in those circumstances forced us to laugh. The rebel coughed up a gobbet of blood. Hans tried him in Swahili, but he was already too far gone.

His agony was impossible to watch. Turning to the nearest man, I said, "Take him into the bush and finish him off." A young, fair-haired chap of about nineteen shot him, but in his nervousness used five shots. A wave of indignation swept through the men, who shouted out, "One's enough, you bloody murderer!"

Probing the psychology of this remark kept me busy for the next ten minutes as we marched up the hill into Watsa.

The air transferred its attention to the middle of the town, and reported that the rebels were fleeing, hundreds of them. Davy Chaloner screamed up to the cross-roads, pumping out lead from his Browning and touching off his bazooka for good measure at likely targets, whilst John-John ran from cover to cover, pursuing the terrified enemy.

Thirty minutes later I stood in the mission in the centre of the town. Bouve signalled the code word to Jacques Noel—Watsa had fallen.

The business of consolidation was not new to us and the Commandos set forth to seize the airfield, the gold-mine and all points of tactical importance. I installed myself in the parlour overlooking the gracious gardens of the mission. A man came slowly up the drive, carrying a small Congolese girl in his arms, a look of great sorrow on his face. It was Sergeant Patterson. He laid her on my desk. The child, who was about seven years old, had been shot through the elbow, the same bullet passing through her stomach. Pieces of grey matter were pushing their way through two places in her flesh. She whimpered with pain. Doctor Flemming shook his head when he saw her. With no drugs and little in the way of theatre facilities, he doubted he could save her, but he would do his best. The poor little soul died in the night.

In the maternity section of the mission a man held up a new-born baby. It was not more than an hour old. John Flemming said it was "a premature—probably five months." It was as ugly as sin, but aroused great interest as we tenderly wrapped it in an army blanket.

John Peters reported the situation on his sector. He had found four Europeans hiding in a house. Two were from the gold-mine, one was a doctor and the other a priest. They sent me their compliments and thanks for their salvation. I am a stickler for protocol and my gorge rose at their lack of common courtesy.

"Arrest them at once and bring them to me here," I told John. Collaboration with the enemy was one charge they would have to clear themselves on, and the murder of thirty-eight Belgian civilians in November must be a matter they knew something about.

"By the way, sir," said John, "shall I place a guard on the hospital? There are fifty or sixty wounded Simbas in one ward and you know what will happen if the A.N.C. get to them first . . . ." I cursed myself for my stupidity. I should have thought of it when we first arrived.

John returned twenty minutes later with the four Europeans sitting on the bonnet of his jeep. Somewhat shamefacedly they faced my baleful gaze and answered my brutal enquiries. They regretted their lapse in etiquette, but protested their innocence on all other charges. They gave me details of the massacre. All the Belgians had been lined up and killed in the forest close by. Nobody had escaped. Hundreds of Congolese had suffered the same fate. It was the sickening pattern as before.

"How come they didn't kill you?" I asked. They were spared because of their usefulness in the gold-mine and the hospital, they explained. It seemed reasonable.

They invited me to dinner that evening, "jugged hare and red wine," they said, the priest adding regretfully that it was all they had left of the church stock. The thought of the church wine stuck in my throat and I declined with thanks.

I shot a silent enquiry at John about the hospital. He shook his head. He was too late. The A.N.C. had got there before him. To kill a man in action is one thing. The savage butchery of a wounded man lying in a hospital bed is another and about as disgusting an act as a human being is capable of. I sent for Commandant Tavernier.

Hans Germani took the mulatto to hospital and John Flemming performed an operation on his leg. He recovered in due course and became a familiar figure in Watsa, hobbling around on his crutches. He had told us the truth and we honoured our side of the bargain. Strangely enough he became quite friendly with some of my men and with 14 Commando after we left.

The town of Watsa is amongst the glories of the Congo. It is high, cool and healthy. The water is pure. The town is laid out with an architectural brilliance and its private houses set deep in the lush green tropical vegetation are a joy to behold. The missions are built in rich red brick, opulent and solid and set the tone of the town, which is quiet and well-bred. I decided that Watsa was eminently suitable as my headquarters.

Any plans, however, that I may have had for establishing myself in beautiful Watsa were shattered the next morning with the arrival of the first F.A.T.A.C. D.C.-3. The airfield is on a hill, which is difficult to negotiate and was rough enough to break the tail wheel of the first plane to land. Watsa was immediately placed out of bounds to all aircraft. As an airfield was essential to my headquarters, I had no alternative but to return at once to Faradje.

I warned Hans we would be leaving straight away. Germani is the untidiest man I have ever met and I marvelled at the state of his room when we came to move. He is the only man I know who could walk into a room stark naked and leave it with enough equipment to fit out two men!

I discussed the tactical position with Jacques in Stan. 6 Commando were still not ready to move. Dungu and Niangara were the last two big towns in the north still holding out and Gombari the last one in the south. He suggested that 5 Commando should do the job, which would make it game and set!

Tavernier with my armour under command, plus one Commando made short work of the Gombari garrison and chalked up another victory for the A.N.C., for the loss of five of his men killed and one of mine wounded. One armoured car had been knocked out by a rocket. Meanwhile we returned to Faradje and prepared plans for the move on Dungu.

We dined that evening with a Congolese priest at the mission. Whilst we were there we witnessed a heartrending sight. A white nun was brought in from the bush by some Congolese, who had befriended her after the rebels had killed the priests in Faradje. All these months they had hidden her deep in the forest, fed her and kept her safe. I went outside to congratulate the men who had done such a noble deed at such risk to themselves. They were all lepers.

We walked back to our quarters in the dark. We took a short cut through the garden and stumbled over a dead body, hands still tied behind his back. John Peters turned the corpse over with his foot and swore profusely. He sent for the guard commander and harangued him for fully ten minutes. Finally, the R.S.M. brought me the report. Captain Peters had brought this man from Watsa for trial. He was the rebel who had ordered the massacre of the Belgians in Watsa. Now he had been shot, trying to escape. It seemed straightforward enough to me, but John was still as mad as a snake. If ever a man should have been kept alive, he explained, it was this one. Before the Belgians were killed in Watsa, he had made them all deliver up their jewellery and money and he was the only one who knew where it had been hidden! The secret had gone with him.

We got down to the plans for attacking Dungu. The first place on our route was Gangala na Bodio. Jacques had warned me that it was quite possible that some white hostages might be held there under guard. Gangala was a village at the entrance to the Garamba National Park, one of the most beautiful game reserves in Africa, and I had given strict orders that the park was not to be touched, even though we knew that the rebels were hiding in it and using it as their larder. The park is a national asset and the day will come when people from all over the world will visit it again.

In the event we found the village deserted, but an incident took place that might have made the photograph of the year. Gangala is the home of the only trained African elephants on the continent and they now demonstrated their prowess. The game guards had shot some buffalo for our men and these were lying on the far bank of the river which runs through the camp. At a word of command from their "mahouts" the elephants swam across the river and dragged the dead buffaloes back through the deep water by the tail and deposited them at the feet of our men.

Force John-John took Dungu that day and Niangara the next with a great show of force and determination. John Peters encouraged the civilian population to return to the towns quickly and promised them protection from the Simbas. Once more the villagers proved to be our safest shield and within days the towns were running themselves again and rebels were brought in from all sides. The stack of enemy arms grew high. Only the airfield at Niangara remained to be cleared. The civilians said that the Simbas had mined it; it was justice, therefore, that they should be used to un-mine it. A gang of them were roped together and marched across the airfield as human mine detectors. Fortunately for them, one of them remembered the plan and knew where they had all been planted. They were all dug up and destroyed.

My sector now stretched over six hundred miles from Aru to Niangara with the Niangara garrison responsible for patrolling to Yakaluku and Doruma on the Sudan border, a further hundred miles north. We were woefully thin on the ground, but the fact that the civilian population was with us turned the scales. In all areas we concentrated on getting the civilians back from the bush, arming some of them through their Chiefs, and using them as an extension of our power. In this we were outstandingly successful.

Aru was controlled by Lieutenant Gerry Joubert, Aba by Lucky Griffin, and Faradje by Adjudant Bouve, who was completely in his element and making a wonderful job of it. Watsa and the gold-mine were being run by Tavernier, Dungu by Jack Maiden and Niangara by John Peters. My corps of "District Commissioners" warmed to their task and their efforts proved popular and successful. It was strange that a quirk of fate should bring back the white man to this part of Africa to restore law and order and stranger still that, in many cases, it should be restored by the hand of South Africans.

Peter Johnstone closed down our base at Bunia and loaded the entire stores on to three brand new Mercedes Benz trucks, which Gino had spirited out of the air. His convoy drove hard and fast all the way to Faradje, stopping only at Aru for a brief rest. It was a first-class effort on Peter's part and we were all happy to be reunited again, even if Faradje was not the best of stations. In his report, Major Johnstone described how the Congolese Chief of Police from Bunia had accompanied them as far as Adi, but when crossing the bridge, the other side of it, he had inadvertently stepped on a mine and killed himself. I cannot say that I was distressed at his untimely end. The story of his cruelty came to my mind. It was he who had ordered thirty rebel prisoners to dig a massive hole in the ground and had machine gunned them as they stood in it. Other prisoners were forced to throw earth on top of them, living or dead until, as one eyewitness described it to me, "the surface of the pit rose and fell like small waves at sea."

As all was quiet along the length of my sector I felt myself free to visit Stanleyville to discuss the next stage in the campaign with Colonel Mulamba and the Commander-in-Chief. I was anxious that the momentum that we had achieved at some cost to ourselves would not be frittered away to dissolve into inaction, resulting from lack of planning at a higher level.

At the same time, I could honestly tell the General that 5 Commando had obeyed his orders to the letter—the border with the Sudan and Uganda was now closed, firmly, finally and irrevocably. It had taken us seven weeks to do it.

# 15

## TRIUMPH AND TRAGEDY

I was on the point of leaving for Stanleyville when the long awaited counter-attack against Aba materialised. Peter Johnstone, who was now in command of the military side of things, repelled the enemy and chased them up as far as the border, where, as always, they dodged into the Sudan and took refuge. In the action we lost two men killed and several wounded.

I decided to put a stop to this nonsense once and for all. John Peters was recalled from Niangara and took command of a strong column, comprising several hundred men from 5 and 14 Commandos, with orders to destroy the enemy up to the Sudan borders. If they ran behind it for cover, he was to pursue them for a reasonable distance and hammer them. I appreciated that this might mean an international incident, a violation of a "neutral border" and so on, but I was prepared to bear the brunt of it when it arose. I was not prepared to have my men killed, merely to observe a one-sided agreement over a hypothetical border, unfenced, unmarked and undetermined.

When I arrived in Stanleyville I received the news. Captain Peters had had a most successful outing. He had chased the rebels over the border and found it necessary to pursue them eight miles to their camp, which he burnt down, killing over eighty of them and destroying their vehicles. I was as pleased as the Congolese authorities were alarmed. There were repercussions in due course from the British Embassy, but the raid was conclusive and the rebels troubled us no more in this manner.

A signal from the Commander-in-Chief invited me to accompany him in his private aircraft on a tour of Orientale Province. A large parade assembled on the tarmac at Stanleyville Aerodrome to greet him. The Congolese Army is superb at ceremonial drill and loves an occasion for brass bands, swords and much saluting. The General's plane was due at 11.00 hours. At noon the large crowd became restless and the troops began to wilt a bit in the hot sun. At 13.00 hours we were distinctly worried for the General's safety. Perhaps, someone suggested, we had been given the wrong E.T.A. Could it not be 11.00 hours Zulu—Greenwich Mean Time—and not 11.00 hours Bravo—local time?

Colonel Mulamba said we were not to worry, we must be patient, he knew what was meant—it was 11.00 hours Bantu! At 13.30 hours he dismissed the parade, a hard decision which I applauded, understanding his difficulties and, of course, as soon as we had returned to the Hotel des Chutes for lunch, the General arrived! Situation normal.

There was an animated scene that evening at Colonel Mulamba's house. A band played on the riverside lawn whilst canoe–loads of tribesmen, dressed in their colourful regalia, paddled in unison and sang songs of praise for General Mobutu. Madame Mulamba showed me a photograph of herself and the Colonel being presented to the Pope and another of her two boys at school in Belgium. The future of the Congo lay in that photograph and similar ones all over the country, I thought.

The General's aircraft was a beautifully appointed D.C.-3, which had been a present from President Kennedy. It was the first time I had been close to the General. I learnt more about him in the course of the tour than a hundred visits to his office could have taught me. I was pleasantly surprised to find that he had a dry sense of humour and a lively wit. Moreover, he was pleasingly modest. He loved to talk of history and had a vivid sense of perspective; he saw clearly the special place which would be given to the events of the moment, when the history of the Congo was written.

Following him around the various army establishments, I came to understand his great love for his army, the A.N.C. Plainly it all stemmed from his seven years' service in the Force Publique. That force, under the Belgians, had been a model administration and one of the finest armies in Africa, staffed as it was by over two thousand Belgians. The General saw the Armée Nationale Congolaise as the natural successors to the Force Publique with all its glories undiminished, but with none of its present failings. There was now a bare handful of Belgian advisers. Nevertheless, the General maintained a deep attachment to the army, his army, which politics will never erase.

Commandant John Powis, a regular Belgian Army officer, was the General's A.D.C. He had kept the substantive rank of Commandant, when I have no doubt he could have assumed the acting rank of Major, had he so wished. Commandant Powis was an aristocrat. He was proud, haughty and disdainful, and did not suffer fools gladly. At the same time he was charming, courteous and efficient. The mainspring of his being was the General, whom he worshipped. The Congo was his first love and he was utterly devoted to its service. He saw an enemy in anybody who was in the slightest bit critical of its shortcomings.

Largely because of this attitude he was extremely unpopular with Belgians of the old school. Many of them dismissed him with the remark that, "He was the first man to open the door for the Congolese", a reference to his appointment as A.D.C. to President Kasavubu at the time of Independence.

Powis had been in command of a Reconnaissance Squadron at Gombari in the days of the Force Publique. During his service, unlike many of his compatriots, he had made a thorough study of the Congolese whom he now understood better than any Belgian I met in the Congo. His philosophy, simply stated, was "help the Congolese to help themselves." He pursued this ideal with the zeal of a visionary and a paternalism in keeping with his high-born station.

To while away the time in the air, the General occasionally told some jokes. The one I enjoyed most was about Mr. Tshombe. Apparently when the General had first related it to Mr. Tshombe, the Prime Minister had laughed until tears ran down his cheeks. Mr. Tshombe could enjoy a joke, even against himself.

The General began by emphasising that the whole thing was, of course, apocryphal. Mr. Tshombe was on a visit to Paris and had been invited to visit an establishment of some note, where the ladies were reputed to be remarkable for their talent. Madame was proud of her protégées and introduced the most accomplished to the Prime Minister and left them discreetly alone. Madame, however, being human and feminine, naturally could not resist the temptation to eavesdrop. After a few moments, to her utter astonishment, she heard her number one girl exclaim, "Absolument pas!" as she dashed from the room in high dudgeon. The same thing happened with Mesdemoiselles numbers two and three. Overcome with curiosity, Madame begged Mr. Tshombe to tell her what had made the girls so irate and whatever could it be that they had refused to do. In all her years in the business this had never happened before.

. After much persuasion and promises not to tell, the Prime Minister was forced to give up his secret.

"They won't take Congolese francs," he said.

The plane circled around Faradje. The General gasped. All down the side of the red murram runway a seething mass of humanity had gathered to pay homage to the Commander-in-Chief. The General inspected the Guards of Honour and addressed the vast crowd from the back of a Land-Rover. He was a brilliant speaker and his sincerity carried conviction. The people clapped politely.

Adjudant Bouve took him down the runway to inspect five hundred Simba prisoners, seated in three ranks, their hands tied behind their backs. Bouve, with a wry sense of humour, had made them dress themselves in their Simba uniform—a palm leaf around their middles and another wrapped around their heads. The General and Colonel Mulamba walked down the long lines of cross-legged rebels, stopping now and then to talk with one.

"If you are Simbas," he commanded, "let me hear you roar!" The Simbas let out an imitation lion's roar to the great amusement of the crowd.

Bouve had separated a small group of *Jeunesse* from the main body. None was over twelve years of age. Mulamba, a fatherly type, patted one fierce little warrior of eight on his curly head and asked him if the Simbas had given him a rifle to fight with. "Yes, sir," said the bold boy, "it was a point thirty." "And did you fire it at anybody?" "No, sir, it was too big and went off with such a big bang."

We toured the town in a motorcade and the crowd screamed out their delight at seeing the General. He inspected the gaol and was shown the prisoners, whom we had classified into three grades. First, the hard core rebels and murderers, who would be tried as criminals in proper courts of justice. Then the ones who had joined the rebels because everybody else did. These we had already tried and sentenced to work on the roads and airfield and other public places to make reparation to the State. Lastly there were *les imbeciles*.

The *jeunesse* were the chief concern of the General. He foresaw great difficulties in the rehabilitation of lads of fourteen, fifteen, and sixteen, who had fired rifles, even killed people, and been part of an exciting rebel movement. How could they be persuaded to settle down? We presented him with our answer. In a corner of the town under some trees a tribal court was in session before a large crowd. A boy's name was called. He stepped forward to be confronted by his father, who stripped him in front of the tribe—a disgrace of some magnitude—and then belaboured him with a stick until he cried in public. The young lad went off, presumably chastened. Parental control within the framework of the tribe seemed to me the only solution.

The visit ended with an inspection of our lines and a personal interview with six men from my command, at my request. Adjutant Bouve was raised to the rank of Lieutenant and told to continue his excellent work in the civil administration of Faradje. "Lucky" Griffin was likewise congratulated for his work in Aba. Commandant Tavernier was commended for his spirited leadership of 14 Commando and R.S.M. Cassidy for his bravery at Golu and elsewhere. Volunteer Murray Grobler was told by the General that he would be compensated for the damage done to his farm and his good service in 5 Commando was noted with appreciation. Finally, Captain Peters was shown in. I read the citation for his exceptional bravery at the Nzoro. The General hedged a bit when I suggested that suitable recognition would be an immediate promotion to Commandant. He reminded me that these things ought normally to go through the proper channels for his decision, etc. I told him how the Kings of England often raised squires to knighthood on the field of battle and he grasped the point at once. Captain Peters now became Commandant Peters—with effect from 1st May, added the General. He had a neat mind.

Back at the airstrip we took photographs to record the visit and the General flew off once more for Paulis. We said good-bye with the warm feeling that earlier misunderstandings between us had blown away and that a new era had dawned for 5 Commando. It was certainly so. Perhaps one day I would be able to implement my cherished plan of raising a Congolese 5 Commando, identical in every respect to us, trained and taught in our ways, which I would leave behind to take our place and keep the peace when finally we left the scene. I could conceive no finer memorial to the bravery and prowess of my men than that. But it was not to be.

In my short absence on tour with the General, all had not been well. The enemy had attacked Niangara in great strength and, using civilians as a shield, they had crossed the bridge and begun shooting. In less than five minutes the place was deserted, and Force John-John turned out to meet the rebels. John Peters had run from the other side of town to see a solid phalanx of Simbas approaching down a narrow road. Flinging a grenade into the middle of them and shouting the only words he knew in French—"Avancez les mercenaires"—his men joined battle. After some bitter fighting, the rebels were pushed back over the bridge, leaving eighty dead behind them.

In the early stages of the raid Davy Chaloner had been wounded in the arm, but continued to fire his machine gun. Seconds later a burst of fire hit him again and he was killed. Poor Davy was a fighter to the end. If he had to choose a way to go, I am sure it would not have been otherwise. Our casualties were heavy in this action and included Volunteer Smallberger, a brave youngster who had joined 5 Commando purely for adventure. A week before he died, unbeknown to him, his grandfather had left him a fortune in South Africa.

A few days later I received a letter by special courier from the Commander in Chief. It was dated the 11th May 1965, and read;

"My dear Colonel,
I am delighted to tell you how much I have been agreeably surprised by my visit to Faradje on the 6th May 1965.
The turn-out, the discipline and the impeccable presentation of the troops under your command, the excellent spirit which animates them, the resounding success that you have achieved in executing in record time and with a minimum of losses the different missions which I have confided in you, the sealing of the frontiers of the Sudan and Uganda, are so many proofs of your exceptional qualities as a commander.
Moreover, I am glad to express my particular satisfaction for the manner in which you have carried out your principal mission, namely: PACIFICATION.
To put the population back to work, to feed them, to assure the proper functioning of the hospitals and the schools, to reinstate the workings of a sound administration, to re-establish the means of communication, in a word, to wipe out practically all memory of the rebellion, such were the principal matters which occupied you.
The day will come, when the history of this country will be

written. The tragic epoch of the fight against the rebellion will occupy
in it a very long chapter, at the centre of which you will be give a
place of honour.
Believe me, my dear Colonel, with the most cordial sentiments.
Commander in Chief
Mobutu J.D.
General Major."

Any doubt which may have lingered in my mind that the General
did not appreciate 5 Commando were thus pleasantly swept aside.

At Group Headquarters Jacques Noel was busy putting the finishing touches to his plan for Operation "Violettes Imperiales." Briefly,
this involved the seizure of two large towns, Buta and Bondo, all
that remained of any great importance in the Province. There were
thought to be many white hostages in both places and almost definitely thirty-eight Catholic priests at Buta. With this operation 3
Group would cut off finally the rebel line of communication from
the outskirts of Stan, through Bondo to the Central African Republic
and through Buta to the Sudan. It was an operation of some importance and encompassed both 5 and 6 Commandos, as well as the
A.N.C.
The role of 5 Commando would be a six hundred-kilometre dash
to Bili and Bondo, crossing two big rivers on the way. 6 Commando
would seize Poko and Buta at the same time. 6 Commando was
stationed in Paulis and had as its strike force a composite unit known
as "Premier Choc," which may have been very romantic in French,
but sounded odd in English, and gave rise to some mirth amongst
the ruffians of 5 Commando. "First Shock", as we called them, were
commanded by a Frenchman, Commandant Bob Denard, a soldier
of some ability and a well respected leader. They were equipped well
enough to make us regard ourselves as rather shabby country cousins.
Unfortunately the whole of 6 Commando and First Shock suffered
from a marked inability to get off their big fat bottoms and the
operation was being strangled at birth for the lack of co-operation.
The patient Jacques had revised the date of the operation three
times already and now finally gave it out as 25th May, and there
would be a final briefing at Paulis on 24th May. The idea of a six-
hundred kilometre dash across country, behind enemy lines, sounded
rather romantic to me and I went back to my room at the Hotel des
Chutes to study the maps.

The Hotel had been converted into an Officers' Mess for 3 Group and was run extremely well. One feature of the bathrooms appealed to my sense of the bizarre. For some reason the lavatory seat was placed on a plinth, one foot above the surrounding floor, which gave it a pleasing throne-like effect!

Later that afternoon I was recalled to Headquarters urgently. Bad news awaited me. Lieutenant Gerry Joubert had led a patrol from Niangara to Poko and been killed with one of his men, as they entered the town. Gerry Joubert had taken over 52 Commando recently and was rapidly making a good unit out of his men, mostly Germans, who had been somewhat demoralised by the death of their three previous commanders. Gerry was the fourth. I felt his loss keenly, as he had the makings of a first-class officer and a natural leader of men. The two of them were buried in Niangara alongside Davy Chaloner.

The other news was no less disturbing and its ill effects echoed down the corridors of Q.G.-A.N.C. in Leopoldville and destroyed in one fell stroke all the goodwill and understanding that had been built up so laboriously between the A.N.C. and 5 Commando, but more particularly between the General and myself. I read the signal containing the grim news. It said:

> "Regret advise you Congolese Adjudant François was killed last night reputedly by eight men 57 Commando at a party in Paulis stop holding men in prison Niangara pending court enquiry and your return stop Jack Maiden."

The repercussions were immediate. Colonel Mulamba, who was never one to prejudge any situation, gave me the official A.N.C. account of the killing and asked me to look into it at once. Jacques Noel informed me that as a result of the death of the Adjudant, the Katangese troops in Paulis had refused to take part in "Violettes Imperiales." The Adjudant was their acknowledged leader and they would not go into battle with anybody else.

The facts were plain enough. Eight men had attended a Katangese party in Paulis. There had been an altercation, when one of them asked to play the drums and was refused. The Sergeant in charge of the eight, a level-headed youngster, then ordered his men to leave the room. On the verandah the argument continued, shots were fired and the Adjudant was killed. Who fired first, and why, were things which would have to come out at a Court of Enquiry.

I caught an early plane to Faradje in the morning. The trip normally takes two hours twenty minutes in a D.C.-3, but after three hours I realised that we were lost. I could tell from the ground below that we were now comfortably inside the Sudan and I thought with anguish of the Sudanese jet fighters, which had recently been seen flying over Aba. Navigation in the Congo is by no means easy and eventually we turned round to fly due south to find the line of the River Dungu. As though the situation was not miserable enough, one engine cut out, causing an alarming drop in altitude, when the pilot, a cool customer, decided to get back to Paulis as quickly as he could, picked up the railway line and followed it in to the town. We returned to Stan later that day, having spent an uncomfortable six hours in the air. However, we made it the next day.

I now made the necessary moves in preparation for Operation Violettes Imperiales, placed Major Johnstone in command of the long sector from Faradje to Aru and issued a warning order to move my Headquarters from Faradje to Niangara. My final task was to write John Peters a letter. John had left Niangara for seven days' compassionate leave and had taken an escort of eight men from 57 Commando to Paulis, where he had boarded the plane, and given them permission to stay the night and return to Niangara the following day. This was contrary to a 3 Group order, which stated that no 5 Commando men were to visit Paulis. I was aware that John had not intended to disobey the spirit of the order and it was indeed necessary for him to have an escort as far as Paulis, but the tragic consequences which ensued from allowing the men to stay overnight made my letter and its unhappy contents doubly necessary. I wrote:

Dear John
    The death of Adjudant François of the A.N.C., allegedly at the hands of some of the men under your command, whether by accident or deliberately, must redound to the discredit of 5 Commando.
    The fact that white mercenaries have killed a Congolese *sous-officier*, regardless of the circumstances, will go hard with them at their trial, if only because it will be necessary for the Court to show that both white and black soldiers are treated exactly alike under Congolese military law. If anything, I fear they are likely to be treated harder.
    You are aware that the men were visiting Paulis contrary to a Brigade order expressly forbidding it, and I regret, therefore, that I must ask you, as their commander and the one ultimately responsible for their behaviour, not to return to 5 Commando until

such time as the case has been heard and you receive the General's specific consent to re-engagement."

It was a harsh letter to write, but in the circumstances it was clearly my duty to do so. It is the way of the army—the man who commands carries the responsibility. I realised with some sorrow that in sending the letter, I was at the same time cutting off my right arm in the campaign about to begin, and on a strictly personal level, appearing ungrateful for all that John Peters had done for 5 Commando and for me. There was no alternative. Even in a mercenary army, justice must appear to be done.

I had one small case to deal with at my Headquarters at Faradje and then I could call it a day. During my absence on tour with the General, the Sergeant of military police had seen fit to use my personal jeep to tow another vehicle, which needed repair. Notwithstanding that the towed vehicle was totally devoid of brakes, the gallant Sergeant had raced along at forty miles an hour until his progress was arrested by a palm tree. Both vehicles were a total loss. The driver of the towed vehicle was a young Englishman from Lancashire, Sergeant Douglas-Holden.

"Tell me, Sergeant Douglas-Holden," I said, "how did you react to being towed through the air at forty miles an hour, knowing your vehicle had no brakes?"

"Apprehensive, sir, that's what I was, distinctly apprehensive." How can you reprimand a man like that?

# 16

## VIOLETTES IMPERIALES

We moved to Niangara the next day. I stopped at Dungu on the way to visit 54 Commando, who were living in some style at the castle. The castle was a replica of one in Belgium and had been erected, so they said, at the whim of a Belgian Administrator some years ago. It overlooked the Dungu River and was a magnificent pile, complete with moat, keeps, secret passages, baronial hall and portcullis. The dungeon was dank and damp, as befits castle dungeons, and was used to house one or two of the viler rebels before they were finally executed. Lieutenant Wepener, who had now fully recovered from his concussion in January, was Lord of the Manor and ran the place like a medieval despot.

Niangara was hot and humid. We had left the open plains of Kibali-Ituri and its green hospitable fields for the closeness of the equatorial jungle once again. 5 Commando ran the town, assisted by a company of local police, and a civil administration, which was headed by a young Senator who had emerged from the bush after being on the run from the rebels for the last five months. He returned to his work with infectious energy and an unbridled hatred for all rebels. He dispensed justice with a heavy hand and from time to time I found it necessary to restrain his enthusiasm for the firing squad. 5 Commando was running the town utilities, including the electricity plant and the water pumping station, so that when the news finally leaked out that we would be leaving shortly, the towns-people were greatly distressed. The Senator approached me at Bishop's House, where I was living, and presented a "loyal address", begging us to remain and to continue with the administration of the area. It was a gratifying moment and I was able to alleviate his fears, when I explained that Lieutenant Lucien-Brun would be the new

P

"District Commissioner" and that we were not deserting them entirely.

Niangara lies on the old slave train route from the interior of the Congo to the Sudan. Wherever the Arabs went in those days, they planted mango trees, in much the same way as the Portuguese planted cashew trees in Mozambique. Today, as a result, Niangara is lined with enormous mango trees and now in late May, overripe mangoes littered the roadway, so that it was impossible to walk more than two steps without treading on one.

I attended a final briefing in Paulis for Operation Violettes Imperiales, which would now begin on 29th May, said Jacques firmly, with or without 6 Commando. The R.S.M. showed me around Paulis after the O Group and took me to see the Governor's house. In the garden a ferocious looking chimpanzee stood under a tree. It ambled up to us, dripping saliva from its mouth, and stopped short, checked by a heavy chain around its waist. I was surprised. My previous experience of chimpanzees had led me to believe that they were mild little creatures who liked their tea with children on a Sunday afternoon at the London Zoo. Not this one, said the R.S.M., and went on to tell me how the A.N.C. had bound and gagged a rebel lieutenant and thrown him to this animal for their amusement. The chimpanzee had torn off the rebel's genitals and left him to bleed to death.

I was woefully short of officers. Peters had gone, Roy Larsen was sick, Wepener had completed his contract. Fortunately Jack Carton-Barber and Ben Louw had returned to the unit to make up my strength for the operation about to begin. In addition, 3 Group had attached to me a Belgian wireless operator named Joe Saeys, whom they had promoted to the rank of lieutenant for the occasion and, as they said, "to compensate him for being attached to 5 Commando!" Joe was the most aggressive and militant Belgian I knew and he fitted into the unit perfectly.

The column comprised one hundred and ten men and an A.N.C. bridging unit under command, plus two armoured cars. We travelled as light as possible in order to cross the rivers in our path on our own pontoons.

The column was formed up ready to move at 04.45 hours on 29th May and stayed only to listen to the opening round of the Clay-Liston fight, which was being broadcast by the Voice of America.

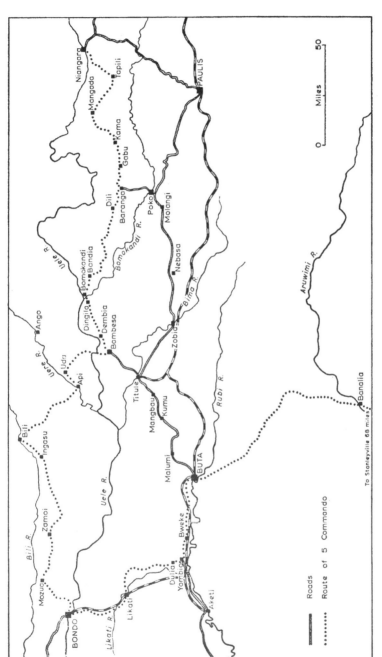

6. ORIENTALE: Operation Violette Imperiales

As this lasted a disappointingly short time, it did not detain us long. Commando leaders reported three deserters from the column, resulting, I presumed, from the long wait between actions when nerves tend to become a little worn. We started up and pulled quietly away into the dawn to begin our 630-kilometre dash across country. A thrill of excitement ran through the column as we passed over the last bridge separating us from the enemy and we faced the day with brave hearts and the comforting knowledge that two Ferret scout cars, a platoon of 81 mm. mortars and one hundred resolute men would take some stopping.

The first 230 kilometres would be the worst, according to my reckoning, but once we were across the Bomakandi River, I knew we would have the element of surprise on our side with all the safety that went with it. At Tapili we had some trouble with elephant traps and ran into a severe ambush further on, when our leading Ferret was struck by a bazooka rocket and was nearly written off. Fortunately, a jerry-can of water, strapped to the front of the car, took most of the shock, but some pieces holed the radiator and held us up for a while.

Ben Louw caught the guards hopping at the Bomakandi River, after which we raced across the bridge, avoided some skilfully prepared elephant traps and cleaned up the town of Dingila just as it was getting dark. Thirty kilometres further on we halted for the night, after cutting the adjacent telephone wires to Bambesa and put out an ambush party for the night. The rebels did most of their travelling at night to avoid our air by day and at two in the morning a rebel truck fell into our ambush. They obviously did not know we were coming. Neither did Bambesa.

Early next morning we stood in the centre of the town, hardly able to believe our eyes. A full scale Simba parade was taking place outside the "Territoire" building, not two hundred yards away from our leading vehicle. The Ferrets dashed towards them, spitting lead, but their fire was damnably inaccurate.

By the time Jack Carton-Barber's men got to the scene, the rebels had vanished into thin air. To add to their disappointment, said Jack, the office safe was too heavy to put on their truck! We searched the office for papers, however, and discovered the minutes of a meeting held on 29th April, at which Christopher Gbenye had presided and all the local chiefs were present.

Some prisoners showed us the little used road to the south bank of the Uele River, which was running over a mile wide. The ferry refused to function, and I began to miss Tom Harrison. Our bridging unit built a pontoon and with outboard motors, temperamental as ever, ferried us across one at a time. By the end of the day we were across.

The crossing of the Api River, a further sixty kilometres on, the next morning gave us no difficulty and we now stood poised ready for an attack on Bili. We knew for certain that two Norwegian missionaries, Mr. Johannes Holte and his wife, Greta, were both held captive by the Simbas in Bili. Mrs. Holte owed her life to the fact that she ran the dispensary for the rebels. We burst into Bili at four in the afternoon, crossed the river in a rush and surrounded the mission at the top of the hill within minutes. It was deserted. Inside the mission house some coffee on the stove was still hot and a Bible lay open where someone had been interrupted reading it. It was obvious the Holtes had been taken away the minute the Simbas heard us coming. We searched the area thoroughly, calling out their names, but there was no sign of them. I gave them little hope, but left Ben Louw there with his Commando, in case they should return under cover of darkness.

Two lorries full of Simbas crashed into our outpost that night. We got the first lot with our bazookas, but the second disappeared into the bush. I expected an attack at the dawn stand-to from those that escaped, but nothing happened. At stand-down Ben Louw signalled that the Holtes had just walked in from the bush! They were in a distressed condition after suffering a night of terror at the hands of a Simba guard, who had deserted them at four in the morning presumably after he had heard the shooting coming from our ambush.

I entered the mission house just as the two missionaries were giving thanks to God for their salvation. I did not want to hurry them, but I explained that we were trying to reach Bondo that day and how important it was that we should do so. I watched them as they bade farewell to the scenes of their labours of so many years, heartbreak and disappointment, resignation and disillusionment in their faces. With a last longing look at all they had laboured so long to build up, they walked slowly down the hill with me to the river. They knew they would never return again.

I explained that they must now join our column and accept all its hazards as though they were part of 5 Commando. They were an

odd sight in the next few days, taking cover behind rocks and ant
hills when the bullets were flying, but they never complained. There
was certainly a Divine Providence watching over them and, though
they had lived through some frightful times in the last six months,
they had come through alive. Mr. Holte had suffered at the hands of
the rebels, who had beaten him within an inch of his life on two
occasions. The very thought of Bili and the rebels was a nightmare
to him. Especially the rebel leader, a lunatic savage, who called
himself, "Charles de Gaulle"!

I was hurrying the Holtes across the river when heavy firing
broke out from the town. I dashed down to my command post to
find that the rebels who had escaped our ambush during the night
had counter-attacked, killing one of our men and seriously wounding
another. I lifted the blanket. It was Sergeant Norrie Douglas-
Holden. He had held off a band of rebels whilst his men clambered
to safety and lost his life doing it. Doctor Flemming operated on the
wounded man and thought he would survive. We were too far for
helicopter evacuation and he had to take a chance on it. We dug a
grave in the Bili cemetery for the Sergeant and buried him with full
military honours. I see him now, Norrie Douglas-Holden, his
happy face and sense of fun making the best of the dullest situations.
God rest you, lad.

It was 188 kilometres to Bondo and already ten o'clock. We would
have to go fast if we were to reach the town before nightfall. We left
Bili cautiously and on foot; my tactics were invariably to march
after every halt. This time it proved providential. The rebels were
lying in wait for us half a mile down the road and we fought a quick
battle, leaving their bodies lying on the road as a grim reminder that
we had passed.

The column accelerated and at times was travelling at over fifty
kilometres an hour, a tremendous speed through the African bush.
As we drew nearer to Bondo, the population, which had been well
indoctrinated with Communist propaganda, came out to give us the
Lumumba salute, mistaking us for Russians! Further on, gangs of
*Jeunesse* threw spears at our trucks as we sped by. At 18.30 hours it
was beginning to get dark. I looked at my map. We were a bare ten
kilometres from Bondo. I thought we could just do it before daylight
failed, but the column ground maddeningly to a halt. I ran to the
front. The leading Ferret was boiling and had blown a cylinder
head gasket. The radiator had finally given in. The other Ferret was

already being towed. I was in a cleft stick. To abandon the Ferrets and go on now would mean doing the last few kilometres in the dark, with all the risks of night ambush. At the same time, if we stayed where we were for the night, we would lose the element of surprise so vital to us. Mr. Holte warned me that the final approach to Bondo was through heavily populated villages which lined both sides of the road. It was a deciding factor. I halted the column. The lives of thirty hostages hung on the decision.

During the night the enemy crossed the river with the hostages. Many of them were never seen again.

The town of Bondo is an important trading post on the north bank of the Uele River. A large ferry, capable of carrying 35 tons, connects it with the railway on the south bank, which runs to Aketi and Buta. Bondo had been seized by the rebels early in September, but the Europeans had been allowed to go about their business in the normal manner until the fall of Stan, after which they had been rounded up and held as hostages. Bondo had been the scene of some unprintable savagery in late November and I had made a careful note of the atrocities perpetrated by the leader of the rebels in this area. He would get short shrift from us when we finally caught up with him. He was now in another town where he professed to be favourably inclined towards the Europeans, but the record of his cruelty at Bondo would take some expunging from the book of crimes.

The Simbas crowded around this man at the landing stage last November, as the Europeans were brought before him for summary trial. Most of them were shot and their bodies flung into the river, but for one man he had a special fate. He was forced to watch whilst his wife, a pretty young girl of twenty-three, was raped in front of his eyes. After that he was killed and his body thrown into the river. The next man, a Belgian, was bound hand and foot, placed in a sack and thrown into the water, alive. Little did the barbarians know that by a miracle he freed himself and groped his way to the bank. Late that night, he crept back into the town and tapped at his friend's window. His friend was one of the few who had been spared, and only because he was the mechanic in charge of the ferry. With a pounding heart his friend hid him in the attic of his house, where he lived for the next six months! Food and water were passed to him through a tiny trap-door and he was kept alive. Time after time the rebels searched the house, but his faithful friend stopped them from looking in the attic.

On the morning of the first June, the sole surviving European in Bondo—the same mechanic—staggered into my Headquarters and led me quickly to his house, where we released the Belgian in the attic. He was as white as a sheet and unable to speak. He could barely walk. Captain Flemming quietened him with drugs and let him sleep. When he awoke he had so much to say he collapsed again in tears. Finally, he told us that unless he could find his wife and children, he would prefer to die. They had been taken out of Bondo the night before.

He joined our column and soldiered with us for the next four weeks with one purpose only in his mind—to find his family. He was a man of incredible courage and strength of mind and we admired him greatly. A month later, after heartbreaking disappointment, false trails and the agony of finding the remains of other hostages, his prayers were answered. His wife and two children were discovered, safe and sound, deep in the bush south of Buta—and he was on the very patrol which found them!

At nine I received a signal from Jacques to abandon Bondo and make for Buta with all speed. We would have to cross the river and pass through the small town of Likati, where normally there were Europeans. They were all Greeks and Portuguese.

The crossing was difficult and the engine kept breaking down, but we had most of the column across by two in the afternoon. At three the enemy put in a counter-attack and Volunteer Dyson was killed in the action. The Reverend Holte buried him in the mission grounds.

I was steering the barge myself, wishing to heaven Tom Harrison was still with us. I realised that the last crossing, when we must abandon the town, would be the most dangerous and we would be sitting ducks for the enemy as we crossed. Ben Louw's unit were the rearguard and ran on to the ferry as I gave the signal for covering fire to come down from the other bank. Everybody took cover under the vehicles as the barrage began. I felt remarkably lonely on the somewhat exposed bridge, when a man came up from below and stood next to me, as though to share the dangers. He pressed a 50-franc silver coin into my hand. "That's for luck, sir," he said. It was Sergeant Columbic.

Bullets twanged against the steel superstructure and whined off into the air sideways. The strong current carried the barge down towards the enemy—and the engine cut! The Belgian in the engine room worked frantically to start it again, as we drifted helplessly downstream. At the last minute it spluttered into life and twenty minutes later we grounded on the other bank and disembarked safely.

6 Commando with "First Shock" in the lead had finally emerged from Paulis with much caution and little enthusiasm for the fight. They had taken Poko and were now on the road to Buta, but they would have to hurry if they were to be there before us. In any case, I feared for the lives of the Buta hostages. The whole campaign had been so well advertised and delayed so many times that I gave them little chance of being alive.

We reached the outskirts of Likati exactly at nine the next morning. On the way we had run the gauntlet of ambushes, all of which evaporated in the face of our determination not to be held up. The mission was deserted and the house alongside it, which was known to be that of a Portuguese trader and his wife, had just been evacuated. The milk was still hot on the table. I felt the first flutter of fear for the people of Likati. We cleared the town in double quick time and pushed on down to the bridge. At the other end of it I saw what I thought was a sack, leaning up against the iron railings. Volunteer Mandy signalled frantically to me from the leading armoured car, as he accelerated and took up a covering position. I drew level with the end of the bridge. It was not a sack, it was a young man bent double on his hands and knees, a spear sticking out of his intestines, grey rolls of them lying on the ground beside him. He had been dead a few minutes. At the end of the bridge a woman of twenty-five lay on the ground, a spear sticking out of her back. A groan came from the long grass on the other side. A man lay mortally wounded with a spear wound in his chest. He was still alive. Doctor Flemming worked on him and he managed to gasp out that the Simbas had heard us coming, had ordered them out of their house and forced them to march barefoot down to the bridge. The other two had then been killed. The doctor gave him a blood transfusion, but held out little hope.

One of my men took some photographs of the girl lying in the grass, her skirt torn from her body. With a sudden burst of temper I took the camera from him and flung it in the river. I ordered the column to search the rest of the houses which were a mile down the road, fearing the worst and knowing full well what we would find. The Simbas had received orders to kill all whites, I was certain of it. Portuguese and Greek traders are traditionally neutral in Congolese fighting, and the sight of these three Portuguese convinced me that all whites were in mortal danger.

We found them by the side of the road.

An old Greek was dead from bullet wounds. Close by a young man lay butchered with a spear. Another lay dying in the bush next to his twelve-year-old daughter. She had been killed by a bullet through the heart. The little girl looked beautiful in death, her curly black hair and white skin typical of her people. Her father was still alive, shot through the shoulder and one lung, stab wounds in his back. He pointed to his house. The mother lay in one room, beaten, bruised, clinging desperately to life, despite a gash in her chest and arm. Her son, aged eight, lay on the verandah. The medical orderlies in the unit worked flat out to save the mother and father, while the doctor gave his whole attention to the little boy. A spear had been thrust into his back and twisted out, leaving a gaping wound the size of a man's fist next to his vertebrae. The lad talked to the doctor in English and joked with the soldiers. One of my men saluted him, with tears in his eyes, and received a shaky salute back. An hour later John Flemming stood up and said, "That's it, my lad. Lie still for a few moments and you'll be quite all right." The brave little fellow had no chance. A minute later he shivered and died.

Whether mental telepathy exists or not I do not know, but at that precise moment his mother, who was in another room uttered a piercing scream and cried out that her child was dead.

We went through the houses and the shops. One of my men came out of the old Greek's house, carrying a portable radio and some loot. My anger welled up at this callous act and I drew my pistol on the man in my rage.

Feelings were running high the length of the column. I stopped by the truck as my men were loading the bodies of the dead girl and her brother, their pathetically small bodies wrapped in blankets. There were many men there with sons and daughters the same age. They were all thinking the same thing. One of them was Sergeant-Major Burger, a professional heavy-weight boxer and a fine soldier. Tears stood in his eyes. Someone shouted from the back of the column—"The prisoners are escaping!" Fifteen rebels we had captured in Bondo had broken loose and were making a dash for the bush. The Sergeant-Major looked at me and held up his F.N. rifle. I nodded. The crackle of fire broke out along the column and the prisoners rolled over one by one. Nobody bothered to go and look at them.

We resumed the march considerably subdued and thoughtful. An unspoken order ran down the column—kill everything that moves. There is no stimulus like revenge and the column swept forward, searing the countryside with the bright flame of retribution. We halted at dusk at the cross-roads, seventy-four kilometres west of Buta.

I had reported the events of the day in "Flash" signals to Jacques, but now that I had time to think, I was even more convinced that the rebels had issued a general order to kill all whites. I signalled Stan:

> "In view my conviction all whites this area doomed to death strongly suggest immediate leaflet drop on Buta warning Mukondo penalty for harming hostages will be death of five thousand rebels now in our hands and further that every rebel now in Buta will be guilty of murder and hunted down and destroyed even if it takes years."

Later that evening we received a signal from Jacques advising us that leaflets had already been dropped. He was sorry, but my suggestion had not been well received. The leaflets, which had been dropped, had been printed some days ago and offered safe conduct to all rebels who now surrendered. They would be treated honourably as prisoners of war—they had Colonel Mulamba's word for it. Mukondo was warned not to touch the hostages. No penalties were mentioned.

I realised that the leaflet drop was futile and a waste of time. Any message which failed to mention personal reprisal stood not the slightest chance. Once again we were according savages gentlemanly treatment, when nothing they had done from start to finish of the campaign warranted it.

We buried the seven at the cross-roads at first light, the Reverend Holte officiating. A dejected John Flemming and three medical orderlies had lost their fight.

We crashed into Buta at ten that morning to find it completely deserted. 6 Commando arrived from the east an hour later. We were all too late. There was no sign of the hostages, but a soutane by the river's edge told us the worst had already happened. A Swiss man appeared out of the bush. He confirmed that the thirty-eight priests had been led away to the bridge the previous evening and killed. They sang as they marched to their death, he said. Then there was a rattle of gunfire and their bodies were thrown into the river. I held the Swiss for further questioning.

We cleared the airstrip and a plane arrived shortly afterwards to evacuate the Greek man and wife. He died in the plane before reaching Paulis, leaving the woman as the sole survivor of the massacre at Likati, her own family completely wiped out.

That evening my men led in a young woman with three small children, clutching to her skirt. She had been hiding in the bush and now that the firing had stopped, she came forward. She knew nothing of the enemy and his movements or of the massacre, she said. She wore a look of resignation, which said, "I have seen the worst life can offer; nothing more can hurt or surprise me now."

'Can you tell me how you come to be the only person left in Buta safe and well, whilst all others have been taken away and killed?" I asked, not unkindly.

She shook her head. She ran away at the right time, she whispered, avoiding my eyes.

"Did you perhaps have any special protection?" I asked, trying not to be harsh. She began to cry. Piece by piece the cruel story came out. They were going to kill the children. She gave her body for their safety. She had to, she wept, she had to.

She smiled wanly with a flicker of hope in her brave eyes, when I told her there was not a woman in the world that would not applaud her sacrifice.

3 Group Headquarters now ordered my column to proceed south to open the road to Banalia and then to return to Stan. We had covered a distance of over one thousand kilometres since we set out from Niangara. I handed over to Jack Maiden, and said farewell for the time being to my gallant little band. They had done well and acquitted themselves like men.

Two days later I boarded a plane for Leopoldville to visit the Commander-in-Chief and the Prime Minister. I was the only passenger in the D.C.-4, but lying in the middle of the plane was a stretcher case—the sole survivor of the Likati massacre.

The bruises had come out all over her face and she was barely recognisable. She lifted her eyebrows when she saw me, her eyes swimming with tears. I knelt down next to her and talked about everything, but the tragedy. I took her limp hand in mine. Her well worn and pathetic little wedding band brought a lump to my throat. Her mouth was so swollen, she could hardly speak. I bent close to listen to her.

"Colonel," she said, "why has God done this to me?"

On 26th May the leaders of the recently formed O.C.A.M. group—the French-speaking countries of Africa—had all voted that the Congo should be allowed membership, and President Houphouet-Boigny of the Ivory Coast had raised his voice in protest against Ghana and Egypt for blocking Mr. Tshombe's admission to O.A.U.

Mr. Tshombe was as ebullient as ever. He was delighted with the course of events in Orientale and saw the beginning of the end in the province. Elections had been held, when they had almost ruled them out as a possibility for months to come. But he was concerned about the position in the south. The rebels were still receiving massive aid from Burundi and across the Lake from Tanzania. Something would have to be done about the Ruzizi Valley and Lake Tanganyika, he said. The communists must be stopped before they turned the Congo into a battleground. He reminded me that Chou en Lai had said that if he could take the Congo, he would have the whole of Africa.

We discussed the political situation within the Congo and the resounding victory he had won recently in the parliamentary elections. He had certainly led the country back along the path to prosperity and peace, but he thought it would be years before the Congo recovered from the economic disruption caused by the rebellion.

I thought this was as good a time as any to indicate that I would not be renewing my contract, which expired shortly. He was alarmed at the prospect—which flattered me—and asked me to stay. "Complete your work," he said, "the job is still only half done."

I explained that I had been away from home for almost a year and that I was exhausted, both mentally and physically, from campaigning in the Congo. He nodded sympathetically. A way must be found, he said.

I went through it all with the Commander-in-Chief, who was

adamant that I should stay for yet another contract. We discussed the military situation. The threat of communist infiltration into the Congo and the establishment of a "presence" via the Burundi border and across Lake Tanganyika into the Fizi Baraka pocket were matters which were exercising his mind. There was still a big battle to be won. He held out the carrot. Suppose I were to have command of that campaign to close those borders, just as I had done in the north, how would I go about it. I fell for it. I would make a base at Albertville, I said. There lies the answer to your personal problem, my dear Colonel, he said. We give you a nice house for your wife and family and you will not be in a hurry to leave us. I laughed. It was neatly done.

Alastair was to be offered the same terms, and in the end, but with some reluctance on my part, I agreed to a further six months' contract, to expire when I had overcome the rebel resistance in the Fizi Baraka pocket. I advised the General that it would be wise to raise a second battalion for 5 Commando, which could be under command of Major Johnstone, to police the north in case the enemy got any ideas when they saw us depart for the south. He agreed.

I made a quick visit to General Bobozo in Elizabethville, as the new 5 Commando would fall under his command, and made tentative arrangements for the reception of the men at Albertville in about six weeks' time. Another new unit, another lot of recruitment, training and heartache—for the third time of asking! John Latz wondered if I was sane. In the small hours of the morning, I wondered myself.

Catching a Boeing once more from Leopoldville, I winged my way south to enjoy a full month's leave in glorious Durban.

# 17

## ALBERTVILLE AGAIN

The Fizi Baraka pocket of resistance covered an area twice the size of Wales. It stretched from Uvira at the top of Lake Tanganyika south along the coast for one hundred and fifty miles to Kabimba, which was thirty miles north of Albertville, and inland to Kasongo on the Lualaba. It was a land of sudden escarpments, rushing rivers and twisting tracks. For well over a year now the enemy had been allowed to defend this mountain fastness, unmolested by the A.N.C.

The rebels were receiving massive communist aid from across Lake Tanganyika via Dar es Salaam and Kigoma, the port on the Lake roughly opposite Albertville. Most of the equipment was of Chinese origin and included land mines, machine guns, 76-mm. cannons, and a good supply of "bamboo bazookas"—the Chinese equivalent of the American rocket launcher.[1]

In recent months observers had noticed a subtle change in the type of resistance which the rebels were offering the Leopoldville Government. Whereas it had been of a reasonably passive nature— "what we have, we hold"—now it was becoming more aggressive. The change coincided with the arrival in the area of a contingent of Cuban advisers, specially trained in the arts of guerilla warfare. The price of assistance would undoubtedly be the establishment of a communist presence in the Congo, and the Fizi Baraka pocket represented the ideal terrain for such a manoeuvre. Any doubts that were entertained about the truth of the reports concerning the

---

[1] Chinese small arms are in many cases exact copies of American weapons but with one significant difference—they are always one millimetre greater in the bore. Thus the American 81 mm mortar has an exact counterpart in the Chinese 82 mm mortar, the 75 mm recoilless rifle (cannon) in the Chinese 76 mm recoilless rifle. By this means they are able to use our ammunition but we cannot use theirs in our weapons.

Cubans vanished with the discovery of a dead Cuban after the recent rebel raid on Bendera. His diary and passport confirmed that he had travelled from Havana via Prague and Peking, in both of which places he had undergone extensive training. An entry in the diary had the clarion ring of truth, where he described that the Congolese rebels "were too damned lazy to carry the 76-mm. cannon and its heavy shells!"

Jacques Noel was now at G 3 (Operations) in Leo and quickly outlined to me the tactical picture in the Fizi-Baraka pocket. Fizi was the main administrative centre and Baraka was its port, thirty-five miles away, nestling in the crook of Burton Bay. The enemy, said Jacques, were a very different proposition from the ones we had fought in the north. These were the Bahembi, a fierce tribe who had consistently defied the Government in the past and resisted nearly all attempts by missionaries to convert them. They were apparently untameable. They had a reputation for gold and diamond smuggling and were a secretive and insular clan. They were proud, independent and warlike and revelled in tribal fighting. In a word, they were the Irish of the Congo! But the most gloomy aspect of the situation was that the entire civilian population was behind the rebel movement to a man. We could expect no help in that direction.

The terrain was entirely in their favour as defenders. The approach to the redoubt from the Albertville end twisted up along two lengthy escarpments at Lulimba, which the rebels had turned into a veritable fortress. Apart from that, the country could only be entered by mountain tracks or by invading the coastline.

It had the earmarks of a rough and bitter campaign. The rebels were obviously well equipped, well trained, properly led and determined. They would rely on their military skill, rather than put their faith in the half-baked doctrine of Mulele. The long term threat of Communism in Africa loomed large and ominous; the rebels were the catspaw. I foresaw that we would require a 5 Commando trained to a very much higher standard than hitherto, with better equipment and a more professional outlook, if we were to succeed in ridding the Congo of this malignant parasite.

Unfortunately all was not well with our recruitment. Darby de Jaeger had already warned me that we had scraped the bottom of the barrel in South Africa and he was not optimistic about the possibility of raising six hundred men for our new battalions. I

1. A training session led by Mike Hoare in Kamina, Katanga province, September 1964. (*Alamy*)

2. The 5 Commando letterhead in 1966.

3. A 5 Commando jeep with additional decoration. (*Photos by Bob Houcke, a French pilot who worked for the CIA-sponsored Congolese Airforce*)

4. The beachhead at Baraka, 1965. (*Photo by Bob Houcke*)

5. In September–October 1965, any injured 5 Commando men were medevacked by chopper to the outskirts of Albertville, and thence to hospital by ambulance. (*Photo by Bob Houcke*)

6. Sgt Tim Dreyer, left, and the chopper pilot Bob Houcke at Albertville airport. At this time, Houcke was flying injured 5 Commando men to Albertville in a Bell 47G3B1 helicopter with floats to facilitate safer flying over Lake Tanganyika. The CIA had provided the Congo with an air force comprising T28s, B26s, C46s and choppers. Note two B26 bombers in the background. (*Photo by Bob Houcke*)

7. A T28 in Isiro (previously named Paulis) in the north-east of the Congo. (*Photo by Bob Houcke*)

8. Mike Hoare, standing left, and the wounded John Peters, standing right, supervise the evacuation of the wounded after the battle of Baraka in September 1965. (*Photo by Bob Houcke*)

9. Injured 5 Commando volunteer being flown out of Baraka to Albertville, end of 1965. (*Photo by Bob Houcke*)

10. The dropping zone (DZ) in Albertville was beside a church as it was the closest place to land near the hospital. (*Photo by Bob Houcke*)

began at once to consider the United Kingdom as a possible source of volunteers. I had desisted in the past in order to comply with a request made by the British Embassy in Leopoldville, who thought recruitment in the United Kingdom might embarrass Her Majesty's Government, but I had received enough written applications from London alone to paper the walls of a five-roomed house and almost as many from America. United States citizens, however, were ruled out by virtue of their loss of citizenship should they enlist in a foreign army.

Volunteers as such were not lacking, but it was a question now of recruiting the right type. The problem became acute within the next few weeks and finally I made the wrong decision and persevered in South Africa, rather than breaking fresh ground elsewhere. It was a costly error.

I toured G.H.Q. and pestered the various departments with my special needs, particularly radio, and discussed my problems with the new Chief of Technical Assistance, Lieut.-Colonel Goosens, an unsmiling, pessimistic and perpetually harassed Belgian, who was nevertheless helpful and efficient. I was not surprised to hear that his nickname was *Sans Souris*. I was never at my ease in G.H.Q. and was glad to leave for Albertville the next day, filled with a steady determination to come to grips with the rebels once and for all. The knowledge that a successful campaign to crush Communist infiltration in the Congo would change the course of history, buoyed me up and strengthened my resolution. It was a worth-while task.

My aircraft circled wide over Lake Tanganyika, casting a shadow on the shimmering blue water beneath us. The mighty lake had risen over twenty feet in recent years and I could see the cleft in its side, through which the beautiful pure water poured wantonly away to become the Lukuga River.

I stood on the tarmac recovering my soul after the long swift journey at 20,000 feet, touched by a spasm of nostalgia. Across the bay in a southerly direction I could see Rutuku and Malembe, the scenes of our exploits barely a year ago. There was the Filtisaf Clinic, where Nestler and Kohlert had been killed. It all looked so different now.

A recent rain had washed the atmosphere clean and Kigoma lay clear across the bay, a distance of over forty miles. The air was soft

Q

and balmy and exuded a lazy feeling of well-being. I was shown to a comfortable room at the Hotel du Lac, own bath and view of the lake. Some of my officers were similarly quartered. It was delightfully soft and feminine, but it was not war. I decided to put an end to this make believe existence straight away. The coming campaign would call for an exceptional degree of fitness and an attitude of mind, which could never survive the luxury of hotel bedrooms, and which could only sap the sinews of our stern resolve. The Hotel du Lac saw us no more. It was not a popular move.

Commanders are frequently described as puritans. The greatest of these in current times is that great soldier, Field Marshal Montgomery, whom I admire unrestrainedly. (I have been described as looking like "Monty" and also, as one who dislikes him; the former may be true, but the latter is certainly not.)

In my view no commander can be successful unless he leads a personal life completely beyond reproach. This must give rise to a reputation for puritanism, I suppose. Certainly it entails eschewing the flesh pots, if only to set the right example. Example is everything. The rank and file in any army have a passionate desire to respect their leaders and they feel disillusioned when they turn out to be mere mortals like themselves, with feet of clay. (Nothing in the foregoing, however, should be construed as a description of myself as a Commander! On the contrary, I regret, I care very much for the vices of the world and show a marked addiction to some of them. But not to smoking, which I abhor.)

Alastair had been busy preparing the Lubuye Mission for the reception of our new unit of 350 men and the "barracks", parade ground and playing fields were adequate for our purpose and provided the best conditions we had known in the Congo. A rifle range was improvised by the water's edge and the surrounding countryside, hilly and well laced with streams, was ideal for the training of troops in infantry tactics. The food was excellent and included Capitaine straight from the Lake. Beer was easily obtainable, Simba once again, and Albertville had all the makings of a first-class station.

The town of Albertville itself is strung out along a lake front road, edged with palm trees and bordered on the lake side by the railway line and on the other by a row of windowless shops with large wooden shutters, most of which are run by Indians. The hill behind the road is the main residential area, with glorious views of the Lake. It was one of the few places in the Congo in which there was no shortage of anything—except fresh milk—and a brisk trade was carried on across the Lake with Kigoma and by rail with Rhodesia via Elizabethville.

For my part, the only disappointment was the absence of the promised house. I had by now discarded the vision of the two sentries, but I felt cheated that the house should have been completely overlooked. After all, it had been fundamental to my agreement with General Mobutu. However, I was saved from violent reaction by the kindness of Monsieur van der Oostyn, the Managing Director of Filtisaf, a local textile company, who very kindly placed a small house at my disposal, another for Alastair and similar ones for use as an Officers' Mess.

Once more we were busy phasing out the old 5 Commando and bringing in the new, this time to a two-battalion strength. Major Johnstone waited patiently in the north for his unit to arrive to hold the six-hundred-mile sector from Aru to Niangara. We were so hard pressed for men that we were never able to do him justice, but he managed to fulfil his role by dint of much struggle and determination.

The new arrivals were disappointing, and I was obliged to send home over three hundred for various reasons. They just simply would not do for the campaign ahead of us which, I kept repeating, would demand the fittest and best trained soldiers we could lay our hands on. Anything short of that would result in catastrophe. This was going to be war, not the kid stakes we had been engaged in most of our time in the Congo. I found this attitude extremely difficult to get through to those who arrived with grape-like varicose veins, fingers missing, glass eyes, pot bellies, expensive red noses and permanently dry throats. As to the dope fiends and confirmed alcoholics, they went back on the same plane that brought them.

A few of the old 5 Commando came again for a further term. I made a ritual of interviewing every man personally on arrival. There was something familiar about the tall Dane, who stood before me. I flicked through my memory file. Oh, yes!

"Aren't you the chap that I found boiling down some rebel skulls at Bikili last year?" I asked.

He fidgeted nervously.

"Yes, sir."

"Well, beat it, my boy, I don't want your type in my unit."

"But, sir, I promise you I've given it up!"

For Lent, I presumed. He went back. Pity, but there was no knowing what a man of that temperament might do next! Fortunately one or two of my former officers and N.C.O.s came again. Amongst these was Sergeant Columbic, a Jewish lad, who was immediately raised to lieutenant. Ron Columbic was a large, easy-going chap with a fine physique, barrel chest and happy-go-lucky manner. He had the modesty which often goes hand-in-hand with great physical strength, and was one of the few officers able to lead by sheer force of personality, an unusual gift. His favourite expression was "There's a luck." Brave Ron, his luck deserted him in the end. His inseparable companion was Sergeant Tim Dreyer, a fierce moustachioed Afrikaner, a giant of a man, who put the fear of God into the recruits, but got results.

Hans von Lieres, fully recovered from his wounds for the second time, now returned to a third contract. I slapped him into an office straight away to take over administration, protesting volubly that he was a soldier and not a scribbler. I gave strict orders that he was not to go within a hundred miles of the front. He was definitely accident prone!

Barry Hobbins was now a Captain, Graham Hogan had returned after a long holiday and took over a Commando, Sergeant Braham from Kenya became an officer to lead the armour, and Sergeant Duka, the only American in the unit, was promoted second lieutenant to assist him. Howard Carter took over Signals as a lieutenant.

Apart from the seven rifle Commandos, the signals and the armour, my responsibilities included "The Navy." This was a small force of thirty 5 Commando men, reputedly all web-footed, who manned an eighty-foot gunboat called *Ermans* and six high powered P.T. boats capable of a silent thirty knots. Their specific task was interdiction. They were to be the means of closing the border with Tanzania. The Navy developed a great esprit de corps and came under the eventual command of Curly Gurnell, another third term man, who was promoted Lieutenant. The skipper of the *Ermans* was Sergeant Peddle, who had until recently been second mate on an Australian ship.

Twelve T-28s were busy training at the aerodrome and the pilots were the best group of Cubans yet. Four B-26s would be available to us for the actual operation, but with their longer range they were based elsewhere. The most welcome addition to the air force was a Bell helicopter, capable of lifting two lying wounded and this was flown by an adventurous young Frenchman. Tragedy overtook the air force soon after our arrival. A T-28 failed on take-off and flipped over on to its back in five foot of water, drowning the Cuban Chief pilot, Mario.

The intensive training programme placed the main emphasis on physical fitness and weapon training. Equipment and transport poured in from Leopoldville and by the middle of August we were unusually well found in this respect. The second phase of our training could now begin.

Kabimba was a small port thirty miles north of Albertville, which owed its existence to a cement factory called Cimental. The rebels were just the other side of the hills overlooking the harbour, which made them suitable for advanced training in recce and fighting patrols. As there was always the possibility of bumping the enemy, there was a touch of reality about it all. One Commando at a time used Kabimba for this purpose.

Sixty-five kilometres up the main road towards Lulimba there was a large hydro-electric power station, defended by one battalion of the A.N.C. The whole area was mountainous and heavily wooded and made a perfect training ground for cross-country marching. The A.N.C. unit was sustained by a twice monthly convoy of rations, which was frequently ambushed. The last one had been completely wiped out ten kilometres from Bendera about a week ago. It was necessary to send another and this time we provided the escort as a training measure. Dave Braham commanded the column, which comprised six Ferrets, one Commando of infantry, and an umbrella of T-28s for the whole length of the journey. They returned the next day without mishap.

Difficulties once more arose with the men's pay. The delays involved were already bad enough, but the new Belgian Staff in Stanleyville aggravated the matter by insisting that our pay section should be based there, rather than with the unit. This involved a further delay and I refused to comply with the unreasonable request. But it was too late, the damage had already been done and I was faced once again with mutiny.

My sympathies were entirely with the men in this instance. They had come to fight for money, and when after a reasonable lapse of time money was not forthcoming, they struck. I flew off to Leopoldville to see the General, determined that as far as I was concerned, the A.N.C. could either pay the men properly or find a new commander. I was sick to death of the whole problem. I laid my ultimatum on the desk—pay within seven days, using a more efficient system, or I would call it a day. On the seventh day the money was paid into a bank in Johannesburg. There was never any question of the A.N.C. welshing on the contract, it was entirely a matter of someone, somewhere along the line, suppressing the necessary authority to pay. The reasons for this would have made interesting reading, I had no doubt.

Pay was a headache in the middle of my unit problems, but pay was why we were there and pay we had to have, timeously, as the lawyers say. During my leave I had received an alarming telegram from Leopoldville, advising me that our Paymaster had run off with the unit payroll, totalling 55 million Congolese francs, a tidy sum. The court case had been disposed of before my return and the Paymaster found not guilty, but reprimanded. Doctor Brenhardt, who had been languishing in Faradje, decided to have a week-end in Leo and persuaded the Paymaster to accompany him. The Paymaster was a conscientious man and decided to take the payroll with him, "For," as he explained, "I could hardly leave that amount of money lying about, could I?" Of course not. The large green tin boxes, stuffed with bank fresh notes, posed something of a transport problem, but this was happily solved by the timely assistance of Major Dick Kohlbrand, Colonel Raudstein's second in command at the U.S. Embassy. Not knowing what was in the boxes, he generously suggested that these should be carried to Leo in a C-130 leaving Stan that day, and to make it all quite legal, he would put his name on the boxes.

At three the next morning the telephone rang in the Kohlbrand household. It was Knut Raudstein.

"Kohlbrand?"

"Sir?" Dick says he saluted.

"It may interest you to know that you have just involved the United States Government in the theft of 55 million Congolese francs!" Dick says he fainted. When he recovered, the voice was saying, "Find it, and find it quick. Good night."

He did, and Dick was able to dine out on the story for the next three weeks, but his favourite nightmare remains the sight of a C-130 ramp descending to reveal a stack of large green tin boxes, all marked "Major Kohlbrand—handle with care."

Congolese francs were never a problem for us in the Congo, although the cost of living seemed to have risen a few points during the last year. This was borne out by one of my Lieutenants, who had just spent two days in Leopoldville, doing the round of the night spots and complained bitterly at the cost of loving.

"It's cost me over thirty thousand francs for the week-end!" he told me.

"I hope you've got something to show for it," I replied.

"Gosh, Colonel," he said, "I hope I haven't!"

On my return to Albertville, the Wild Goose[1] flag was flying at half mast. Lieutenant Graham Hogan and Volunteers Nolte and Rademeyer had been killed the previous day in an ambush this side of Bendera, in exactly the same spot as the A.N.C. convoy of a few weeks ago. Graham had been sent with two Ferret scout cars to escort a Belgian Adjudant Chef and his three assistants to Bendera. The whole operation had been handled too lightly. Unsuspectingly, Graham and his boys rolled along, turrets open, almost at journey's end. Suddenly, an enemy bazooka hissed through the air, to explode on the leading Ferret, while machine guns opened up on one side of the road. Seven out of the eight people in the convoy were killed. The sole survivor was Volunteer Trevelyan, a youngster of twenty-one.

If the A.N.C. had issued medals to 5 Commando for bravery, Trevelyan would have received the highest decoration available. He was driving the second Ferret when his gunner, Rademeyer, was killed by a burst of machine gun fire. A bazooka rocket struck the back of the vehicle and exploded two Jerry cans of petrol, which ought never to have been there. The blazing petrol seeped through into the cockpit, turning it into a flaming inferno. Trevelyan was trapped inside by his gunner's body blocking the turret escape. Getting out of the small driver's hatch in front of him, he engaged

---

[1] The Wild Goose was the badge of 5 Commando and every man wore a patch on his left shoulder showing that he was a member of the unit. I took the badge from the history of the most famous mercenaries of all time—the 19,000 Irishmen "who were the vanguard of the "Wild Geese", the scores of thousands of Irish who were to seek their fortune in foreign armies in the course of the eighteenth century." (Christopher Duffy's interesting book *The Wild Goose and the Eagle* tells their story.)

the enemy with his F.N. rifle and fought them off. He then went to
the assistance of the other Ferret, but both the lieutenant and his
driver had been killed instantly. A hand grenade had landed in the
middle of the jeep they were escorting, killing the Belgian Adjudant
Chef and his three assistants outright.

Trevelyan then marched several kilometres towards Bendera on his
own to get help from the A.N.C. It was a stirring feat of bravery and
I commended him heartily for his action.

The loss of a fine officer and two good men saddened the unit.
We resumed our training, chastened and a shade less confident in
our invincibility.

The men were coming forward nicely now, but I was again
desperately short of officers and N.C.O.s. I cast about for any old
5 Commando men, who could be brought back in a hurry. Commandant Peters returned from Salisbury, R.S.M. Cassidy from
Scotland, Lieutenant Pete Ross-Smith from Bulawayo, Lieutenant
Sam Smallman from South West Africa, and finally, and to my
great joy, Lieutenant George Schroeder from Johannesburg.

Thus reinforced, I felt ready for the fray.


The tactical position in the Fizi-Baraka pocket was unfavourable
to us, but had the saving grace that it allowed freedom for
manoeuvre. The enemy were contained in their mountain stronghold and did not look like emerging from it at the moment. The
initiative lay entirely with us. The total inaction on the part of the
A.N.C. during the last year, which was quite inexcusable, had
allowed the enemy to build up unassailable positions at Lulimba and
further west at Kabambare. A complete rebel chain of command
existed to our certain knowledge, with Fizi at its centre. By their
very nature, the Bahembi might have been happy to continue their
untroubled "Sinn Fein" existence, but with the advent of the
Cubans, a new and more militant note was being struck. The enemy
were moving towards the attack.

On our side we had 5 Commando, rapidly reaching a good
standard of training, and two battalions of A.N.C., one at Bendera
and the other at Lulimba, both on all accounts anxious to get up and
go.

I studied the terrain and air photographs. Aerial reconnaissance
revealed a network of tortuous paths, many bridges, fast running
streams and much wooded and hilly country. The Lake ended

abruptly in a rocky coastline, which shot up three or four thousand feet at an impossible gradient.

At first blush it was obvious that motorised warfare was impracticable. I began seriously to consider the possibilities of a cross-country column, operating out of a series of strongholds supplied by air—in fact, a "Wingate column." This would mean a large number of porters, but they were available in another part of the Congo. It was feasible from every viewpoint, in theory anyway. The idea appealed to me greatly and I tried out an exercise at once, to see how the men would react to this type of warfare, spiked as it is with hardship and difficulty. I studied Lieutenant Fielding's report on his first cross–country trip with 51 Commando. It was disappointing. Further exercises convinced me that we could never reach the standard of training required for an operation of this type in the time available. Furthermore, the logistical support on which the whole thing would stand or fall, would only be available for the actual show and not at all during training. Reluctantly, I ruled it out. There is something infinitely romantic about a column of men, striking off over the mountains led by a compass needle and the will of a determined man, and the thought died hard with me.

I looked now at the Lake. We had overwhelming superiority on the water and in the air and the idea that we might land a sizeable force somewhere behind the enemy lines took root in my mind and flowered into a simple plan.

Amphibious operations are traditionally bedevilled with unthought of hitches in their actual execution, but the advantages of striking the enemy by surprise in his rear and destroying simultaneously his nerve centre and his means of supply, convinced me that it was the only course of action to pursue. I thrashed it out every way, until satisfied beyond a peradventure that we could do it and do it without loss. Compared with a frontal assault on the Lulimba escarpment, it was a thousand times safer.

One of the major problems would be security. Albertville had a thousand ears and the C.F.L. boats traded daily with Kigoma, which was also the port for the enemy supplying Baraka. If the plan leaked out and we were met by a reception committee, it would prove ruinously expensive. I decided to keep the plan strictly to myself and to make it known to my inner circle three days before we were due to push off, and to the men only when we were actually embarked. As a "deception" I allowed it to get around that 5

Commando was preparing for an overland march and issued papers from my office, marked Top Secret "Operation Wingate." Some of these were allowed to fall off a truck in town and within a week, the story was well established that we would be striking the enemy over the tops of the mountains near Bendera and Lulimba.

I visited the C.F.L. authorities. They were delighted to help. I reserved three ships, sufficient for an assault force of two hundred men and an initial landing of eighteen vehicles. For the vehicles I required the conversion of one of their flat top barges, which they must fit out with ramps long enough to reach across to shallow water. C.F.L., to their credit, undertook to do it all without fuss or bother and with no questions asked.

*Ermans* was fitted with radar, effective to thirty miles and so was one of the P.T. boats. Curly Gurnell assured me he would put us down on the right beach, regardless of the conditions. As the Lake is placid at night 364 days of the year, I had no qualms on this score. Having decided on my plan of attack in principle and seen that it was quite workable, I left it in abeyance, with every intention of taking it up again about the middle of September, ten days before D day.

The area in which we were operating was known as "Operations South—Ops Sud," and in due course Lieut.-Colonel Hardenne arrived in Albertville, as Chief of Staff to Ops Sud. Roger Hardenne was a Belgian regular Army Officer in the Parachute Regiment and had been trained at Fort Leavenworth in the United States. He was a good-looking man of about forty, fresh faced, dashing, keen, and anxious not to step on anyone's toes. He knew his job and tackled it with enthusiasm, as yet unblunted by Congo lethargy.

"Wireless sets?" he asked me one day. "How many would you like for your battalion? I am sure I can get as many as you want." After three weeks, four came trickling through. He was very new to the Congo.

Slowly, I watched him being worn down by the inefficiency of his subordinates, his working day getting longer and longer, until I feared he might collapse under the strain. As soon as the campaign began, however, he took on a new lease of life and won through, his bright eyes and happy disposition helping him through the sticky places.

Colonel Kakuji, who commanded Ops Sud, was a small bantam

cock of a man, pleasant and intelligent. Our relationship was normally harmonious, except for the one occasion when I felt justifiably angry. Despite my urgent reminders, the Congolese Chef de Protocol had not included 5 Commando in the wreath-laying ceremony at the war memorial to mark the anniversary of the relief of Albertville. No mention was made of the two Germans from 5 Commando, who had given their lives. Undismayed, we held our own parade immediately after the official one, at which we were ignored. My twenty Germans, led by Lieutenant von Lieres, then laid two enormous wreaths to mark the day.

We had not forgotten.

In the last few days a wave of panic had swept through the town. The civilians were scared of rebel attack, once 5 Commando pulled out and nothing would persuade them the probability was remote and could easily be handled by our reserve Commando. Injudicious statements by various technical advisers convinced them trouble was on the way and many packed their bags and left. Some of the staff at Ops Sud contributed to the wave of panic, with a view to having the area declared a "danger area" for pay purposes, when a special daily bonus became payable.

My wife had every confidence in what we were doing and decided to stay in the Filtisaf camp with the baby, if only to set a good example. I went a long way towards calming some troubled breasts. Later General Mobutu sent her a personal letter, thanking her for her spirit. He said, "*Alors qu'un vent de panique soufflait sur Albertville, et que le plupart des civils parlaient de quitter les lieux, au depart du 5me Commando pour Fizi ; vous avez décidé de rester sur place, donnant à tous, un bel exemple de sang froid et de sérénité.*" It was a gracious tribute and I thanked him for it.

It was Friday, 24th September, and I sat back from my desk. I was working on my plan to attack the enemy, when a visitor from Leopoldville was announced. It was Lieut.-Colonel Goosens.

He began by enquiring if I had fully considered the heavy responsibility which rested upon me for the safety of the people of Albertville, once 5 Commando went forward to the attack. I assured him I had. He then ventured some advice on a suitable plan of campaign. Going to the wall map, he drew a triangle—Albertville, Kabimba and across to the road to Bendera. His advice, of which I was cautioned to take great heed, was that we should begin by clearing this triangle, slowly and thoroughly, ridding it of the enemy, step by step.

"How long would you allow for that?" I asked innocently.

"Two months."

"After that?"

"Move further north." He drew in another advance line to run through Bendera.

"And how long for that?"

"You should finish that by February."

"And Fizi-Baraka?"

"By next March or April."

I thanked him for the suggestion, promised I would give it every consideration, assured him I was aware of my great responsibilities and showed him to the door. The guard presented arms, as he drove off.

Under my blotter lay my detailed plan for seizing Fizi, Baraka, and Lulimba simultaneously on 27th September—in exactly three days' time!

# 18

## OPERATION BANZI[1]

My helicopter hovered over the tiny port of Kabimba. I counted the ships. They were all there, the tug *Ulindi*, the long barge *Uvira*, and the flat topped *Crabbe*. *Ermans* stood off, outside the harbour, its six P.T. boats milling around it in a flurry of foam.

The men had been ferried up from Albertville all through the day and were now under cover, resting. Security was vital to the operation and, as far as the local population were concerned, the boats were here to load cement.

The first Commando embarked an hour after dusk and loading of the vehicles, eighteen in all, began in the glare of arc lamps. All went smoothly until eleven that night, when a power failure threatened to wreck the whole plan. A Ferret hung immobile in the air for over three hours, until the crane started again with a jerk. At four in the morning everything was loaded, six jeeps were lashed down with steel ropes on top of *Crabbe*, and the balance of the vehicles and armour chocked down securely on *Uvira*'s deck. The men slept where they could.

By first light we were well into the middle of the lake, out of sight of land, and steaming due north. The tug towed *Uvira* and she towed *Crabbe*. *Ermans* towed the six P.T. boats. The convoy made an impressive sight as six T-28s and two B-26s flew overhead on their way to soften up Baraka and the villages to the north of it. Two hundred voices raised a cheer, as they dipped their wings in salute.

At dawn the next morning we would strike Baraka.

I lay in my bunk and thought over the events of the last few days. I was confident that my plan to seize Fizi and Baraka was sound.

[1] "Banzi' was the *nom de plume* used by General Mobutu when he was a journalist.

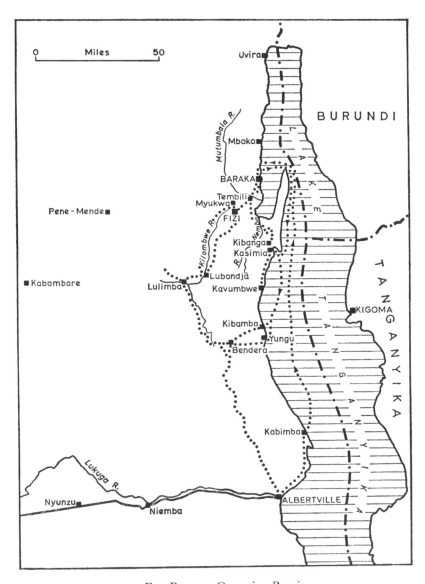

7. Fɪᴢɪ-Bᴀʀᴀᴋᴀ: Operation Banzi

From a military point of view, it was supremely simple and aggressive. On the other hand, it was burdened with political overtones, some of which had been completely beyond my comprehension. In the last few hours, however, much had become clear to me.

President Kasavubu had jolted Leopoldville out of its unaccustomed political calm with the announcement that the new Congolese Parliament would assemble towards the end of September. For fourteen months Mr. Tshombe had ruled the Congo, virtually on his own, and it was plain that some new edict was about to issue. My chief concern was whether the Prime Minister would be dismissed by the President, a power well within his purview and clearly permitted in the Constitution. Tshombe's mounting popularity and his success in putting down the rebellion, led one to suppose that he would be the Congo's next President after the February elections. This probability would only increase the chances of his early removal from power, if President Kasavubu's normal tactics were to run to form.

If Mr. Tshombe went, two matters would be of the greatest importance to us. The first was the distinct probability that the new Government might treat with the rebels. For some time now we had heard rumours that the President was considering talks with the rebel leaders and that the former Congolese Prime Minister, Cyrille Adoulla, had contacted Gbenye and Kanza in Rome. As Adoulla was now in Leopoldville and Kasavubu was well disposed towards him, it was not improbable that something might come of it. The second was that the new régime might take a very different view of white mercenary troops and our future could be uncertain and even fraught with danger.

I was so concerned with these aspects of the political situation that I sent John Latz to see Mr. Tshombe on my behalf, expressly to ask him this question—"Will the Government now or in the near future treat with the rebels?" If the answer was "Yes," or even "Probably, yes," I would call off the attack on Fizi and Baraka. It would be madness to risk our lives on a Monday, to treat with the rebels on a Tuesday, and I said as much.

Latz hurried back with the reply, which reached me the day we left Albertville. Mr. Tshombe was certain that no Congolese Government would ever deal with the rebels, now or in the future; he asked us to press on as quickly as we could to end the rebellion, even though he saw in this a threat to his own office; the future of

the Congo was the paramount consideration; his future, he regretted, looked a trifle uncertain, but he hoped for the best; he
wished me luck.

It was typical of Mr. Tshombe that he should put his country
above his personal ambition and I had a presentiment that the end
was near for him as Prime Minister.

On a national level, the capture of Fizi and Baraka would be
heralded as the end of the rebellion. Internationally, it would have
immediate repercussions. Those countries which had been nourish-
ing the rebel cause, notably Tanzania, Sudan and Uganda, would
cease to comfort and aid the rebels overnight. Armed with these
facts, President Kasavubu could tell the new Parliament, with a
certain amount of truth, that the rebellion was over and that Mr.
Tshombe's writ had run its course. His task had been completed
and this was the time to remove him and replace him with somebody
better suited to the next and more peaceful phase in the development
of the Congo.

I realised, with some dismay, that my urgent action and abnormal
haste to capture Fizi and Baraka, whilst militarily sound, would by
its very success endanger Mr. Tshombe's continued existence as
Prime Minister of the Congo. It was an unfortunate dilemma, but
the die was already cast and I saw my duty clearly. There was no
turning back.

My unit was divided into two groups of one hundred, Force
John-John under Commandant Peters and Force Oscar under
Captain Hugh van Oppens, an Englishman despite his Belgian
sounding name. Hugh was tall, handsome and authoritative.
Command was nothing new to him and he had soldiered all his life,
more recently in Korea. He had an odd, but endearing mannerism—
he would pause before answering a question, with an introspective
"Um—yes" and a twirl of his long moustache.[1]

Our medical arrangements were rather better than usual and a
helicopter had been placed under command for the evacuation of
the wounded. The unit Medical Officer was a young doctor of about
thirty, named Couve de Murville, a distant relative of the French
Foreign Minister, I was informed. He was well read, extremely

----

[1] Hugh van Oppens was killed at Mboko, north of Baraka, on 13th May 1966. He
was second in command of the unit at the time and was due to take command in a few
weeks.

amusing, and knew his job, but lived in his private world of femurs and bacilli and thwarted every attempt at conversion to regimental soldiering. "C.O.'s met his Waterloo!" said Peters one morning, confronted by the doctor on a ceremonial parade, gaiters on back to front and equipment festooned about him like presents on a Christmas tree. For all that "Couve de Mouve" was always there, no matter how hard the battle and always completely oblivious of the danger. I often wondered if the mere fact of concentrating on one's special duty—doctoring or signalling—helped one overcome fear.

The most dangerous and important task in the whole operation had been given to John Peters. He had carefully chosen six others to form a Beach Reconnaissance party. Their job would be to paddle ashore to reconnoitre the beach I had chosen for the landing. They would put up lights to signify all was well. They had rehearsed their role, until they were letter perfect, and it was impossible to see them until they were twenty yards from the beach, and then only if you knew they were coming. They had paired off—Ron Columbic and Tim Dreyer, Sergeant Hammond and Sergeant Mansfield, Lieutenant Smallman and Lieutenant Braham. John had rehearsed them, dryshod and wetshod, until they were absolutely confident they could land without a sound. The brave little group won my admiration, but every one of them was destined to be killed or wounded in the next few days.

The selected beach was eight kilometres north of Baraka. I had flown over the whole area in a B-26 to make a personal reconnaissance of possible landing places. A road ran fifty yards from the water's edge and there were some villages about a mile away. The whole area was densely populated. We took a series of aerial photographs and the beach stood out clearly. On a radar screen it would be easy to find—it was just below the same parallel as the end of the Ubware Peninsula.

Just before dusk, we hove-to, half-way to Baraka, and an O Group assembled on the mess deck of *Ulindi*. All the crews of the P.T. boats were present and these were now controlled by the Beachmaster, Hans von Lieres. He had steadfastly refused to be left behind and in the end I had weakened. Three journalists were also present. At the very moment when we were leaving Albertville, they had asked permission to join the column, not knowing where we were going, or even what we were about to do. One was John

Spicer of the Argus Group in Southern Africa and the other two were Bob Rogers of N.B.C. and Don Steffan of C.B.S. It was an awkward decision, but as they had already learnt too much, I was obliged to let them come. I did not regret it; they were all three exceptionally brave and aided rather than hindered the operation.

I gave out my plan. Our force of two hundred men would land eight kilometres north of Baraka and attack the town at first light. Simultaneously, Alastair with one hundred men, who were now well on their way, would attack Lulimba frontally to cause a diversion. After the capture of Baraka, the next phase would be a dash to Fizi by Force John-John. Finally we would attack the Lulimba fortress from both front and rear.

I gave out the detailed orders for the landing. At 01.30 hours in the morning, the Beach Recce Party, under John Peters, would push off. On their "all clear" signal, the first wave of five P.T. boats would leave *Ulindi*. By dawn the whole force would be ashore. The vehicle barge *Crabbe* would land at first light and, as soon as the jeeps were landed, we would race into Baraka and take it by surprise. I would wait for dawn before advancing, because I wanted to be covered by the strong air support which was due over us at first light.

I expected everything to go wrong, knowing that amphibious operations are peculiarly prone to mishap and a prey to the unexpected, but the plan was simple and there was a lot of latitude for error. In any case, everyone would know the general intention and could execute it independently if necessary. It would be a pitch black night, as there was no moon that night. Already it had clouded over and there was every prospect we would get ashore with total surprise. I ended by saying:

"Tonight, gentlemen, will be a long night. In the stillness of the small hours of tomorrow morning, you may like to remember that Sir Winston Churchill, that great warrior, once said, 'Enterprises of great pith and moment rely for their execution on men of courage.' This is certainly such an enterprise and you are certainly such men. Or that the late President Kennedy once remarked, 'Victory has a hundred fathers, defeat is an orphan.' Gentlemen, tomorrow at breakfast time, I hope we shall all be victorious fathers!"

As there was nothing more to be done, I turned in for some rest, leaving orders to be awakened at ten o'clock when I would transfer to the Gunboat *Ermans* to command the operation. I slept soundly.

My batman woke me at ten with a hot cup of coffee. Half of it was in the saucer. The weather had changed and the ship was rolling badly. I stepped outside. A loose tarpaulin was thrashing the deck rail, as the ship moved defiantly into the teeth of a fierce storm. Huge waves crashed over the bows as lightning flashed across the sky and rain lashed the lifeboat above me. I made my way unsteadily to the bridge, where the Belgian Captain was staring into the night, everything blacked out. "*C'est incroyable!*" he said. He was afraid the storm would get worse and the seas steeper off the end of the Ubware, where there was always a swell coming out of Burton Bay. He thought it might last for a full day. My heart sank. What damnable luck! Of all nights in the year for a storm, it had to be the one we had chosen for our landing. Perhaps it would be calmer inshore? The Captain made no comment.

The P.T. boat alongside rose and fell ten feet. I jumped in at the top of the rise and got aboard *Ermans*. Sergeant Peddle was at the helm, as one of his men peered into the radar screen, the only light on the bridge. We were fifteen miles from our assembly area and already we were nearly two hours late. I went below to find the Beach Recce party. John Peters and his men were all blacked out with burnt cork, ready to go ashore, but John was suffering agonies of sea sickness. He dashed to the rail and heaved up. Others around him did the same. The little *Ermans* carried considerable top hamper and the strong cross wind caused her to pitch and roll in a corkscrew motion. The tug signalled that she would have to go even slower, her hawser was under tremendous strain towing the two barges, and vehicles on *Crabbe* were in some danger of sliding off.

By three in the morning we reached the end of the Ubware. The seas were enormous and the wind strengthened to a half gale. I ordered Peddle to get in closer to the shore, hoping for quieter water. I would have to make a decision in the next few minutes and I seriously considered calling the whole thing off. The wind eased a fraction and I decided to carry on.

I consulted with John.

"Do you think you can make it in this weather, John?"

"We'll try. Anything to get off this bloody ship." He ran to the rail again.

The little party pushed off in total blackness in Curly Gurnell's P.T. boat at exactly 03.30 hours. We were two hours behind schedule. My signaller kept contact with them for the first five minutes, but after that—nothing.

A mile from the shore the beach recce party transferred themselves to an assault boat, which they had towed behind them. Curly gave them a compass bearing, indicated the general direction of the beach ahead and waved them good-bye, disappearing into the black night around them. Seconds later Curly's engine cut out and his radar and wireless went out of order. He drifted helplessly for the next two hours, battling to start his motor again. The beach party paddled slowly forward in absolute silence, lifted by each successive wave, flung madly forward and then dropped into its trough. Several of them were sick. John was in the stern, vomiting between strokes. The shoreline came in sight, a thin white line of surf crashing on the sand. It was not the right beach, but they grounded. Without a word they completed their drill and at the end of fifteen minutes erected their beach lights and tried to contact us on their radio. All was clear, but their lights were too dim and their radio too weak to reach us!

On *Ermans* I was worried. John had been gone for over an hour and Curly had not returned. In another half hour it would be getting light. I had no alternative but to release the first wave and hope they would pick up John's lights closer in. I gave the order for the convoy to close with the shore at full speed. It was a race against daylight now and the last thing I wanted was to be caught in the open, trying to land on a defended beach.

Hugh van Oppens commanded the first wave, and Hans was in contact with me the whole way. They reached the shore just as daylight broke and simultaneously the enemy opened up. Tracers arced out towards the ships and yellow flashes lit the sky. The first wave got ashore and were pinned down by enemy machine gun and mortar fire, but Hugh made his way to a hut and fired it—it was the best homing signal we could have wished for.

Back came the P.T. boats, flat out at maximum speed, their hulls lifting right out of the water. My headquarters were in the second wave and we flashed towards the shore, enemy bullets falling wide of us. Within minutes we were over the side into five feet of water and on to firm ground. Patrols pushed straight up to the road, through a field overgrown with manioc, and established a small beach-head. John made his way to us, whilst the remaining waves came ashore. By 05.15 hours the last wave hit the beach and the whole unit was contained within the beach-head. 5 Commando had landed.

I enlarged the perimeter to half a mile, waiting for *Crabbe* to come in and offload the six jeeps. The landing went off without a hitch, down went the ramps and the jeeps raced through the manioc on to the road like greyhounds released from their traps.

As soon as my air arrived phase two could begin. Force Oscar would push down the road with all speed, John-John to bring up the rear; Oscar to take Baraka first and consolidate; then John-John to crash on to Fizi to take it by surprise.

There was no wireless contact with base and the cloud level was so low, I realised after a few minutes, that we would get no air that morning, possibly none that day. There was no point in waiting. I gave Hugh the word to go.

It was not my lucky day. No air and the night approach had been almost disastrous. We had already lost the power of surprise, on which I had counted so heavily, but we were committed and there was nothing for it, but to go like hell.

Hugh hit the enemy four kilometres from Baraka, as his jeep crashed into cover. A parrot, clinging to the mirror in another jeep, screamed out with rage as he was flung off his perch. A fierce fight ensued and the enemy fled, leaving their dead behind. Volunteer Madden was seriously wounded in the stomach and the groin, and despite everything Doctor Couve did for him, he died. We burnt down the village and a long column of smoke ascended into the sky, a grim warning to the defenders of Baraka that we were on our way. With a shout of joy, Dave Braham and Skinny Coleman (a 250-pound Rhodesian) swept past us in two Ferret armoured cars to give Hugh a spearhead of steel. The pace quickened, as the marching men were ferried to the front of the column, clinging to jeeps and scout cars.

Torrential rain fell and I stopped the advance at the entrance to Baraka, where one road led left down to the port and another right to by-pass the town. We sheltered under a dripping mango tree, as the enemy kept up heavy machine gun fire, slicing the leaves off the tree from time to time.

The port was now vital to us. Our reserves of ammunition had run dangerously low and without immediate replenishment, we might have to withdraw. John-John moved down the by-pass road to engage the enemy and a fantastic exchange of fire took place. Advancing relentlessly along the track past the huge Cotonco warehouses, we made our way to the port, scouts running through the dense bush, probing every likely enemy defence. Force Oscar held the centre of the town, whilst a small party dashed down to the shore to bring in the boats with the much needed ammunition.

A beach party under Hans von Lieres cleared a landing place and signalled the convoy to close on the beach.

So long as we held the port, we could deal with the enemy when it suited us, but supplies and ammunition were first priority. I decided to hold a small perimeter. The enemy were reckoned to be about two thousand strong and the pressure on John-John's flank was too great. He regrouped to fall back when Lieutenant Columbic, in the act of rallying his unit, was hit by a burst of machine gun fire. He dropped to the ground. Tim Dreyer ripped off his shirt and applied a field dressing, but the bullet had pierced his heart and Ron Columbic knew he was going. "There's a luck, Tim," he said with a faint smile. "This is it." They were the last words he uttered.

At the cross-roads Dave Braham and John Peters were caught in a hail of bullets and both wounded. John refused morphine and continued to direct the battle, until weak with loss of blood, Sammy Smallman took over and sent John down to the clearing station. Force John-John withdrew step by step. Smallman, who was a stickler for the book, rejoiced in the drill-like precision of the movement.

Back on the beach, four P.T. boats rushed in at thirty knots, slewed round as though skiing on Durban Bay, and began to throw boxes of small arms ammunition into the water. My men dashed out to gather them up. The enemy, seeing that help was reaching us, put in a counter-attack on the beach and a hail of lead forced every man to take cover and dig. The P.T. boats withdrew to a safe distance, whilst Hans set up a 60 mm. mortar in a trench and ranged in on the enemy. Ten yards from the water's edge I lay in a shallow trench, while a few feet away the three journalists dug in with their hands. Bullets whistled dangerously overhead. Bob Rogers called out, "If I should stop one now, I know just what my wife will say—he died trying to grow up!"

It was touch and go. The barge was standing well off the beach, waiting for our signal to come in. If we could not offload it, we would be in serious trouble. Two Commandos were already out of ammunition and all reserves had gone. An enemy heavy machine gun was scouring our beach from about two hundred yards' range and it would have been suicide to unload the barge in the face of it. I tried to pinpoint its position. The fire seemed to be coming from the mission immediately to our front. Bob Rogers wormed his way through the sand to me. "Don't want to interfere, Colonel, but how about getting the gunboat to hit the mission with its cannon, while we engage them from here. That ought to silence them for a while and we can get the barge unloaded."

It was the answer. Bob Rogers had been an officer in the U.S. Army and had forgotten nothing. I radioed *Ermans* and Peddle brought her in close, opposite the big building. With a spout of flame fifteen feet long, she loosed off an armour piercing 75-mm. shell which struck the gable end, blowing it into a hundred pieces. The enemy ran and our mortars spread grief amongst them, as they made for the village behind.

At the same time, the barge nosed its way in and a human chain of men waded out, up to their necks, crying out encouragement to the exposed crew, clinging to the top of the barge, and in the next few minutes the precious ammunition was being manhandled ashore. Machine gun bullets lashed the water and hit the barge, with a clang. One man was hit and the water around him ran red. It was too hot to hold and I ordered the barge to be abandoned now the ammunition was off. Runners took the boxes to the edge of the perimeter, where it arrived just in time. Now that we had closed in on a small perimeter, we fired only when we saw the enemy and conserved every round, but the enemy kept up a never-ending fusillade of shots.

An hour later I was confident we could hold Baraka. I inspected the perimeter defences at dusk. Every man was dug in and determined nothing would budge him in the night. Back at my H.Q. I counted the cost. Lieutenant Columbic, Volunteers Rall, Ellis and Madden had been killed and seven wounded. It was a fearful loss. The enemy losses were one hundred and twenty killed and an unknown number wounded. The body of their commander, Wasochi Abedi, lay outside my H..Q for identification.

We repulsed a dawn attack with little difficulty. The day of storms had been swept away and a clear blue sky showed overhead. I established contact with Ops Sud, who told us that the aeroplanes

were on their way. Thirty minutes later six T-28s swooped down
low over our position and began to strafe the enemy. As though to
make up for their absence the previous day, the Cubans put on a
show of aerobatics to beat any flying display, their white wings
flashing in the sunlight. An aggressive spirit now surged through the
men and fighting patrols went out, intent on avenging the death of
our four men. Meanwhile, I gave orders to clear a field of fire outside
our small perimeter to a distance of two hundred yards. This meant
levelling concrete buildings, filling stations and shops. The ex-
Johannesburg miners were in their element as great explosions of
dynamite blasted off throughout the day.

Colonel Hardenne reported that all had not gone well at Lulimba.
Alastair's force had met with tremendous resistance and he had
contented himself with creating the maximum diversion, according
to plan. I decided to withdraw him and bring his force to Baraka as
soon as possible. The strength of the enemy at Baraka had been
something of a surprise to me and for the advance on Fizi, I would
need at least four hundred more men—three hundred being A.N.C.
Meanwhile, I intended to hold a small perimeter and to patrol
actively outside it by day.

The enemy were very different from anything we had ever met
before. They wore equipment, employed normal field tactics, and
answered to whistle signals. They were obviously being led by
trained officers. We intercepted wireless messages in Spanish. One
of my signallers was a Spaniard and said that the language used was
very poor class Spanish, and it seemed clear that the defence of
Baraka was being organised by the Cubans.

Dawn and dusk, as regular as clockwork, they put in their formal
attacks, which were notable for the lack of noise and shouting, the
usual hallmarks of rebel activity. On the fifth day the pattern
changed. A vast mob of rebels attacked from the Cotonco end of
Baraka, screaming and yelling "*Mai* Mulele" and advancing down
the road in a solid mass, doped full of their *dawa*. We held our fire
until they could receive the full benefit of every shot. They broke
and fled, astonished that the bullets did not turn to water. I realised
at once that the reversion to type could only mean one thing—the
Cubans had gone!

I began at once to make plans for a swift advance on Fizi.

# 19

## THE LAST BATTLE

The arrival of Major Wicks at Baraka with four hundred men heralded the beginning of the end. During the past week we had been subjected to suicidal onslaughts by the enemy, who sought to fling us back into the Lake, but our well defended perimeter, bristling with machine gun posts and mortar proof shelters, was sturdy enough to withstand the strongest attacks. The ferocity of the enemy astounded us and the strength of their forces far exceeded my estimation. Later I discovered that Baraka was to the rebels an almost holy place, transcending purely military considerations. The very name signified something between "Good Luck" and "Fate".[1]

The next phase of the operation for 5 Commando could now begin. Our immediate task was to clear the road to Fizi, then to strike Lubondja, the key to the Lulimba fortress, and finally, to reduce the Lulimba garrison from the rear. When this was done, the enemy would be contained within a semi-circle, whose diameter rested on the coast. The centre of the circle was Yungu, a small port nestling at the foot of precipitous cliffs, and thought to be the headquarters and training ground for the Cuban advisers. Whilst 5 Commando attacked Lulimba, the A.N.C. battalion at Bendera would advance over the tops of the hills to capture Yungu. That should put paid to the rebel effort in the Fizi Baraka pocket; but it seemed obvious to me that the enemy would withdraw into the hills to continue their struggle as guerillas, if their Cuban advisers had taught them anything. The last thing I expected the rebels to do was to stand and

[1] "Baraka is a term used among the Berbers to indicate the quality of holiness of people and things . . . it is inherent in corn, bread, trees, especially palms and olives, wells, springs, stones, rocks, caves, sometimes animals or birds. Finally, it must always be remembered, for offence is easy, that Baraka is extremely sensitive to pollution, and is spoilt, e.g. by contact with infidels"—*Encyclopaedia Brittanica.*

fight and destroy themselves, in preference to melting away into the hills; but I had already been proven wrong at Baraka.

The main feature on the road to Fizi was the Mutumbala Bridge, sixteen kilometres south of Baraka. The bridge itself was a four-span concrete affair with one span on the point of collapse, the pier beneath it having sunk into the sand. We began our advance once more, cautiously and in expectation of great resistance. Two hundred men spread out along four main axes of advance and scoured the countryside on foot, meeting little opposition until we reached the Mutumbala Bridge. Our strong air once more flattened all rebel positions at Tembele, a village on the south side of the river, which overlooked the bridge and was the focal point of roads from the coast and Ubware Peninsula.

During the night Lieutenant Pete Ross-Smith took a fighting patrol, crossed the bridge and seized Tembele with an admirable display of fighting spirit and dash. The road to Fizi was now clear ahead and by lunch-time we had brushed minor resistance aside and found ourselves at the bottom of the seven-kilometre escarpment leading into the town. Lieutenant Bekker climbed the steep hill in thirty minutes and signalled the "All clear" to dash into Fizi. The column rolled into the town on the afternoon of 10th October to find it completely deserted. Patrols went out at once and established that the enemy were in some strength fourteen kilometres to the northwest.

Fizi was the brainchild of a Belgian administrator, who saw in its unique position a healthy and convenient administrative centre. It was a model village, cold and bracing, and from its commanding position, four thousand feet above the plain, one could see the Lake thirty-five kilometres away. From a military standpoint it could have been made almost impregnable, but now that it had been abandoned by the enemy without a shot being fired, I realised the enemy did not intend to fight, but would employ traditional guerilla tactics.

We did not tarry in Fizi, but left a small garrison to defend it and pressed hard for Lubondja the next morning, without waiting for our blood to cool. The main column had trouble with bridges, which had been hastily destroyed, whilst a second column under Captain George Schroeder made its way down a parallel track, ten kilometres west of us on the other side of the Kilombwe River. This track came out conveniently at the back entrance to the Lulimba fortress. The speed of our advance had once more taken the enemy unawares and in one village we completely surprised them. In the fighting which ensued, Lieutenant Borrodaile despatched a rebel officer with his own spear, after being narrowly missed by a bazooka rocket. By late the next afternoon, we signalled Ops Sud we were in Lubondja. Schroeder's column, however, was having difficulty with the last twenty kilometres of the track.

I contacted Alastair at Fizi on my G.R.C. 9. As Fizi was so high above sea level, signal reception was excellent for a change. He had just been visited by General Bobozo, who had arrived in the Bell Helicopter, and had given him the startling news. Mr. Tshombe had been dismissed by President Kasavubu! Although I had half expected it, now that it arrived I was deeply shocked. The news ran like wildfire through the Commandos with much speculation as to our future.

At dawn the next day, 9 Commando of the A.N.C. advanced out of the village of Lulimba to attack the fortress frontally, as we raced in from the rear. The pincer movement worked magnificently and by three in the afternoon the two forces joined up and the enemy were completely overthrown. Vast quantities of heavy ammunition had been abandoned and a small number of 76 mm. cannons and heavy machine guns captured, but very few rebels were actually killed. This was significant and their tactics began to add up. The fortress was yet another position they could have held for weeks, even in the face of strong attack, had they been so minded.

Whilst I took the main column, John Peters was sent to join up with George Schroeder, who was now having bridge trouble. John's column ran into a small skirmish and once more John suffered a wound in his leg, this time from an exploding hand grenade. He was evacuated to Albertville the next morning by helicopter and I went with him to discuss matters with the Chief of Staff at first hand. The Bendera battalion had not moved out, as planned, and there would be a further delay of about ten days. I suggested that, in the meantime, 5 Commando could advance to the southern end of the Ubware Peninsula and seize the town of Kasimia, which would draw the net tighter around the remaining rebels. My force could then make its way down the coast in the direction of Kavumbwe, and beyond, at the same time as the Bendera battalion put in its attack on Yungu.

Personal reconnaissance was required. I flew over the southern tip of the Ubware in a D.C.-3 piloted by the same Belgian captain who had been piloting the day we got lost over Faradje. This time he promised not to lose me, but flew slowly over the enemy at five hundred feet, to fill me with the greatest misgivings for our safety. I felt it was only a matter of time before something solid came up to greet us from below. In the meantime, I had a perfect view.

The track from Tembele to the southern end of the Ubware was motorable as far as the Nemba River, approximately half the distance but the river was broad and deep and there was no bridge across it. From there to the coast and Kasimia, the village in which we were interested, the track meandered north for some distance and might be as long as forty kilometres. The country was open and undulating and was, in fact, an old hunting ground much visited by the Belgians in this area, looking for a little sport. From the air, it seemed to present little difficulty to a column of men on foot, and the direct cross-country distance could not be more than twenty-five kilometres.

We flew over Fizi and Alastair reported that Tim Dreyer and Sergeant Hammond had both been wounded the previous day in an ambush and had been evacuated to Albertville by helicopters. The Beach Party was beginning to thin out. There was only Sammy Smallman and Sergeant Mansfield left, who had not been wounded or killed.

On the way home we took a last look at Kasimia. As the plane banked at about three hundred feet to turn south, a series of unnerving bangs resounded through the fuselage. We had been hit by a number of ·50 explosive bullets fired from immediately below us! I opened the cabin door to find the plane full of smoke with jagged holes strung across the aluminium, two feet apart. "Pas problem—," said Captain Laurent, a cool customer, as he waggled various parts of the contraption to see that everything was still functioning correctly. I admit to being a devout coward in the air and my happiest moment in any flight is when I am stepping out of the infernal machine. I was never happier to see Albertville than on this occasion.

The Chief of Staff called a final conference to tie up the ends of the operation which was about to begin. All was set for the *coup de grâce*, and Lieut.-Colonel Hardenne handled it in a masterly fashion. In addition to the two-pronged attack on Yungu, he had placed the Navy off the coast to capture those who might try to make a getaway.

My plan to capture Kasimia was to use fifty hand–picked men, capable of the long march across country, who would hit the village from the rear. At the same time, our main force under Hans von Lieres would stand off the coast with the Navy and await our signal to come in. I led the small band and a finer bunch of tough and resolute men I have never commanded. There was considerable risk involved in the raid, as there could be no possibility of evacuating any wounded, who would simply have to take their chance. I realised, as we set off at dawn from Tembele, that it would be my last battle.

We should be able to reach the line of the Nemba River in our vehicles without trouble and we started out in the usual manner with our armour leading. Traditionally Dave Braham would reconnoitre each village by fire, as his Ferrets led into them, but this morning for some reason he did not. It was an almost fatal omission. Half-way through the first village, a bare three kilometres from Tembele, the enemy opened up on our three-vehicle convoy at point-blank range. A shower of bullets crashed into my windshield as we were caught in the cross fire of two light machine guns. My men dashed for cover as Hugh van Oppens and I flung ourselves out of the cab for mother earth. I lay on the grass verge, my head hard up against a tree, as bullets kicked up the dust around me. A young volunteer lying next to me slithered back and dropped his rifle, a bullet had shattered his wrist. It was an ugly situation, saved by the coolness and courage of Lieutenant Bekker, who rallied his men and went for the enemy. It was a heart lifting display of fighting spirit. The rebels were no match for us, even when they had every advantage on their side, and Bekker pursued them relentlessly. The casualties were four seriously wounded, including my driver, Sergeant Hoy, who received a bullet in the thigh which shattered his femur. It was incredible that nobody had been killed. Hugh and I had been lucky to get away with it.

We reached the Nemba River just before dusk. The raiding party separated themselves from the escort and prepared to swim the fast flowing Nemba. It was a balmy evening and we strung out in single file to march until our clothes were dry. There was no sign of the enemy—we had total surprise. I called a halt about nine o'clock and decided to doss down for the night in a deserted village at the top of a hill. The sentries were warned not to fire, the power of surprise was with us and therein lay our strength. At two in the morning I heard a muffled scream, as our sentry drove his bayonet into a rebel, who had crept through the long grass to the edge of the huts.

I had a presentiment of attack arising out of this incident and gave the order to move from the village an hour before dawn. We were hardly on our way, when a barrage of mortar bombs fell on the huts we had just evacuated!

After four hours' pleasant marching, we came to the point where the track meandered off to the north, and this was the place for us to start our cross–country march on a compass bearing. We deployed in diamond formation, covering a front of about four hundred yards. Of all infantry tactics, the one which never ceases to thrill me is the sight of a strong body of men making their course relentlessly across country, using covered lines of approach, and brushing aside every obstacle in their path, until they reach their objective. From an enemy point of view, I have no doubt it must be a terrifying sight, particularly where the sunlight glistens on a fixed bayonet, and I am not surprised defenders often cut and run, when they know they are being outflanked by a number of men on foot.

The bounds were nicely spaced and the march took us through rolling downs, lush valleys, and open fields overlooked by small knolls covered with palm trees. An occasional stream gave us difficulty, but refreshed us at the same time. Volunteer Ross-Johnstone, one of our forward scouts, fought out a gun duel with a well dressed rebel, who was carrying a message from the Ubware garrison to Tembele, and got the better of the exchange. When I arrived the other scout, Volunteer Sylvester, a Greek, had already laid claim to the rebel's elegant pair of boots and was busy trying them on.

By three in the afternoon we were well placed behind the village of Kibanga, which was close to Kasimia. It was a set-piece attack with mortar support and a timed first wave. In twenty minutes it was all over and the Navy came in fast to close with the shore on our signal. As they steamed in, the enemy on the tip of the Ubware opened up with their 76 mm. cannons and 82 mm. mortars and forced us off the beach. The Navy, in a moment of panic, let loose the vehicle barge, *Crabbe*, which they had been towing, and this crashed into some rocks and stuck fast. No apparent damage was done and we rescued it later, after we had silenced the enemy, but it was an accident we were shortly to regret vehemently.

Early the next morning we pushed south for Kavumbwe along

the coast, using our P.T. boats to leap-frog us along the shore. We captured vast stocks of ammunition and several weapons, including the heavy ·50 Browning which had fired on the D.C.-3! Late that afternoon we captured Kavumbwe and took over the Protestant Mission, which was deserted. Two days later, a strong enemy counter-attack on the village resulted in the death of Sergeant Mansfield, with two others wounded. That left Sammy Smallman as the only member of the Beach Party still unscathed, but poor Sam, the strict disciplinarian and lover of the book, met his death a few days later at Fizi. With him went the last of that brave little band—the Beach Recce Party. I salute you all.

I flew over the peninsula. It was well held at both ends, but there could be no question of clearing it in the sense that we could start one end and work our way to the other. A spine of densely wooded hills ran down the middle, making progress impossible, while the villages clung to the shore and were connected to each other by small tracks. Hugh van Oppens commanded the attack on the southern end of the Ubware and he and George Schroeder reported total success by nightfall, but with one disappointment—the attractive village at the tip of the peninsula turned out to be a leper colony!

I now gave Captain Schroeder his own force to command, as I had been greatly impressed with his ability for some time. George had a background of regular army soldiering in the South African Army Parachute Regiment and was tall, handsome and knowledge-able. His success stemmed mainly from his ability to command and impart confidence to his men, who followed him with devotion. For all round excellence in soldiering, I would have chosen George Schroeder as the finest man I met in the Congo.

As our main task was now complete, and we awaited the result of the attack on Yungu by the A.N.C. battalion, I thought it reasonable to leave Force Oscar to hold Kavumbwe, Kasimia and the tip of the Ubware, whilst concentrating the balance of 5 Commando at Baraka. From there, we could take it in turn to have a short rest in Albertville. Our wireless code name for Albertville was Paradise[1] and that was just what it would seem like now.

---

[1] Our Albertville Base S.S.B. was manned by Vol. Daniels, a diminutive and some-what lachrymose soldier. Alastair told me how he heard Daniels try for several hours to make contact with me in Baraka until he was on the point of tears. Dejected and miserable and with a running nose he was heard to say, "Hullo Queen, hullo Queen . . . this is Paradise, this is Paradise."

We embarked on the tug *Ulindi*, which towed the barge *Crabbe*, fully laden with six jeeps, arms, ammunition and a mountain of paraphernalia, and set sail for Baraka. Late that night a loud explosion occurred in the bowels of the ship and all lights went out. At the same time there was a distinct jerk in the towing cable. Hans von Lieres reported, almost immediately, that *Crabbe* was sinking. Ten men were clinging to the barge precariously as we winched it in alongside, trying carefully not to disturb its distinct list to port. The ship's pumps were out of commission and there was no course open to us, other than to offload and abandon the barge. Working in the light of powerful clusters, we took off everything movable, but two hours later, half full of water, she turned turtle and slid away from the ship. As dawn broke we tried to sink her with gunfire. It was only a barge carrying six jeeps, but she was still a ship, which had served us faithfully and seen us through some stirring times. As she went down at last, the Belgian Captain of the *Ulindi* stiffened to attention and saluted.

Whilst the final act of the drama was being played out in the hills around Yungu and the two A.N.C. battalions, reinforced by resolute Belgian mercenary officers, closed in on the last remaining rebel stronghold in the Fizi-Baraka pocket, political events of an earth-shaking nature were taking place in Leopoldville. As these had a direct bearing on the men of 5 Commando, I resolved once more to visit General Mobutu.

The dismissal of Mr. Tshombe had touched off a wave of speculation amongst the men in my unit as to our future, so to put all minds at rest I sent off a signal to the Commander-in-Chief, asking for a categorical statement that the new Government would continue to honour our contract and that there was no intention to abrogate it in any way. The assurance I sought was sent to me at once and for the moment we were relieved. That the request for such an assurance was timely, the events of the next few days was to show.

The removal of Mr. Tshombe had come as a blow to most members of the western world, where he was seen as the one man who was able to restore stability to a Congo, chronically prone to unrest. The reasons for his dismissal from office and replacement by his former colleague, Mr. Evariste Kimba,[1] were things which were

[1] Evariste Kimba was appointed Prime Minister by President Kasavubu after the dismissal of Mr. Tshombe. He had previously been very close to Mr. Tshombe and in 1960 was Foreign Minister in the Independent State of Katanga. His appointment as

but dimly understood in the capitals of the west, but nearer home it was known to be a political manoeuvre designed to rid Kasavubu of his foremost rival for the Presidency. There was little doubt that Mr. Tshombe would have been successful in the February elections. Mr. Tshombe's personal popularity was fast becoming a legend in Leopoldville and everywhere he went, flanked and preceded as a general rule by a posse of motor-cycle outriders, sirens screaming, he was greeted as the Saviour of the Congo. Everybody knew Mr. Tshombe—not one in a hundred Congolese could have recognised the President. He shunned publicity and ruled with an olympian detachment from the seclusion of his Mount Stanley home on the banks of the Congo River.

There is an old Congo saying that if one watches the Congo River long enough, the bodies of one's enemies will eventually go floating by. Kasavubu had been watching the Congo River as President for the last five years, during which time four Prime Ministers had gone floating by. President Kasavubu appeared to conduct the affairs of the Congo with a masterly inactivity, consulting nobody and achieving little. In the past, this may have been the result of certain restrictions placed on him by the Constitution, but the new Loi Fundamentale gave the President supreme and absolute power. It was generally assumed that the President must now take a more active part in Congolese politics or lose his position as leader by default. The population was not left to speculate on this possibility for very long. Assisted by the able Mr. Victor Nendaka, the Minister of Security, the President decided to show his teeth.

The Organisation for African Unity was due to hold its much heralded meeting in Accra on 21st October. President Nkrumah had erected a special building for the conference, with a view to impressing other African States, but despite the advance publicity, the show opened with a thud. The delegates stayed away in their thousands! Almost with one accord, the French speaking countries of Africa decided to boycott the meeting in protest against Nkrumah's policy of giving aid to the dissident elements in their countries. In addition, the members of O.C.A.M. had all resolved that it was high time the "Redeemer" was cut down to size.

---

Prime Minister seems to have marked the end of the friendship and Mr. Tshombe did not lend him his support. On 2nd June 1966 Kimba and three other former Cabinet Ministers were hanged in the Grand Place in Kinshasa for taking part in a plot to kill President Mobutu.

S

Nevertheless, this was the occasion chosen by the President of the Congo to make a pronunciamento. His obvious intention was to ingratiate himself with the members of O.A.U., wipe out the sins of the past perpetrated by Mr. Tshombe—for instance, the hiring of mercenaries—and put an end to the estrangement which existed between the two brother Congos, Leopoldville and Brazzaville. His statement was brief and to the point—the Congo rebellion was at an end and the white mercenaries could now be sent home; secondly, the river traffic between Brazzaville and Leopoldville would be reopened after negotiations.

It was the combination of these two statements which hurried me on my way to the General. It was absurd, from the strictly military viewpoint, to send home the mercenaries at the very moment when final victory was within the General's grasp. The reopening of the Congo River crossing to Brazzaville was merely an open invitation to a flood of Communist infiltrators and a calculated act of stupidity, nullifying everything we had been trying to do in the eastern Congo to keep them out.

The General was furious. He had not been consulted about the withdrawal of the mercenaries from his army and he felt bitter in consequence. I had known all along that the General tolerated our presence in the A.N.C. only for the very real results which the Congo gained by our employment, but he was not going to permit our dismissal at the wrong moment. The President's statement at Accra had been made entirely without the knowledge or prior agreement of the Commander-in-Chief. He demanded at once to have it rebutted. The unfortunate task fell to the new Prime Minister, Mr. Kimba, who duly explained over Radio Leopoldville that what the President actually meant was that European mercenaries, who were not part of the A.N.C., were to be sent home, and that there was no intention of sending the others home until the Congo had been thoroughly pacified. It would have been difficult to determine exactly to whom Mr. Kimba was referring, but he managed to smooth over the breach and an outward peace was restored.

The episode was important in that it showed plainly that the President had emerged from his cocoon and intended to use his almost dictatorial powers without consultation with the Commander-in-Chief, or anybody else. This caused a rift in the lute of friendship between Kasavubu and Mobutu and their hitherto cordial, if somewhat remote, relationship underwent a marked and noticeable estrangement.

It is possible that the President regretted his unilateral action, for a few days later it was announced, somewhat unexpectedly, that Kasavubu had decided to raise Major-General Mobutu to the rank of Lieut.-General, with effect from 1st January 1965. Perhaps it was a douceur, perhaps not. Another body of opinion held that it was a necessary promotion, in order to make the Commander-in-Chief senior to the new Belgian General, who was now about to arrive in the Congo. I favoured the former supposition.

Aided and abetted by Mr. Nendaka, who was becoming exceedingly active, the President concluded his talks with the Brazzaville Congo and, in due course, the ferry service between the two cities across the mile wide Congo River began again. The entente was heralded as a political triumph for Kasavubu. General Mobutu, however, was fully aware of the dangers inherent in the situation. I represented to him that we were not happy risking our lives to keep out Communist infiltration in the east of the Congo, only to have the same result, by invitation, in the west and very heart of the country.

The General was well advised of the explosive situation that existed in the many large communes of the City of Leopoldville, and appreciated the dangers arising from the fact that one and a quarter million Congolese were now living, where in previous and more settled times, four hundred thousand found shelter. A few skilled Communist agitators amongst the many thousand unemployed, most of whom subsisted below the bread line, could blow Leopoldville sky high.

The General was sympathetic to any observations I had to make and gave them all due consideration. He was never too busy to examine a viewpoint, different perhaps from his own, and his ability to sift and weigh the evidence of conflicting reports, marked him in my estimation as a statesman in the foremost rank. I like to think also, that by this time a more personal and friendly relationship had grown up between us and of this I was humbly and justly proud.

Maj.-General Delperdange duly arrived from Belgium and, to mark the occasion of his promotion to Lieut.-General, the Commander-in-Chief invited us both, with many others, to lunch at his residence. I noted with pleasure that it was a large house and had two sentries outside it! I admired the General's home, his new tiled swimming

pool and his sumptuous and graceful mode of living. The General
had an easy manner off-stage and made a happy picture of domes-
ticity, bouncing his delightful little four months' old baby girl on his
knee, whilst chatting inconsequentially to a number of visiting
dignitaries.

Lunch itself was a delightful affair with excellent wines and
delicious meat. My mind flashed guiltily back to Baraka, as I
accepted a second helping of venison and I wondered how my boys
were doing and if the old goats were still holding out!

I foresaw in the arrival of General Delperdange the first step in
the implementation of a new policy in Leo Deux. The Commander-
in-Chief had grown in political stature during the last fifteen months,
out of all proportion to those surrounding him. His successes in the
field and his reorganisation of the Armée Nationale Congolaise,
which now virtually administered two-thirds of the country by
direct military law, placed him in a position of exceptional power.
The day to day management of the Army and the close watch he
maintained on excesses of a financial nature, peccadilloes to which
so many of his subordinates were prone, left him little time for the
greater tasks of leadership. I surmised that the arrival of General
Delperdange was intended to free him to take a greater part in the
running of the country.

The Belgian General was lithe, grey haired and likeable. He had
a quiet sense of humour and the simple touch, which marks out the
truly great amongst soldiers and statesmen. He had abundant
patience—which he would certainly need in the Congo—and was a
good listener. Watching him, I gained the impression of a man with
the restrained energy of a caged panther. He was precisely the man
needed by the Commander-in-Chief for the formidable tasks which
lay ahead.

I had been invited to attend the big formal parade at Camp
Kokolo that morning, at which the Commander-in-Chief would be
formally elevated to the rank of Lieut.-General by the President.
The very fact of the invitation was not lost on me and was accepted
with great pleasure.

General Delperdange picked me up in his car at the Memling
Hotel and took me out to Camp Kokolo, where we separated in
deference to military protocol, he to a seat next to the General, me
to a seat amongst the Lieut.-Colonels. I was the only officer present

in khaki drill, with my sleeves rolled up, all others were immaculate in service dress, black belts and white gloves. I felt like Cinderella.

The parade was at the usual high standard of the A.N.C. on ceremonial occasions, and compared favourably with the Brigade of Guards, which is the greatest compliment I can pay them. Five battalions formed a hollow square around the edge of the parade ground and awaited the President. Fanfares of trumpets announced his arrival. The first boom of an eighty-gun salute blasted out from a far corner of the parade ground. Instinctively one man on the "tribunal" ducked. It was me. The President read the citation, which was markedly short and formal, the troops marched past, officers saluted with drawn swords, there was a special cheer for "Mobutu's Own"—the crack Parachute battalion led by the exceptional Major Bumba—and the parade was over.

# 20

## A FAREWELL TO ARMS

Events had come to pass more or less as we had expected after the fall of Fizi and Baraka. As far as Leopoldville was concerned, the war was over. On an international level, our forecasts had proved correct. Tanzania halted the supply of arms through Kigoma; Uganda made overtures of friendship towards the Congo; the Sudan, too occupied with the rebellion of its own subjects in the south to concern itself further with aiding the Congolese rebels, told them to quit the country at once. Further south, Mr. Ian Smith declared Rhodesia independent of the British Government, but the Congo was too busy with its own affairs to pay more than lip service to the strident O.A.U. resolution that all African States should use force to oust the Smith régime.

In short, the external political position of the Congo was as stable, or not as unstable, as it had been for years. Internally, however, all was not well. As foreseen, the opening of the river crossing to Brazzaville brought turmoil in its wake. Gangs of unruly youths marched down the Boulevard Trente Juin and desecrated the statue of King Leopold II; other gangs burnt the Belgian flag before the House of Assembly; hand grenades exploded in Congolese bars in the communes. That this was the work of Congolese politicians, aided and abetted by factions from across the river, there could be no doubt. Only the gullible were persuaded that the demonstrations were of a truly spontaneous character and had as their origin some deep rooted discontent with the present order. That there was a guiding hand behind it all soon became apparent.

Victor Nendaka chose this moment to pour petrol on the flames of discontent by broadcasting an inflammatory speech in Lingala (the language used by the Armée Nationale Congolaise), in which he attacked Europeans in the Congo generally and Belgians who were employed in the Army Technical Assistance programme specifically. The whole of Leopoldville bubbled with the expectation of political strife and an atmosphere of unrest dropped on the City like a heavily laden rain cloud, due to burst at any moment.

In the middle of this turmoil Mr. Nendaka, as Minister of Security, claimed to have uncovered a plot by certain Belgian officers to bring Mr. Tshombe back into power again. The two officers allegedly involved were summarily dismissed and expelled from the Congo at twenty-four hours' notice. Lieut.-Colonel Lamouline, who was in command of 6 Commando, and Major Protin of the Judge Advocate General's Department were the ones involved. Lamouline was a mild and pleasant man with a singularly confidential manner and, from my knowledge of him, I would have given him a very low rating as an intriguer. In any case, he was within days of the end of his term in the Congo. The handsome Major Protin, the saviour of Manono in 1961, was a highly experienced officer and, in my view, quite incapable of the stupid acts accredited to him. However, they both went at short notice, and it says much for both of them that on their return to Brussels, they denied themselves the pleasure of vituperation through the Press.

This episode, the burning of the Belgian flag, and the acts of hooliganism, which were now occurring with alarming frequency in the City, all added up to one thing. The body politic in Leopoldville was rotten and in need of urgent surgery. The man with the knife was on the way.

It was the evening of 24th November and the anniversary of the Stanleyville massacre. I had just finished my business with the Commander-in-Chief and General Delperdange and noticed that the General's waiting-room was unusually full of senior Army officers. General Bobozo and all other Group Commanders had been called to Leopoldville to attend a routine conference.

At five o'clock the next morning the telephone rang in my bedroom at the Memling. It was John Powis breathlessly asking me if I had heard the news. The General had executed a military *coup d'état*! At the meeting of the Army Commanders the previous evening, it had been decided that the political situation had got out of hand and it was time for the Army to take over. Radio Stanleyville announced that General Mobutu had declared a "State of Exception", had dismissed President Kasavubu and taken over the duties of President himself. Parliament was suspended for the moment, but would meet again later that day to hear the General's plans for the running of the country.

The coup was completely bloodless. Small groups of A.N.C. patrolled the streets and an armed guard was placed on the Post Office, one of whom slept fitfully throughout the day. Leopoldville was calm.

I had lunch with the new President the next day. I formed the distinct impression that the coup had been a decision on the part of the Army Commanders which had generated itself from their deliberations, and was not in any way premeditated. It was an extremely well kept secret and there was not a single European in the know. The ex-President was placed under a mild form of house arrest and had already signified that he was prepared to abide by the results of the coup.

History had repeated itself. For the second time in just over five years General Mobutu, "the weakest strong man in history", had decided to take action to save the Congo from the machinations of its politicians. In his declaration to Congress, which met on the afternoon of 25th November, he said:

> "During the last five years the national politicians have not been able to put an end to the anarchy gripping the Congo. This situation has been deliberately maintained by the politicians and has been exploited by certain foreigners, despite the watchfulness of the Army Headquarters. As a result the Army High Command has taken upon itself the conduct of the State."

The General went on to make certain fundamental dispositions, the first being the declaration of a "Régime of Exception" as from 24th November, and the cessation of the previous Government as from that day. He himself, as Commander-in-Chief, would take over the duties of President, and lastly, the new Government would consist of a maximum number of twenty-two specially chosen delegates.

The Prime Minister was to be Colonel Mulamba and all posts of importance would be given to Army Officers, who would run the country under a Military Government. Lieut.-Colonel Ferdinand Malila, the popular Chief of Staff at A.N.C. Headquarters, was appointed Head of Information Services with direct control over all Broadcasting.

The new Prime Minister began at once to form a Government and within three days he had interviewed the representatives of all the provinces and made a tentative selection of delegates for the General's approval. With surprisingly little fuss or show of emotion, the new Government did as it was told and took over its duties.

Once more, the General had gauged the mood of the population exactly and acted promptly in accordance with what he knew to be their wish, unspoken though it may have been. That drastic action of this sort was necessary had become abundantly evident in Leopoldville in the last few weeks, but that the coup should have been a military one and have taken place so quietly and successfully, came as a surprise to the outside world. It was, however, only a logical development of the situation.

The Army was fortunate in that it had an efficient administration, free from political interference. Its clear-cut methods had been handed down to it by the old Force Publique and a chain of command, good system of communications, and a reasonable standard of discipline obtained throughout. The Army represented, in effect, the only system of administration which had shown itself capable of government, the civilian system having broken down under the strain of events and the junketings of unscrupulous politicians. To make matters worse, the civilian machine had been fraught with office seekers, opportunists, financial mendicants, and politicians whose sole aim in life was not service, but personal aggrandisement.

In fairness to the politicians, it could be said that no pattern of behaviour existed for them to copy, they had received literally no training for executive positions or administrative matters at the higher levels, and to them political appointment represented the ultimate in African sophistication, coupled, as it was seen to be, with instant acclaim, great wealth, and fantastic power.

As part of his general overhaul of the Army during the last fourteen months, the Commander-in-Chief had introduced a Judge Advocate General's Department and placed it under a distinguished Belgian Officer, Colonel Van Hallowen. It was a brilliant move. In the first few months of its existence the J.A.G.'s Department tightened up control throughout the Army and court martialled several highly placed officers and Military Governors for defalcations of large sums of money, many of whom were sentenced to terms of imprisonment exceeding eight years. On the civilian side no strong judiciary existed to deal with matters of this sort, which were reported in the Congolese Press with monotonous regularity. It has been held that an African politician, who begins life with literally nothing, cannot really govern his fellows dispassionately until he places himself beyond the needs of day to day living. I am inclined to agree with this theory, but some Congolese politicians were carrying the thing to absurd limits.

The strong hold the Army had on excesses of this nature assisted it, when the crunch finally came, to emerge as the saviour of the country. The fact that this military coup set the pattern for similar coups throughout Africa, indicated that there was a need for a more stringent self discipline amongst African politicians generally. When the politicians have digested this lesson, so ably taught them by the Army in various countries, one has no doubt that the destinies of their countries will be handed back to them.

It was an unhappy return to Albertville for me. My good friend of three campaigns had been killed the night before in a jeep accident. The gallant Hans von Lieres, after braving battle in all parts of the Congo, had met his death through an unlighted and badly parked truck in the main street of Albertville. Hans had had a presentiment of his death only a few days previously and sent in a resignation, with a request for immediate repatriation. This I had willingly approved, nobody could have done more than he had done for 5 Commando and the Congo, and he was due to leave for Johannesburg the following day.

The mechanics of handing over to John Peters were completed in quick time and all that remained was for me to say good-bye to my men and to return once more to Leopoldville to take leave of the General. I regretted that it was not possible to see my troops individually, strung out as they were in the middle of operations from Baraka to Fizi, but I sent them a farewell message which ended:

"During the course of the four glorious campaigns which we have fought together as comrades in arms, 5 Commando has helped to alter the course of history and change the face of the Congo for the better. It is a record of which we may be justly proud. I salute you all."

I said good-bye to John Peters with very sincere regrets and inadequate thanks for all his efforts on my behalf and for the unit.

It was his responsibility now and I could not have given 5 Commando over into safer hands.

With a last look at the bay and the lake which had held so much adventure, heartbreak and tragedy for me in the last eighteen months, I boarded an aircraft for Leopoldville.

The massive Congo lay calm and peaceful beneath us in the afternoon sun, straddled with lazy brown rivers and startlingly green patches of virgin forest. I had covered the country from end to end many times during my tour of duty and been to out-of-the-way places, which no tourist or settler would have the occasion or wish to visit. The map of the Congo was imprinted indelibly on the soles of my feet; the exciting and colourful land had taken a grip on my imagination and I would be sorry to leave it.

I had made some effort to study the history of the Congo, the better to know its problems, but had succeeded only in scratching the surface of past events and acquainting myself with their complexity. It had been fashionable at one time in Europe, particularly after the war when the Belgians were winning the race to reconstruct their country after years of German occupation, to accuse the Belgians of using the Congo as their milch cow. Whatever the truth of that may be, in my journeying around the Congo I had seen with my own eyes ample evidence of an enormous Belgian investment in the country, both in money and in labour. Beautiful towns and cities with prosperous and thriving industries had been won from the suffocating equatorial jungle. Magnificent schools and missions had arisen, where once there had been nothing but disease and pestilence. Every village now boasted its own clinic. No village was so humble but it possessed its own water pump, invariably marked F.B.I.—a gift from the Belgian people. It was a record of which the Belgian people could be proud.

One thing stood out clearly in my mind—the Belgian presence in the Congo from the earliest beginnings of the Congo Free State, though the era of the Congo Belge from 1908 to the granting of Independence on 30th June 1960, was an epoch of achievement in Africa which no other country can equal.

The fantastic size of the Congo in itself was sufficient to daunt any but the stoutest hearts, but the Belgians had succeeded in bringing stability to the country and had given it an Administration which was the envy of the whole of Africa. Certainly they made their errors. What colonial power did not? If their policy towards the political advancement of the Congolese people erred on the side of paternalism, who could have foretold what tremendous strides the African peoples generally were to make after World War Two? If the premature granting of Independence found the Congolese people untrained and unready to assume the responsibilities of self-government, it was in my mind, a debit to be set against the enormous credit of having led the Congo thus far and of having handed it over economically viable, united and internally at peace.[1]

The troubles which have arisen in the Congo since Independence are of Congolese making. They were not inherited on the formation of the Democratic Republic from the former Congo Belge. This has led some observers to remark that the Congo cannot exist in its present form without the unifying presence of some external power, such as Belgium, for instance. The peoples are too varied and the country too vast, is their general contention. Leopoldville is too remote as the seat of Government for people one thousand miles away in Orientale or Katanga, and the Congolese will never knit their two hundred and twenty odd tribes into a single Congolese people, with one national outlook. The same body of opinion concludes that the Congo is, in fact, not one, but three countries. I am inclined to agree, but with certain reservations. From my small experience of the Congo, I can visualise the country divided into three parts—Orientale and Kivu as one, Katanga another, and the rest as the third. If each were economically viable and self-supporting, this arrangement might prove satisfactory and would certainly fulfil many nationalistic aspirations, but as they are not and never can be, it seems that a Federal form of Government may be the next best thing.

[1] F.B.I.—the Fonds du Bien-Etre Indigène—"was founded in 1947 for the purpose of improving native living conditions in the Congo. Spending at the rate of 300 million francs or 6 million dollars per year on approximately twenty thousand projects, the F.B.I. in its first ten years constructed 28 hospitals, 369 dispensaries, 118 maternity hospitals, 124 consultation centres for children, 15 orphan asylums, 5 sanatoria, and 17 equipped medical centres. It provided 242 ambulances . . . gave 60 million francs to the building and improvement of centres for treating leprosy, established three campaigns for insect examination and hygiene, and distributed 220,000 pounds of powdered milk throughout the Congo. It set up at least one fish breeding centre in each province and its programme totalled 8 such centres and 610 fisheries and ponds. Cattle raising centres were established, and stables and smaller centres were built in smaller communities. Community barns and warehouses were constructed, anti-erosion campaigns undertaken, experiments in light mechanisation for agriculture conducted, and agricultural schools established. This is truly a remarkable record."—Merriam, *Congo : Background of Conflict.*

The effects of the too hasty Independence have certainly been far reaching and calamitious, but it is not too late to make amends. The salvation of the Congo, as I see it, will be the reintroduction of as many Europeans as are prepared to emigrate to the country to become part of the fabric of the Congo, to help the Congolese on the road to political maturity and to teach them the skills of commerce and administration. These immigrants must come with a new mind—not as "*agents sous contrats*", the iniquitous Belgian system[1] —but as settlers, as white Congolese, who will take a pride in their adopted country and who will come not with any superior colonialistic ideas, but with the genuine desire to help the Congolese help themselves; not as masters of the Congolese, but on an equal footing with them in all respects. And there are many thousands of capable and enthusiastic Belgians, Frenchmen, and other French speaking Europeans, who would jump at the chance.

If the Congo is allowed by one means or another to fall a prey to the Communist invasion, which is now beginning, Africa will be the scene of untold misery within the next thirty years. The Congolese may do worse than consider the advisability of encouraging immigration from Europe for settlement in the eastern side of the country, between Bunia and Bukavu, if only as a buffer to counter Communist infiltration and to be a source of strength in time of trouble. The country is certainly hospitable enough and that part of the Congo is undeniably the most beautiful and healthy part of Africa.

I said good-bye to the President the next day. He was busy with his new duties, but never too busy, he said, to welcome me and to thank me for my services to the Congo, which he personally greatly appreciated. Would I come back again if he should ever need me? I answered that one by saying that with the General at the helm, it would never be necessary. I sincerely hoped not, anyway.

He had been expecting me and handed me a letter which I read at once. It said:

[1] The large concessionary companies operating in the Congo recruited their technicians and executives almost exclusively in Belgium and sent them out as "*agents sous contrats*." The usual period was for three years with long leave at the end of it. Many agents came back for a second or third tour but they were never encouraged to settle in the Congo. In addition no white man, or black man, had any vote or say in the future of the country with the result that the agents took a rather detached and disinterested view of Congolese affairs, and regarded the Congo merely as a place to work hard in so that they might save enough money out of their exceptionall good salaries to enable them to return to Belgium for an early retirement.

"My dear Colonel,

It is with a sincere and profound regret that I see you are about to leave the Congo, which you have served for two years, and where so many of your men have fallen in its service.

The Congolese nation owes you a great deal, and will keep of you, a living and very edifying remembrance.

As for myself, and all the Commanders of Army Groups, who have had the honour to have you under their orders, we know that we can always count on you in case of need.

A man of your character cannot remain deaf to the call of his friends.

Furthermore, you will learn with the passing of time and distance, that the Congo is a country that you cannot forget easily. Sooner or later you will return here.

I want you to know that you will always be welcome here and that at all times, my house will be open to you.

That is why I do not say 'Adieu' but 'Au revoir', my dear Colonel Hoare.

President of the Republic
MOBUTU, J. D.
Lieutenant-General."

It was a letter which I appreciated deeply and I took my final leave of the General with every best wish for his success in the future. If the Congo is to succeed in taking its place amongst the great nations of Africa, it will be largely as a result of the efforts of this great man. I left his chamber realising that I had been privileged to spend some short months in the presence of one of the truly great Africans of our time, and one for whom I had nothing but unstinted admiration and praise.

Alastair and I visited Mr. Tshombe at his home at Binza to say farewell. It was a sad occasion. The old smile and the well-known Tshombe affability were still there, but the great diplomat was tired and needed a rest. He would be on his way to Europe in a few days, he said, and we must keep in touch. He liked to know how his friends were getting along.

I shook his hand and thought back to the evening at Kalina, when he had told me I was his man of destiny. So much had happened in the interval, but who could have foreseen that in his moment of triumph he would have been ousted from office, because he had carried out his duties too successfully.

He was standing at his gate as we turned the corner and he waved good-bye. It was something in my life to have known and

**FORCES ARMEES CONGOLAISES**
**ETAT - MAJOR GENERAL**

Leopoldville, le 26 Novembre 1965.

**LE GENERAL**

Mon cher Colonel,

                    C'est avec un sincère et profond regret, que je vous vois quitter cette terre congolaise que vous servez depuis bientôt 2 ans, et où tant des vôtres, sont tombés, en service commandé.

                    La Nation Congolaise vous doit beaucoup, et gardera de vous, un vivant et très édifiant souvenir.

                    Quant à moi, et aux Commandants de groupements, qui ont eu l'honneur de vous avoir sous leurs ordres, nous savons que nous pourrons toujours compter sur vous, en cas de besoin.

                    Un homme de votre trempe, ne peut rester sourd à l'appel de ses amis.

                    De plus, vous apprendrez avec le temps et l'éloignement, que le Congo est une terre qu'on n'oublie pas facilement. Tôt ou tard vous y reviendrez.

                    Sachez que vous y serez toujours le bien-venu, et qu'à tout moment, ma maison vous sera ouverte.

                    C'est pourquoi, je ne vous dis pas "Adieu", mais "Au revoir" cher Colonel HOARE.

                                Le President de la République
                                      MOBUTU, J.D.
                                    Lieutenant-Général

Au Colonel HOARE
    DURBAN
        AFRIQUE DU SUD.

worked with the great man, and I wondered if we would ever meet again. The Congo needed him and I felt sure he would return one day to take his part in the great struggle ahead of the Congolese people.

It was Ndjili again for the last time. The Sabena Boeing waited for us in the watery sun. A loudspeaker announced the departure of Air Congo Flight number Q.C. 466 for Colquilhatville—Boende—Lisala—Bumba—Stanleyville—Bunia. It sounded like a list of 5 Commando Battle Honours. The reception hall was filled with gay and laughing Congolese moving around the length and breadth of their country. Eighteen months ago this would have been impossible.

It was a cold clear morning as we walked across the tarmac. High up in the cloudless sky far above us a long, straggling, strident arrowhead of birds, answering the unknown call of nature, battled their way into the wind.

The Wild Geese were going home.

# APPENDIX 1

## Note on the political history of the Congo

The year 1956 heralded the dawn of political consciousness in the Belgian Congo. Since 1908 the colony had been ruled exclusively from Brussels through a governor-general who legislated by decree. No Congolese had a vote, neither did any of the 10,000 European settlers. There were no politics and no politicians. In 1956, however, political thinking in the Congo received a sudden impetus through the publication in Belgium of a paper entitled "A Thirty-year Plan for the Emancipation of Belgian Africa" by Professor A. J. van Bilsen. This was in fact a time-table for independence.

The paper was enthusiastically received in the Congo by a group of serious minded Catholic students who issued a manifesto accepting the thirty-year period as reasonable and setting out the ultimate aim of a non-racial Congolese nation made up of Congolese and European citizens each on an equal footing.

The manifesto was vigorously challenged by a cultural group called ABAKO, which emerged later as a political party headed by Joseph Kasavubu. They rejected the thirty-year plan and demanded immediate independence for the people of the Lower Congo. Professor Bilsen's "thirty-year plan" stimulated a desire for political expression which then broke out across the face of the Congo in a rash of minor parties mostly with regional or ethnic bases. At this stage there was no truly nationalistic party and such nationalism as was discernable arose from tribal reaction to government from a remote centre and was invariably a form of protest against the artificial unity imposed upon the country by the colonial presence.

The overall political picture in Africa encouraged Congolese political aspirations. Britain had announced her plans for Ghana's independence; France had decided to give autonomy to large areas of Africa; and in nearby Brazzaville President de Gaulle proclaimed that any French possession could have independence that wanted it. Finally in Belgium, the new Government declared that its policy towards the Congo was to be "decolonization".

In due course four main political parties emerged. The ABAKO, essentially a tribal party, had as their main policy immediate independence for the Lower Congo. The CONAKAT, headed by a prominent business man, Mr. Moise Tshombe, was also a tribal grouping, and represented immensely wealthy southern Katanga. Their policy was federation of

T

the provinces peopled by a Belgo-Congolese community. The M.N.C.—Mouvement National Congolais—was the only party to claim a national outlook and it strove to create a nationalism transcending tribal and regional interests which it regarded as old-fashioned. Patrice Lumumba was the leader of this party and had already proved himself to be capable if somewhat unbalanced in his judgement. The P.N.P.—Parti National du Progres—was very moderate in all its aims and advocated a unitary state whilst stressing respect for traditional authority and co-operation with Belgium. Paul Bolya and Albert Delvaux were the leaders.

The extreme views of ABAKO as expressed by Kasavubu caused some concern in Belgium so that when the conference of Independent African Peoples was held in Accra in December 1958 Kasavubu was not permitted to attend. Patrice Lumumba, however, scored a great personal victory and returned to the Congo inspired by President Nkrumah's ideals and methods and convinced that his mission was to lead the Congolese people to independence at once.

Political agitation and considerable unemployment gave rise to an explosive situation in Leopoldville which reached flash-point in January 1959 and resulted in riots, arson and bloodshed. A few days later King Baudouin announced Belgium's intention to confer independence on the Congo and in due course a programme to this effect was published. This was accepted in principle by all parties except ABAKO.

Rioting occurred in Stanleyville in October and Lumumba was imprisoned. Fighting broke out in Kasai and the whole of the Bas Congo seethed with discontent. Many of the European population, which now exceeded 120,000, began to leave the Congo.

In January 1960 Belgium convened a round table conference in Brussels and invited representatives of the fourteen main political parties in the Congo, representatives of the tribal chiefs, and all three political parties in Belgium. Despite the gap in political thinking which existed amongst the Congolese—from the 80 per cent who respected traditional authority to the 20 per cent who were the new leaders of the evolué type—all parties united in their demand for immediate independence.

In the face of this overwhelming and unanimous demand the Belgian Government decided to grant independence to the Congo on 30th June 1960—a bare four months ahead. The decision was greatly influenced by the prevailing sentiment at home, strong pressure from the United Nations and the anti-colonialist attitude adopted by the United States of America. Any delay in granting independence, no matter how obvious it was that it was alarmingly premature, would most certainly have resulted in turmoil and revolt in the Congo.

Dissension arose, however, at the conference, over the proposed constitution. Those parties which favoured a form of federalism—and ABAKO was now one of them—were opposed to the suggested constitution which was entirely in favour of a centralised government—in fact the policy of Lumumba's party, the M.N.C.—but they finally accepted it on the understanding that it was purely a transitional measure and that the Congolese Government itself would ultimately decide on the type of constitution which would suit the country best. The elections for the new government were held a few weeks before independence and resulted in a victory for M.N.C. which could count on 41 votes out of a total of 137 in the lower chamber. Although the results did not give Lumumba's party a clear-cut majority over the remainder of the parties, nevertheless Lumumba was the obvious choice as the first Prime Minister of the Congo and he was summoned to form a government. After an initial failure Lumumba finally succeeded in forming a government drawn from fourteen different parties and nominated Joseph Kasavubu as the first President of the Congo.

On the 30th June 1960, at an impressive Independence Day ceremony, King Baudouin of the Belgians officially handed over the Instruments of Independence to the new Congolese Government and ended fifty-two years of Belgian rule in the Congo.

Within four days of taking office the new government were faced with a major crisis—the mutiny of the Force Publique. All over the country army units arose against their Belgian officers, imprisoned them, raped their wives, and stole their belongings. The root cause of the mutiny was held to be the average soldier's dissatisfaction with his lot. Civilians were thought to have benefited materially by independence but there had been no corresponding improvements for the Army, no increase in salary, no promotions to officer rank and apparently none intended.

Two days later Premier Lumumba broadcast that the senior Belgian officers of the Force Publique were responsible for the mutiny and declared that Belgium was plotting to reannexe the Congo. The immediate result was a mass exodus of Europeans and further rioting. In the absence of any form of law and order the Belgian Government sent Belgian troops to the country to protect the lives and property of its citizens. On their arrival Lumumba denounced them as "forces of aggression" and on 12th July formally requested the U.N. to send military aid to the Congo immediately.

The Security Council passed a resolution calling upon Belgium to withdraw its troops at once and authorised the U.N. to provide a force to keep the peace in the Congo. In the eyes of the world Belgium was thus labelled an aggressor and many of the troubles which arose in the Congo in the course of the next few months flowed from this early misconception.

In Katanga on 11th July, Mr. Moise Tshombe, alarmed by the spread of disorder throughout the Congo seized on the opportunity to declare the Province of Katanga an Independent State, expelled mutinous elements of the Force Publique and raised his own force of gendarmerie.

On 15th July United Nations troops began to arrive and Belgian troops to depart. Prime Minister Lumumba flew off to New York roundly to denounce Belgium as an aggressor at United Nations, attacked Mr. Hammarskold, and returned to the Congo to declare martial law and imprison a number of his political opponents.

Confidence in the Central Government broke down completely and on 7th August ABAKO demanded a Confederation of the Six Provinces, whilst PUNA—a party in opposition to ABAKO and CONAKAT—passed a similar resolution. Two days later the "Mining State of South Kasai" under their leader Albert Kalonji, declared themselves independent of the central government.

On 15th August, Lumumba, dissatisfied with the nature of U.N. aid and their apparent refusal to crush the rebel régimes in Katanga and Kasai on his behalf, appealed to the Russians for military assistance for this very purpose. Russian and Czech technicians poured into Leopoldville and on the 3rd September nineteen Illyushin aircraft arrived in Leo with sufficient transport and equipment to enable Lumumba's troops to march on Kasai. In the fighting which followed over 3,000 Baluba were killed and 300 chiefs and notables done to death for alleged political offences. Lumumba then ordered his army to attack Katanga but his troops were repulsed at the border.

Lumumba had now reached the high water mark of his career. His appeal to Russia for military aid had reacted unfavourably against him wherever moderate councils prevailed and on 5th September President Kasavubu dismissed him in favour of the milder Mr. Ileo. Lumumba fled but was arrested en route for Stanleyville and placed under house arrest in Leopoldville.

On 14th September Colonel Joseph Mobutu, who had been promoted Commander-in-Chief of the Army, disturbed by the administrative chaos which was fast overtaking the country, formed a team of university graduates and students, suspended the Government and declared that his "Administrative College" would run the country for the next four months. At the same time he ordered the Russian and Czech Embassies to close and demanded the withdrawal of the Ghana and Guinea contingents from the U.N. forces in the Congo.

The communist-inclined element in the Government withdrew to far-off Stanleyville where, under the direction of Antoine Gizenga they staged a *coup d'état*, deposed the provincial authorities and set up their own government. Gizenga declared himself the political heir to Patrice Lumumba and claimed that his was the only legal government in the Congo, a claim supported by the Soviet bloc but refuted at the United Nations.

During January Lumumba escaped from custody, was apprehended at Port Francqui and put on an aeroplane for Elizabethville where he arrived half dead having been beaten up by his guards on the way. A month later the Katanga Government announced that he had been shot by tribesmen whilst attempting to escape. The news of his death reverberated around the globe and in many countries Lumumba was proclaimed a martyr of African nationalism.

On 8th March an all-party conference took place at Tananarive on the island of Madagascar. The meeting rejected the U.N. Security Council resolution of 21st February which demanded the immediate withdrawal of foreign political and military advisers, and declared itself in favour of a confederal constitution for the Congo. Finally it demanded the withdrawal of U.N. troops.

The Tananarive Conference marked the turning point in U.N. policy in the Congo. Up until that moment it had performed a somewhat negative role, merely replacing the Belgian forces in order to avoid a vacuum, and trying not to interfere in internal Congolese affairs more than was necessary. Their policy now hardened in favour of a positive intervention in Katanga to force that province to submit to the Leopold-ville Government.

In April the U.N. persuaded President Kasavubu to implement the U.N. resolution of 21st February, at the same time promising him much needed financial assistance. The Tananarive Agreement was repudiated by Kasavubu which led Mr. Tshombe to declare at a conference in Coquilhatville on 23rd April that he had been betrayed. He was promptly arrested and imprisoned near Leopoldville, but finally released two months later at the instigation of Joseph Mobutu.

Katanga was then left in isolation for the moment whilst attempts were made to unify the remainder of the Congo. To this end, and under the guidance of the United Nations, a new government was formed in June headed by Cyrille Adoulla, with the key posts of Vice-Premier and Minister of the Interior going to Antoine Gizenga and Christopher Gbenye respectively, both of whom had been weaned away from Stanley-ville for the purpose. The immediate result was a massive influx of foreign communists into Leopoldville and the reopening of the Russian and Czech Embassies.

Now that the country had apparent unity it tackled the outstanding problem of Katanga's secession. On 28th August Mr. Conor Cruise O'Brien, the U.N. Representative in Katanga, issued an ultimatum to Mr. Tshombe to submit to the Central Government. This was rejected and U.N. troops were ordered to use whatever force was required to arrest mercenary troops and certain Katangese Ministers in Elizabeth-ville. The use of force by the United Nations for the first time in its history created a furore throughout the world and on 17th September the Secretary-General Dag Hammarskold decided to pay Mr Tshombe a personal visit to resolve the whole matter at first hand. As his plane made its final approach to Ndola Airport it crashed into some trees killing everybody on board.

Once more the National Army made an attempt to invade Katanga and was repulsed. Troops from Stanleyville, however, had more success and occupied Albertville, whilst terrorists of the Baluba *jeunesse* harried the north Katanga border and finally perpetrated an appalling crime at Kongolo where they killed twenty-two Catholic priests, most of them Belgians.

In November the U.N. authorised more drastic action to settle the Katanga problem and on 5th December a full scale operation took place against Elizabethville supported by U.N. bombers and fighter aircraft which hit non-military targets as far afield as Kolwezi and Shinkolobwe. U.N. troops were ferried into Elizabethville by United States air transports. Later, the U.N. forces were charged with committing atrocities during the fighting, the most flagrant being the killing of a senior Red Cross official whilst going about his duties in a plainly marked Red Cross car.

Finally, the British Government—who had already refused to supply the U.N. Command with 1,000-lb. bombs for use against Elizabethville—arranged a cease fire and brought Mr. Tshombe and Mr. Adoulla together at Kitona where Mr. Tshombe signed an eight point agreement which purported to end Katanga's secession. Clause five of the agreement stated that Katangese representatives would take part in a government commission to prepare a new constitution.

Gizenga meanwhile had hived off to Stanleyville and once more refused to take part in the present government. Adoula visited the U.N. again February 1963 to drum up support for stronger action against Katanga which was still holding out against the central Government despite the Kitona Agreement. Adoulla met with some success in New York and in particular from the United States Government who were fearful that the existence of a separatist State such as Katanga might be the excuse for communist intervention in the Congo. The U.S. also agreed to give Adoulla substantial financial aid.

United Nations action came to a head in December 1962 when a full scale invasion of Katanga took place by U.N. forces spearheaded by Indian and Ghurka troops, which finally brought the independent state of Katanga to its knees and once more under the control of the central government. Mr. Tshombe then exiled himself voluntarily in Spain.

The separatist movement in Stanleyville, however, continued to defy the Government and gathered around itself its own armed forces—still ostensibly part of the A.N.C.—which rapidly became a byword for terrorism in the whole of Orientale and Kivu provinces.

Early 1964 witnessed the first rumblings of a Communist inspired revolution in the Kwilu Province which blossomed forth into a full scale rebellion in May and June. Two-thirds of the country was under rebel control and the national Army was retreating on all fronts. The U.N. forces were in no mood or position to assist in the internal crisis and at the end of June 1964, after nearly four years in the Congo, they took their departure. Unexpectedly Mr. Tshombe was invited back to be the new Prime Minister of a government which would attempt to reconcile all political parties in the Congo and unify the country.

# APPENDIX 2

Exchange of telegrams between the International Red Cross and members of the Government of the Republique Populaire du Congo on the subject of the Stanleyville hostages.

1. President Gbenye from Mr. Senn, Chief Delegate, International Red Cross, 25th September 1964.
Chief Delegate Senn on board Red Cross plane thanks President Gbenye for welcoming Red Cross Mission. Crew and doctors all Swiss. Senn wishes to meet at the airport [Stanleyville] President Gbenye and Minister Soumiallot and Commander of the Army.

2. Mr. Senn from Government of the R.P.C., 25th September 1964.
You will find at the airport delegate of the Government Minister Soumiallot and Commander of the Army Colonel Opepe.

3. President Gbenye from Mr. Senn, 28th September 1964.
Senn thanks President Gbenye for his reception. He has taken note of his communication over Stan Radio announcing that the Popular Government of the Congo accepts repatriation of foreigners in the following categories: first sickness; second humanitarian cases; third foreigners wishing to leave the Congo for good. We propose to begin evacuation immediately. First the sick, second scholars and students who must begin school elsewhere than Stan, third humanitarian cases. Want you to indicate to us what day we can begin evacuation. Awaiting your reply urgently. Compliments.

4. Mr. Senn from President Gbenye, Stan, 29th September 1964.
Repatriation of foreigners to be at the instance of ad hoc commissions following our mutual agreement. Will inform you as soon as the list is ready. Compliments.

5. President Gbenye from Mr. Senn, Bangui, 29th September 1964.
Senn thanks the President for his reply however after consultations with Geneva he must insist that your Government no longer stops the repatriation of foreigners whom it has agreed are not taking part in the Congolese conflict. In particular we propose 1st October for the departure of the first echelon composed of those sick people whose sickness has been diagnosed beyond doubt and of the young

people who ought to rejoin their schools. You will recall that the actions of the Red Cross cover both parties to the conflict. Compliments.

6. **Mr. Senn from President Gbenye, Stan, 29th September 1964.**
As soon as the ad hoc commission has its first meeting you will be informed of the exact date evacuation first contingent. Compliments.

7. **President Gbenye from Red Cross, Bujumbura, 30th September 1964.**
Senn thanks you for your message announcing repatriation as soon as list established by ad hoc commission [but] after consultation with Geneva he insists that your Government no longer retards the repatriation of the group of foreigners whom it has been agreed are not taking part in the tragic Congolese conflict. We propose the departure of the first echelon of repatriates for first October primo sick people whose diagnosis is established secondo young people who ought to go back to their schools tertio grave humanitarian cases. We propose to employ Red Cross doctors to expedite the lists of the sick. We remind you that Red Cross action is also exercised by our special delegate at Leopoldville in favour of your wounded and prisoners and civilians in the hands of the Government of Leo. We are just as ready to continue to comfort by our means the sufferings of Congolese in the territories under your jurisdiction stop but remind you that all action must be taken without delay repeat without delay in favour of all the victims of the conflict without regard to nationality or race or religion or politics stop world opinion will not understand delays needlessly immobilising doctors and crews and aircraft when other conflicts are soliciting aid from the Red Cross.

8. **Mr. Senn from President Gbenye, Stan, 30th September 1964.**
It will be up to me to determine as soon as the thing will be possible.

9. **President Gbenye from Mr. Senn, 3rd October 1964.**
Your attitude risks wrecking humanitarian action in favour of the R.P.C. Contrary to your opinion organisation of all Red Cross action depends on mutual agreement. Red Cross cannot accept indefinite adjournment. We propose a flight Monday morning 5th October. Bringing equipment dressings and provisions stop awaiting first group composed of your choice of sick people humanitarian cases and students who must be ready for embarkation. Awaiting immediate reply. Compliments.

10. **Mr. Senn from Minister of Defence Gaston Soumiallot, Stan, 3rd October 1964.**
I cannot authorise flight for 5th October. By withdrawing Geneva

doctors you yourself have thwarted formation ad hoc commissions. I am in the process of looking for neutral elements in order to form the commission. The date of the first meeting will be communicated to you in good time. R.P.C. is aware of the humanitarian action of the Red Cross and praises this action. R.P.C. will facilitate all Red Cross missions for the good of humanity. President Gbenye will be absent from Stan and your message to him will be forwarded for his information. Do not wait for a reply before noon in view of difficulties with our means of communication. Compliments.

11. President Gbenye from Dr. Jean Maurice Rubli, Special Envoy, Red Cross Mission, 4th October 1964.

Dr. Rubli, Special Envoy of the International Committee of the Red Cross sends the compliments of President Boissier to President Gbenye. He thanks him again for the manner in which the Red Cross Mission has been received at Stan. He understands all the difficulties which such a Mission represents for President Gbenye. Nevertheless Doctor Rubli must remind him that on 26th September President Gbenye indicated to him that Red Cross action would be able to begin on 5th October at the latest. Senn has asked you on three occasions to shorten the delay because the International Committee of the Red Cross aprpreciated that it has no authority to immobilise doctors and aircraft earnestly requested by other conflicts. In his message of 29th September Senn advised you that the Swiss doctors are at your disposal for the formation of medical commissions with a view to repatriating sick foreigners. He proposed that they should be sent on 1st October from Bujumbura by Red Cross aeroplane where they are still waiting contrary to the assertion of Minister Soumiallot.

I confirm the proposals of Mr. Senn of 3rd October which propose the arrival of Red Cross aeroplane at Stan on 5th October as promised by President Gbenye. This plane will transport first three Swiss doctors, second new load of medicines and provisions. Aeroplane and crew identical to those of first trip. I shall direct the mission myself. In no case can the C.I.C.R. accept any further retardation in the work of its doctors. Dr. Rubli also regrets the delay in sending medicines and provisions of which the people of the R.P.C. has urgent need. We do not understand the new delay in the transport of children to rejoin schools outside the territory under your jurisdiction since this category does not depend on the medical commissions. This new delay risks obstruction of Red Cross action in Leopoldville in favour of your victims in the Congolese conflict. It [the Leo delegation] enjoys every facility and total liberty in its Red Cross work. In no case will the C.I.C.R. allow itself to be held responsible for the development of useless suffering by the victims of the Congolese conflict resulting from repeated adjournments of our actions stop whilst waiting for their departure for Stan our doctors have with the permission of the Burundi Government and according to the wish of President Gbenye attended your wounded in hospital at Bujumbura. We beg you earnestly with every goodwill to accede to our legitimate desires according to the principles of humanitarianism and all international rules on the rights of people. Compliments.

12. **Mr. Senn from Gaston Souliallot, Stan, 5th October 1964.**
President Gbenye being absent from Stan I cannot take grave decision to allow foreign aircraft to land Stan during his absence. If you insist I shall send back to you your medicines because your would-be aid constitutes for us a condition [obliging us] to repatriate foreigners whom you wish to save from American bombardment. I remind you that your arrival in Stan was followed by the bombing of Maniema as was the case in Albertville and Uvira. I fear your arrival in many ways because the Red Cross as an international organisation cannot impose conditions whilst carrying out its humanitarian functions. Wait for President Gbenye to whom I will submit the Red Cross dossier for his decision before any landings of Red Cross planes at Stan and Kindu. Count on your understanding. Compliments.

13. **President Gbenye from Dr. Rubli, 6th October 1964.**
Dr. Rubli Special Envoy of the C.I.C.R. expresses his great astonishment at not having received a reply to his message of 3rd October. He reminds you of his offer to come with Chief Delegate Senn by Red Cross aeroplane on 5th October to discuss our actions. This aeroplane will carry primo three Swiss doctors C.I.C.R. to form the medical commission announced by your government 27 September via radio Stan. These doctors have waited since 27th September for your permission to proceed to Stan. Secundo medicines and provisions which have been ready since 30 September destined for the people of the R.P.C. C.I.C.R. cannot understand why government R.P.C. has adjourned the flight of the Red Cross aeroplane destined to transport Swiss doctors of the Red Cross medicines and provisions [arrange] repatriation grave humanitarian cases and those gravely ill where diagnosis has been established and transport children to schools outside the R.P.C. In effect these actions have a purely humanitarian character and no political or military character.
Dr. Rubli has explained to you that International conventions forbid the retention of foreign civilians who are not participating in the Congolese conflict and has strong reason to consider they are being held as hostages.
We remind you that our delegates at Leo have every freedom of action in favour of your own victims of the Congolese conflict stop we ask that your government accords us the same facilities as those enjoyed by our delegate at Leo.
As our message of 3rd October remained without a reply Dr. Rubli cancelled the Red Cross flight for 5th October. He asks you that we should fix mutually this flight for 6th October. The C.I.C.R. is

recognised and upheld by 102 countries and can no longer accept
new adjournments and hindrances to its purely humanitarian actions.

14. President Gbenye from Mr. Senn, 11th October 1964.
Have seen your telegrams of 3rd and 5th October and beg you to
communicate immediately first possible date for the arrival of the
Red Cross plane at Stan. We shall carry provisions and medicines
as arranged. Beg you to let us know the number of persons selected
by your commission for repatriation on medical grounds and
humanitarian reasons. Last date acceptable for technical and financial
reasons is 14th October morning.

15. President Gbenye from Mr. Senn 13 October 1964.
Senn begs you to communicate to him your reply to his telegram of
Sunday up until 1000 hrs GMT 14th October.

16. President Gbenye from Mr. Senn, 18th October 1964.
According to instructions received from Geneva C.I.C.R. I ask you
to authorise a special flight exclusively in order to deliver to you
provisions and medicines now at Bujumbura in danger of being lost
through prolonged delay in delivery. I confirm that this transport is
entirely independent of all other actions. Aeroplane will call only to
discharge merchandise.

17. President Gbenye from Maître Nicolet, 18th October 1964.
I shall arrive Bujumbura 20th October. Whilst awaiting my arrival
suggest that you receive provisions and medicines ready to be
delivered to you by Red Cross plane without any preliminary or
other conditions. Fraternally.

18. Raymond Nicolet from President Gbenye, 24 October 1964.
No foreigners are to be taken hostage. All rumour is intrigue and
disparagement against the country by American Imperialists.
We have arrested an American major in combat at Yakoma. He
is in good health.
I would have wished for your arrival in the immediate future but
we are cut off from the exterior without air traffic. Our villages are
bombed and burnt by American planes leaving in them many
corpses. Impossible to bury them stop in this insecurity provoked
by American planes I do not like to risk your life in view of the
enormous kindness which you have rendered to my family. If by
misfortune Tshombe's soldiers put their hands on you you will be
eaten raw as was the case with so many others. In 1962 I stopped and
freed eight Belgian soldiers without condition. That ought to
witness my good political faith. The policy of my government is to
assure security of persons and property without distinction of nationality. I have just returned from a tour which is the reason for

the slowness in replying to your message. My kisses to Leopold
and Firmin. Has Christopher gone to Guinea. Fraternally.

19. Announcement over Radio Stan, 24th October 1964.
To the Diplomatic Corps at Usumbura and specially to the Ambas-
sadors of Great Britain, France and Belgium.
We would be grateful to you for your goodwill to forward via the
Embassies at Bujumbura or at Leopoldville or by any other means,
the following message to the Ministers of Foreign Affairs of Federal
Germany, Belgium, Canada, Cyprus, U.S.A., Spain, France,
Luxembourg, Gt. Britain, Greece, Italy, the Low Countries,
Pakistan, Switzerland, and India.
We testify that all foreigners for repatriation in Stanleyville and in
the surrounding regions are at this moment in good health. They
have never been ill treated all are free including expatriate Americans,
save only the five members of the American Consulate at Stan who
are under house arrest. The authorities of Stanleyville guarantee
the safety of all foreigners and assure them protection. The Popular
Government has given the strictest orders to this effect to the Popular
Army and these orders are very well obeyed.
Given at Stan on behalf of the foreigners in Stan by the Consular
Corps of Stanleyville.
Signed: Rombaut, Gerlache, Nothomb, Duque, Massaccesi, Bal-
tazzi, Theocarides, Franken, Van den Broeck.

20. Announcement over Radio Stan by President Gbenye, 31st
October 1964.
The Popular Republic of the Congo has noted the invitation made
by M. Moise Tshombe to the Red Cross Mission inviting them to
come to Stan to see if prisoners of war are being treated according
to the Geneva convention.
The R.P.C. proceeding on its mission of liberation has not seen fit
to make prisoners of war out of its own brothers. All the soldiers of
the A.N.C. who have been captured or who have surrendered their
arms to the Popular Army have been enrolled into it in order to
fight the régime of Mr. Tshombe.
The R.P.C. asks the Red Cross to come to the Congo to visit the
areas bombarded by the Americans and Belgians in order to render
an account of the truth and to denounce to international opinion
the ignoble massacres perpetrated by the Americans and the Belgians
against the innocent population of the R.P.C.

21. Official Communiqué by President Gbenye, 1st November 1964.
As a result of bombings effected by foreigners in the regions liberated
by the Popular Army all Americans and Belgians finding themselves
in the liberated regions are considered as prisoners of war, and this
measure will be applied equally to their allies so long as they attempt
to bomb the R.P.C.

Nevertheless, we remain ready to negotiate these prisoners with the countries actually at war with the Congolese people, but only through the channels of the O.A.U. because we shall never accept assurances or guarantees given by Tshombe, his American mercenaries, Belgians and others.
We empower M. Thomas Kanza to keep in contact with Prime Minister Jomo Kenyatta, President of the Commission of Conciliation O.A.U. and Secretary General O.A.U. M. Dialo Telli who is conducting these negotiations.
We remain ready to welcome the O.A.U. Commission to Stan in order to find an African solution to the Congolese problem and in order to expel from the Congo American soldiers and Belgians who are massacreing the Congolese people.

22. Statement by President Kenyatta concerning foreign civilians in Stanleyville.
A number of nations, both in Africa and outside it, have made representations expressing anxiety for the safety of civilian nationals in the Democratic Republic of the Congo. As soon as I was made aware of this situation I took immediate action by appealing to all authorities in the Congo requesting them to do nothing that would be inhuman towards civilians in their custody. I went further and requested them to facilitate humanitarian work of the International Committee of the Red Cross who were prepared to fly their aircraft into the Congo on receiving a guarantee of security both for their aircraft and personnel.
In reponse, *the authorities concerned assured me that the foreign civilians in Stanleyville were not in danger.*
It appears to me at this stage that I, as Chairman of the ad hoc Commission of the O.A.U. on the Congo, have taken all necessary steps to impress upon the leaders of the fighting forces in the Congo that it is essential that on humanitarian grounds alone the lives of the people concerned should not be endangered.
It should be appreciated that my commission can do no more than use peaceful means in the circumstances. There are factors in the situation which others are in a better position to control to assist in creating an atmosphere in which peace can be restored in the Congo.

23. President Gbenye from Jomo Kenyatta, President O.A.U. Commission.
On 15th November I telegraphed an appeal to you in order that all the civilians who are held in Stanleyville would be treated humanely. Since then I have received some reports that an American Missionary Dr. Paul Carlson is in danger of being executed as a result of espionage.
I make an appeal to your goodwill to save the life of this man in the name of humanity.

24. Jomo Kenyatta, President O.A.U. Commission from President Gbenye.

Have received your message on the subject of the adjournment of the execution of American Major Paul Carlson. We are eager to transmit to you a resolution by the Congolese people made at a popular meeting which reads:

"Congolese people confirm execution American Major Paul Carlson without delay. Inform position President ad hoc Commission that the Congolese people adjourn execution Major Carlson until next Monday."

If during stay granted Washington does not find grounds for negotiation over prisoners of war with the Revolutionary Government the wish of the people will be done that is to say Major Paul Carlson will be executed. We empower Brother Thomas Kanza to make negotiations with you and Dialo Telli Secretary General of the O.A.U. if you cannot arrive Stan."

25. President Gbenye from Ambassador Godley of the United States of America at Leopoldville, 18th November 1964.

Radio Stanleyville has announced the conviction and sentence to death of the missionary doctor Paul Carlson following an accusation of espionage devoid of all foundation.

The Secretary of State of the United States Government has already written to Mr. Jomo Kenyatta President of the ad hoc Commission of the O.A.U. begging him instantly to take measures to prevent this violation of international law and of all the normal codes of humanitarian conduct.

My Government instructs me to inform you once more that it holds the authorities in Stanleyville directly and personally responsible for the security of Dr. Paul Carlson as well as all American citizens finding themselves in the regions under your control.

As you know my Government has supported along with other nations the fruitful efforts of the C.I.C.R. and of the ad hoc Commission of the O.A.U. in order to get your agreement to a humanitarian mission by the Red Cross to Stan and to the arrangements for the protection and the evacuation of innocent civilians.

We are always ready to co-operate in all humanitarian efforts and to discuss any arrangements by intermediaries of these organisations.

26. President Gbenye from Mr. Senn, 18th November 1964.

Radio Stan has announced on 27th October the arrest at Wasolo of a certain Major Paul Carlson accused of espionage and his transfer to Stan for trial by a military tribunal. Following this Radio Stan has announced that Carlson has been condemned to death.

Evidently you have decided to declare the civilian doctor Carlson a combatant and prisoner of war and it follows from this that you accept the strict observation of the Geneva Convention concerning treatment of prisoners of war. I refer especially to the statements concerning legal procedure notably articles 99 to 108 of the Second Convention signed at Geneva 1949 and ratified by the Congolese Parliament in August 1960 with the other treaties and international conventions. On this basis I ask that Mr. Franken in his capacity as local representative of C.I.C.R. should be authorised to act as an observer and be permitted to procure for Carlson all aid mentioned in the Convention.

27. Mr. Senn from President Gbenye, Stan, 18th November 1964
I have received your message à propos execution American Major Carlson. Before making me any proposition I invite you to resuscitate all Congolese massacred by the Americans in the Congo. I remind you that to assure security of property and persons does not signify tolerance of crime.

28. Announcement by President Gbenye over Radio Stan, 19th November 1964.
It is well known that the Americans, the Belgians and the Italians attack us and furnish military aid in men and materials to the puppet government of Mr. Tshombe.
We declare that if the Imperialist forces do not put down their arms before 48 hours [Monday] we cannot answer any more for the lives of foreigners who are detained as prisoners of war and who until now have never been ill-treated.

29. Part of an announcement by President Gbenye over Radio Stan, 20th November 1964.
. . . any attack on Stanleyville will cancel the postponement of the execution of American Major Paul Carlson.
The capture of American Major Paul Carlson proves that the Americans are helping Tshombe with material and men in the internal struggle of the Congo.
At the first attack on Stan Major Carlson will be executed following the wishes of the people.

30. Jomo Kenyatta from President Gbenya, 20th November 1964.
In spite of American promise to negotiate with us the Americans and Belgians have attacked us on two fronts today, namely Punia and Basoko. The wrath of the people has limits.
We inform you that we have transferred from Stan the repatriate Americans and Belgians whilst waiting for the end of negotiations.

31. Part of an announcement made by President Gbenye over Radio Stan on Sunday evening, 22 November 1964.
. . . to Albertville, M. Senn delegate of the Red Cross, has visited the area and evacuated civilians who wanted to leave. After his

departure the town was bombarded because the plans of the town were delivered to the rebels of Tshombe and the town retaken by them. This treason by the Red Cross is because they are in the service of the American Imperialists.

This is why we refuse to let the Red Cross come to Stanleyville!

*Author's Note.* For the record it should be remembered that the Red Cross Mission arrived in Albertville some time in July 1964 for the sole purpose of distributing medicines. Foreigners who left the town did so by permission of the rebel authorities. The Red Cross Mission left Albertville on 24th July. Albertville suffered its first air attack on 25th August 1964.

# APPENDIX 3
## A lecture on Man Management and Leadership

Every man under your command is a separate entity. Every man under your command is different. Each one has his own personality, his own background, his own likes and dislikes, troubles and fears. There is no general pattern. Your first step in man management will be in trying to understand in what way each of your men is different and what makes him tick.

The first thing you will discover is that every man has a name and prefers to be called by it. Nobody likes to be spoken to as "Hey, you!", or worse still, as "Hey, you with the square head!" We live in the age of the personality cult. The world of commerce has already appreciated this fact to its advantage. Is it not heart-warming to be greeted by your name by the head waiter at your favourite restaurant? Makes you feel a little important, does it not? Begin, therefore, by learning the name of every man under your command. It pays dividends. A man's reaction is not, as you might suppose, surprise that you should know his name—it goes much deeper than that; he feels that you have gone to some trouble to learn it; he feels you care; he is no longer a number—now he is an entity. This is the basis of man management, the ability to care.

You will find the study of men to be an absorbing task. You will be astounded that you understand some of your men so easily. You appear to be on "the same wavelength" as it were. They know at once what you are talking about or trying to say, almost instinctively. Others, on the other hand, always seem to be difficult and contrary, express totally different opinions from yours and you find it difficult to communicate with them. This does not necessarily mean that you are right and they are wrong. To understand these soldiers you will need to know their minds, their backgrounds, and why they take certain attitudes. Some men are even more difficult and are what I call "prickly pears", hornery cusses, who just refuse to be understood. Frequently, these men are tough and independent. A weak leader will accept that they are awkward and will avoid them altogether or give in to them whenever their paths cross. This is an error. You must recognise strength in personality, even if it makes your life a little harder. So often I have found these "prickly pears" to be the ones who are still in there fighting, when all others have fled—for the basic reason that they are obstinate and will not give in. These are priceless qualities in a soldier which must be encouraged, rather than weakened.

Be careful that you do not confuse the "prickly pear", who is a pearl

U

without a price, with the man who is truly impossible. There used to be a saying in the British Army that there were no bad men only bad leaders. This is a large slice of baloney. Think back to the beginnings of this unit for some examples. We began with some of the most incredible soldiers of all time. What can you do with a confirmed junky? How can you lead a habitual drunkard? My advice is—don't even try. Your duty as a commander begins and ends by recognising them quickly and getting them out of your unit before they do any damage.

You will notice that men respond willingly to some leaders and not to others. If you make a study of the methods of the successful ones, you will find that they invariably have confidence in themselves, show enthusiasm even for the most menial tasks, have a sense of humour, and are proficient at soldiering. A lot depends on the way you go about things. Tone of voice, for instance, is most important. One tone, which you will use when you are "on duty", will indicate to your men—they will know you just as well as you know them—that you mean business, no fooling, get on with the job, lads. Be the same every day, not easy-going and playful one day and hard as nails the next. This confuses the men, understandably.

The bed-rock of man management, however, is discipline. Nothing is more certain than that you will obtain the best results with your men if you insist on a high standard of discipline. You will soon find that your men, all men, prefer to be led firmly with discipline. It results in fairer treatment for one thing and every man knows what to expect and where he stands. Once you have decided on your standard of discipline—and this is really a matter to suit your personality and may vary from "iron hand" tactics to the other end of the scale, where you merely insist that your orders are carried out—you must apply the golden rule of consistency. My advice in this regard is to take no chances and to be "Regimental". Be hard, but fair. Strangely enough, men take a pride in being treated hard. Let your men know that when you are "on parade", you are very much "on parade". Off parade, you can perhaps relax a little. This will depend on the strength of your personality. But watch it. More man management problems arise off duty than on. It is totally impossible to spend a night drinking with your men and yet expect them to answer your commands the next day. Familiarity breeds contempt. Human nature works that way and, whilst some of your men will appreciate the difference between off duty and on, there will always be a few who will wreck the thing for you on the parade ground.

With regard to familiarity, should you use Christian names? On parade, definitely not. Off parade, everything will depend on the circumstances. I do not think, however, that an occasion can ever arise where your juniors should address you by your Christian name. And whilst on this subject—make no favourites. This leads to endless discontent and can be as hard on the man favoured, as it is unfair on the others. Keep your relationship formal.

Man management is, I think you will agree, something which we can all learn. We do not have to be greatly gifted to do it. But how do we become leaders of men? We become leaders of men, in the first instance, by showing that we are worthy of being followed. Men will only follow a man they respect. Let us study how we can earn the respect which will turn us into leaders.

We begin with self-discipline. Let me give you an example. The rules, which are laid down for your men, must be obeyed equally by you, regardless of the privileges which may go with your rank. If P.T. parade is at o6.oo hours, then you should appear on it and not be lying in bed, encouraging your men from the warmth of your blankets. Your personal behaviour will come under the closest scrutiny. Men have an inbred desire to respect their leader and excessive self-indulgence will wreck that ideal. No man will follow a booze artist—except perhaps into a pub! —no matter what excellent company he may be. This does not mean that you must be puritanical, but your standard of personal behaviour must be above average.

Next will come a thorough knowledge of your job. Anything you ask your men to do, you must be capable of doing yourself, from marching fifty miles in full equipment to stripping a machine gun. You must be technically superior in all facets of soldiering. You must be as fit, if not fitter, than your men. You must demonstrate to your men that "you know your stuff". This will impart confidence, which in its turn, will instill a sense of respect and build up your powers of leadership.

Let me stress the great importance of being able to communicate with your men. The best way to impress your personality on your men is by frequent talks and discussions. You must practise the art of public speaking and develop a facility for getting your message across clearly and concisely. You must learn to instruct, for teaching will be one of your main occupations as a leader.

There are many rewards attached to leadership, but the friendship of your men is not one of them. Leadership is, generally speaking, a lonely task. It has to be so. It is impossible for a good leader to be chummy with his men and yet subject them to his orders, many of which will be unpopular, even harsh. The comradeship of men in the ranks is a warm and a rewarding feeling, a rare sensation known only to soldiers who have roughed it and braved battle together. Many men recognise this and stay in the ranks, preferring comradeship to the joy of command, which is a different thing altogether. I mention this, so that you will be warned against the cardinal error of trying to curry favour with your men or seeking popularity. It never works. The best you can hope for is the respect of your men, and this can be a considerable reward in itself.

Now let me deal with two aspects of leadership in practice. Firstly, the good leader is one who cares for his men. On active service, the average soldier is usually completely reliant on his leaders for a variety of things, from the supply of food to ammunition. The good leader looks after the welfare and comfort of his troops. He sees they are billeted reasonably, have blankets and food, and receive their share of any creature comforts which are available. He ensures that guard rosters are arranged fairly and that "willing horses" are not given too great a burden to carry. The health of his men and their morale must be his constant anxiety. He does not nurse them, but makes himself available at all times to help them care for themselves and represents their case at higher levels whenever necessary. He cares about them.

Imagine that you are riding along in convoy and suddenly you run into an ambush. Bullets are flying everywhere and confusion and panic grip the column. This is the "moment of truth" for you as a leader. Every man will look to you for leadership. In this moment you will stand or fall in their eyes. How will you react? My advice to you is simply this. Anticipate every situation which can arise in battle and think out your reaction to it, well in advance. The split second which you gain can be decisive. As soon as trouble strikes, shout out an order. It matters little what it is, so long as you let your men know you are in command. "Take cover!", for instance—obvious enough and something which they will do in any event, but the fact that you have reacted immediately to the situation and given an order, is a relief to your men. Instinctively, every man will obey. Your next order is eagerly awaited. Go on and lead firmly. Do not let your men flounder around, wondering if they should take the initiative, something they have heard so much about. Invariably this leads them into trouble. This is your job. You must lead. You must tell them what to do.

Finally, let me say something about that powerful emotion, "sympathy". Watch out for it. It has no place on the battlefield. A stern, even a harsh, word to a wounded man will often induce in him a fighting spirit, which will react to his own advantage. I have seen many a man die from an overdose of sympathy. Sympathy, no matter how well meant, must be carefully controlled on the field of battle. In the Casualty Station it may be a different thing.

Let me recap. To manage your men well you must know them. You must know them intimately, beginning with their names and ending with their private histories. This is the very core of man management. To lead men you must gain their respect. To do this, you will have to show them you are worthy of it. You must, at the same time, be as fit as any of them and technically better than all of them. This way you will impart confidence. Finally, to lead conclusively in battle, you must show yourself to be their leader when the crunch comes. In the moment of truth, when they look to you for leadership, you must not fail them.

Let me end by saying that a leader is only as good as the sum of his men; but let me also assure you that a good leader can raise this sum to the power of ten, by caring for his men, setting a good example, and leading with a firm hand.

# APPENDIX 4

## 5 Commando rules for battle[1]

1. Pray God daily.
2. Make a fetish of personal cleanliness; take pride in your appearance, even in the midst of battle; shave every day without fail.
3. Clean and protect your weapons always. They must be bright clean and slightly oiled. Examine your ammunition frequently. Check and clean your magazine springs and lips.
4. Soldiers in pairs; look after each other; be faithful to your mate. Be loyal to your leaders.
5. Tell no lies in battle. All information must be accurate or your unit will suffer. Exaggerate to your girl friends later, but NEVER, NEVER in battle.
6. Be ready to move at a moment's notice. Mark all your equipment. Keep it handy at all times. At night develop a routine for finding it.
7. Look after your vehicle. Fill it with petrol before resting. Clean it. Do not overload unnecessarily.
8. Take no unnecesary risks.
9. Stand-to dawn and dusk. At night have confidence in your sentries; post as few as the situation demands.
10. Be aggressive in action—chivalrous in victory—stubborn in defence.

[1] The student of military affairs will no doubt notice a similarity between these rules and those of Major Rogers, which he devised for his Rangers in Canada.

# INDEX

## A

Aba, 176, 189, 191, 194, 199, 200 ff., 213, 215, 219, 223
ABAKO, 31, 289, 290, 292
Accra, 143, 273, 274, 290
*Actualitiés Africaines*, 31
Adi, 199, 213
Adoulla, C., 19, 255, 293, 294
*Affreux, les*, 15, 68, 173
African Inland Mission, 199, 205
*Agents sous contrats*, 285
Air Congo, 37
Aketi, 76, 79, 103, 111, 167, 231
Albert, Lake, 179, 180, 183
Albertville, 21, 23, 24, 29, 37, 39, 40, 41, 42, 43, 46, 48, 50, 75, 238, 239, 240, 241, 242, 245, 247, 249, 250, 251, 253, 257, 267, 271, 282, 293
Algeria, 142, 143, 171, 176, 194, 195, 202
Ambesi, 192
Angola, 25
Api River, 229
A.P.L, 23, 24, 53, 75, 77, 82, 90
Aru, 176, 180, 189, 192, 193, 194, 195, 197, 204, 213, 223, 243
Aruwimi River, 154
Attwood, W., 113
Avakubi, 163, 164, 166, 170

## B

Bafwasende, 154, 157, 159, 161, 162, 163, 164, 166
Bahembi, 240, 248

Baluba, 292, 293
Bambesa, 228
Banalia, 79, 154, 157, 158, 159, 236
Bangala, Lieut.-Col., 39, 55
Banzi, 253
Baraka, 238, 239, 240, 248, 249, 252, 253, 255, 256, 257, 258, 261, 263, 264, 265, 266, 271, 272, 276, 278, 282
Basson, F., 120, 124, 131, 179
Baudouin, King, 290, 291
Baudoinville, 39, 41, 42
Bayeke, 28
Beach Reconnaissance (Recce) Party, 257, 258, 259, 268, 271
Bekker, Lieut., 266, 269
Belgian Paratroop Regt., 110, 113, 115, 118, 122, 123, 129, 130, 141, 142, 144, 184, 250
Bell helicopter, 245, 267
Ben Bella, 88
Bendera, 240, 245, 247, 248, 250, 251, 252, 267
Beni, 103, 169
Bikili, 67, 77, 78, 81, 156, 243
Bili, 221, 229, 230
Binza, 44, 145
Blume, A., 38, 39, 42, 46, 51, 54, 55
Bobozo, L., 40, 41, 46, 59, 238, 267, 279
Boende, 77, 78, 81, 82, 103, 156
Bolya, P., 290
Bomakandi River, 228
Bomili, 157, 161
Bondekwe, S., 112
Bondo, 221, 229, 230, 231, 232, 234

Borrodaile, B., 267
Bouve, F., 183, 185, 186, 199, 209, 213, 218, 219
Bouzin, E., 63
Boyulu, 163, 164
Braham, D., 244, 245, 257, 261, 262, 269
Brazzaville, 44, 63, 274, 275, 278, 289
Brenhardt, J., 178, 246
Bridge, E., 45, 48, 51, 52, 53, 56, 57, 58
Brock, Vol., 200, 202
Bubu, "Major", 122
Bukavu, 21, 69, 75, 82, 83, 166, 285
Bulloch, J., 101, 102, 165, 174
Bumba, Major, 277
Bumba, 76, 82
Bunia, 169, 173, 176, 177, 179, 182, 183, 185, 190, 197, 213, 285
Burger, C., 234, 235
Burke, Mrs. C., 163
Burton Bay, 240, 259
Burundi, 142, 171, 237, 238
Buta, 79, 167, 221, 231, 232, 233, 235, 236
Butembo, 83, 169
B-26 aircraft, 73, 203, 208, 244, 253, 257

C

Calistrat, F., 79, 92, 99, 109, 114
Carlson, Dr. P., 78, 112, 123
Carnegie, D., 195
Carter, H., 159, 207, 244
Carton-Barber, J., 61, 71, 88, 94, 96, 97, 98, 99, 108, 109, 110, 124, 125, 144, 147, 150, 159, 160, 226, 228
Cassidy, S., 166, 181, 182, 189, 190, 191, 193, 194, 195, 199, 201, 219, 248
C.B.S., 117, 258
Central African Republic, 221
C.F.L., 249, 250

Chaloner, D., 197, 201, 208, 209, 220, 222
Chanu, C., 53, 58
Chasseurs Ardennais, 85
Chinese arms, 239
Chinese Communism, 20, 22, 112
Chou en Lai, 237
Christie, E., 131
Churchill, Sir Winston, 258
Cimental, 245
Clare-White (consul), 137
Clay, G., 117, 120, 124, 131
Clingerman (consul), 126, 132
Closset, Capt., 71
Cochaux, Commdt., 39, 40, 41
Coetzee, Vol., 177
Coleman, "Skinny", 261
Columbic, R., 232, 244, 257, 262, 263
Communism, 14, 37, 142, 143, 175, 176, 194, 195, 196, 237, 240, 241, 274, 275, 285
CONAKAT, 289, 292
Congolese franc, 19, 31, 218, 246, 247
Congo River, 23, 77, 111, 274, 275
Cooper, "Gary", 98, 155
Coquilhatville, 24, 69, 75, 77, 81, 293
Cotonco, 262, 264
Couve de Murville, Capt., 256, 261
Cramer, J., 158
Cubans, 73, 91, 114, 118, 119, 180, 239, 240, 244, 248, 264, 265
C-130 aircraft, 37, 38, 126, 128, 130, 170, 185, 246

D

Daniels, Vol., 271
Dar es Salaam, 176, 239
Davisterre, P., 31
De Beer, Vol., 185
De Jaeger, D., 63, 81, 99, 173, 240
Delperdange, Maj.-Gen., 275, 276, 279

H

I

J

K

# Also by Greenhill Books

'Fascinating images that expose the poisonous reality of Hitler's Germany.'
DAN SNOW

# HITLER'S
## THIRD REICH
### IN 100 OBJECTS

# ROGER MOORHOUSE
Foreword by
RICHARD OVERY

# MORTAR GUNNER
## ON THE
# EASTERN FRONT

VOLUME I:
FROM THE MOSCOW WINTER OFFENSIVE
TO OPERATION ZITADELLE

THE MEMOIR OF
## DR HANS HEINZ REHFELDT

# RADIO
# OPERATOR
## ON THE
# EASTERN FRONT

## AN ILLUSTRATED MEMOIR, 1940–1949

### ERHARD STEINIGER

FOREWORD BY ANTHONY TUCKER-JONES